THE BISHOPS

THE BISHOPS

A Study of Leaders in the Church Today

FRANK LONGFORD

SIDGWICK & JACKSON
LONDON

All photographs are reproduced by kind permission of Niall Macleod except for the photograph of the Archbishop of Cardiff, which is reproduced by kind permission of Gerald Green Studios, and the photograph of the Archbishop of Birmingham, which is reproduced by kind permission of Neils McGuiness (*Newspix*)

First published in Great Britain in 1986 by Sidgwick and Jackson Limited

Copyright © 1986 by Frank Longford

ISBN 0–283–99279–4

Typeset by Hewer Text Composition Services, Edinburgh

Printed in Great Britain by
The Garden City Press Limited, Letchworth, Hertfordshire SG6 1JS
for Sidgwick and Jackson Limited
1 Tavistock Chambers, Bloomsbury Way, London WC1A 2SG

For Elizabeth

Contents

CONTENTS

Acknowledgements

My grateful thanks go in the first place to the thirteen Anglican and ten Catholic bishops who so kindly allowed me to interview them. Also to the members of their staff who helped me in all sorts of ways.

I had help from too many others to thank them all adequately. Among Anglicans I cannot refrain from mentioning Joy Meacham, Press Officer at Church House, and those associated with her. My old friend and comrade in the struggle against pornogaphy, Professor Sir Norman Anderson, helped me to understand many things about the Church of England not easily comprehensible without his assistance.

Another old friend on the Catholic side, Bishop Agnellus Andrew, kindly read the proofs. I am very grateful also to Monsignor George Leonard of Archbishop's House, and Monsignor Hook of the Catholic Media Office, for their wise counsel.

I have benefited in full measure from the writings of Clifford Longley of *The Times*, and other excellent religious journalists.

In preparing the manuscript, I must begin by thanking Carey Smith and Katrina Ure of Sidgwick and Jackson. I take the opportunity of thanking Carey for all her help, too long unacknowledged, with my book on Pope John Paul II. My closest adviser for many years has been Gwen Keeble. For many years also Barbara Winch, Matthew Oliver and more recently Kitty Chapman have been indispensable to the production of the manuscript.

Elizabeth comes first and last as always.

Preface

Bishops are integral to the Roman Catholic and Anglican communions. These Churches are not alone in possessing bishops, but most of the Reformed Churches brought them to an end. Where they have survived, as in the Scandinavian and Lutheran scene, 'they have sometimes been convenient but they are in no sense necessary or basic to the Church' (Peter Moore, *Bishops, But What Kind?*). The situation is, of course, totally different in the Roman Catholic and Anglican Churches, which come under review in this book, and for that matter in the Orthodox Churches.

The Roman Catholic Church has not had in recent years a better or more instructive friend than Bishop Moorman, who was Anglican Bishop of Ripon until his retirement in 1975. 'Episcopacy is not', he writes in an essay which appears in *Bishops, But What Kind?*, 'something which gradually grew up in the Church and which, having proved itself unworthy of its great office, could easily be dispensed with. It is something which goes back to Christ himself, and is fundamental to the work which the Church is created to perform in the world.'

Some uncertainty hangs over the first Christian century. It seems, however, to be generally accepted that by the middle of the second century a threefold form of ministry – bishop, priest, and deacon – had emerged in the Church and indeed was firmly established. In the Tridentine Canon of the Latin Mass, Peter, Linus, Cletus, and Clement are listed as the first Bishops of Rome. They span the last thirty years of the first Christian century. Bishops in short have from the earliest times been an indispensable part of the Christian system.

'Episcopacy' means oversight. The group of Christ's immediate followers was small and nurtured by the Apostles themselves. It was only as the group grew that development of that oversight was required. During the 1,900 years that have passed since then, the enormous expansion of Christian populations, and correspondingly of priests and overseeing bishops, has gone on unremittingly.

The sixteenth century saw the Reformation, which involved the tragic disruption of the Church. The breach between East and West had occurred five centuries earlier. The apostolic succession, the descent from the Apostles and ultimately from Christ, was gravely threatened. The Catholic Hierarchy, the collective presence of the Catholic bishops, came to an end in England with the death of Mary in 1558 and was not restored until 1850. The succession was preserved abroad, however. When Elizabeth came to the throne, Archbishop Parker was consecrated by four 'Protestant bishops' who had been installed in the reigns of Henry VIII and Edward VI. Other bishops were consecrated, and the vacancies were filled. 'Thus, here also', writes Bishop Moorman, 'the Apostolic Succession was preserved.'

Today we have moved a long way from the point where the bishop can have any personal knowledge of those for whom he is pastorally responsible. Yet pastoral care of his flock is supposed to be the basis of the bishop's ministry. How can the possibility be restored to the bishop of rendering a truly pastoral service to all within his diocese? Suggestions are plentiful. More delegation of administrative duties? Smaller dioceses? More suffragans or auxiliaries? The first two of these have plenty of advocates; the third would appear to have very few.

How far is synodical government in the Church of England compatible with the episcopal principle – that is, government by those to whom a sacred power has been handed down through the Apostles from Christ? This issue does not arise at present within the Roman Catholic Church. The emphasis now being laid on the increased role of the laity, however, may raise, in time to come, similar problems. In the Church of England there is a strenuous argument about the measure of doctrinal unity that the bishops should exemplify. The Roman Catholic and Orthodox Churches have an easier time in this respect. But the Anglican tradition of liberty will not be lightly tampered with. As far as I can judge, few, if any, Anglican bishops agree with the more controversial utterances of the Bishop of Durham, but not more than one or two would wish to penalize him even if they thought the remarks unsuitable in a bishop.

The happiest event since the Reformation has been the Second Vatican Council of 1962–5 in Rome, originally announced in 1959 and followed by the valiant visit of Archbishop Fisher to Rome the following year. Pope John XXIII told the 2,540 bishops that this was an opportunity for the Church to bring herself up to date where required. He spoke with notable sympathy for those who were not of the Catholic world. Paul VI, who succeeded him while the council was in progress, carried on the work of radical reform. The vision of Christian unity has ever since provided a stirring prospect.

The book that follows is called *The Bishops*. Certain limitations should be made plain at the outset. The present study does not pretend to provide a general assessment of Christianity in the world today. Such a project would, of course, involve a full treatment of the Orthodox and Free Churches. Much more attention would need to be paid to the international aspects of the Anglican and, still more, of the Roman Catholic Church.

For the purpose of this book, I have interviewed eleven Anglican bishops in England, eight Catholic bishops in England and Wales, the Church of Ireland and Catholic Primates of Ireland, a Scottish Episcopalian bishop, and a Scottish archbishop. Why did I choose these eleven Anglican bishops in England out of forty-three diocesan bishops and sixty-four suffragan? The Archbishops of Canterbury and York and the Bishop of London chose themselves. The seething controversies aroused by the Bishop of Durham made him an inevitable choice (Durham is, in any case, one of the most senior bishoprics). The Bishop of Chichester, as Chairman of the Church Union, is recognized as a semi-official leader of the Anglo-Catholics. The retiring Bishop of Norwich was, at the time I interviewed him, the best-known evangelical, which he himself describes as meaning 'passionately concerned with the Christian gospel'. He was also a very popular speaker in the House of Lords.

The Bishop of Salisbury is Chairman of the Doctrine Commission. The Bishop of Bradford, a fairly recent appointment, is an equally strong evangelical and is usually referred to as the 'one working-man bishop'. His background and education are certainly very different from those of my other selections. The Bishops of Birmingham and

PREFACE

Liverpool have made notable contributions to public discussion in recent years. The Bishop of Bath and Wells represents a unique episcopal tradition. I apologize to all the other bishops who might so well have been chosen.

Of the eight Catholics chosen in England and Wales, one is a cardinal and four others are archbishops. Bishop Harris of Middlesbrough occupied a unique position in matters of social welfare. Bishop Clark of East Anglia was, for many years, the Catholic co-Chairman of ARCIC (the Anglican–Roman Catholic International Commission). Bishop Murphy-O'Connor of Arundel and Brighton, currently Catholic co-Chairman of ARCIC, is my own bishop in Sussex. Once again, I apologize to all the admirable bishops not selected – diocesan bishops, not to mention auxiliaries.

PART I

THE ANGLICAN BISHOPS

Introduction to Part I

'The Church of England is news', announced the *Church of England Year Book for 1984*, covering the year 1983. The satisfaction was understandable. 'Time was', the report continued, 'when the serious purposes of the Church of England demanded the minimum of attention.' But for four or five years there had been an increasing interest in and concern with the Church and in particular with the doings of the General Synod. It is necessary to begin the modern story with the end of the Second World War.

The history of the Church of England from 1945 to 1980 has been divided by Paul Welsby in his valuable short history into three periods: first, 1945–59; second, the 1960s; and third, the 1970s. The first period roughly coincides with the archbishopric of Dr Fisher, the second and half of the third with that of Dr Ramsey. Dr Coggan and Dr Runcie followed, in 1974 and 1980 respectively. The first period saw enormous tasks of reconstruction successfully performed, particularly in the field of education. There was a general and cordial acceptance of the welfare state, which embodied many ideas that had been floating about in Anglican circles. It happens that I myself was personal assistant to Sir William Beveridge, whose famous Report was published in 1942. Beveridge married soon afterwards. His old friend, William Temple, then Archbishop of Canterbury, took a great interest in the Report and performed a service of blessing after the wedding in a register office. The fact that Beveridge had not been baptized made it impossible for the Archbishop to marry them in church. Temple had been a socialist and was still a powerful social reformer. The enthusiasm of the Church of England, and for that matter of the Catholic Church in England, was diluted only by the recognition that material security was not everything. 'Beveridge is not enough.'

3

On the theological side, the main sensation was provided by the Bishop of Birmingham, Dr Barnes, with his *Rise of Christianity* (1947) and other works. He was taken to task by Archbishop Fisher a good deal more severely than has hitherto been the fate of the present Bishop of Durham.

A wide influence was exerted by the monthly journal *Theology*, which from 1939 to 1964 was under the impressive editorship of Dr Alec Vidler. Fundamental matters, however, such as belief in God or in Christ were seldom discussed in its pages, as if these theological foundations were secure and might be taken for granted. There was an atmosphere of confidence and security. Even those who did write about God, Christology, or the Church did so as though the basis of belief was unquestionably right. The radical issues that arose so suddenly in the 1960s took many theologians by surprise.

I turn to the relationship between the Churches. A speech by the Archbishop of Canterbury in the University Church, Cambridge, delivered on 3 November 1946, has been treated as 'momentous'. It initiated an unparalleled search for unity among the Protestant Churches. In the end, this particular search for unity ran into the sand. The attitude of the Roman Catholic Church during the 1940s and 1950s kept Protestants at a considerable distance. There was, however, an immense change in Catholic attitudes towards other Christian Churches with the coming of Pope John XXIII in 1958.

In my eyes the Second Vatican Council, which sat from 1962 to 1965 ('Vatican II'), was the most memorable event in the long history of the Roman Catholic Church. Be that as it may, no one can deny that a whole new friendliness was exhibited towards other Churches from Pope John onwards.

In 1960, after the Vatican Council had been summoned, but before it had met, Archbishop Fisher took the gallant step of visiting the Pope. He was not made particularly welcome except by the Pope himself. He faced the possibility of considerable criticism among his own followers, but he broke the ice in historic fashion. By 1961, when the issue of Christian unity was debated in the House of Lords, there was only one dissentient voice, that of the doughty old Baptist, then leader of the Labour peers, Lord Alexander of Hillsborough.

He interrupted Archbishop Fisher repeatedly, finally demanding: 'Tell me this, is the Church of England Catholic or Protestant?'

4

Fisher sweetly replied, 'Both,' to the infinite disgust of Alexander.

Alexander apart, the Archbishop's visit to Rome was praised on all sides.

Throughout the 1960s and 1970s the search for unity between the Roman and Anglican Churches continued steadily. The visit of the Pope to Canterbury in 1982 was a triumphant success and put the seal for the time being on twenty years of mutual endeavour.

The 1960s seem to be going down in history as the years of the permissive society. They are also known as the 'swinging sixties'. The social legislation was symbolized by liberalization of the laws relating to abortion, homosexuality, and divorce. In popular music it was the age of the Beatles. A sexual revolution making sex before marriage the norm rather than the exception in wide circles moved forward during these years. The coming of cheap and easy contraceptives removed one of the strongest arguments against promiscuous sex.

The Church reflected the general air of ethical disturbance. The most dramatic event was the publication of Dr John Robinson's *Honest to God* (1963), which sold in vast quantities at home and abroad. The controversy aroused was violent. 'It is not every day', said the *Church Times* (22 March 1963), 'that a bishop goes on public record as apparently denying almost every Christian doctrine of the Church in which he holds office.' The Archbishop of Canterbury, Dr Ramsey, reacted harshly – too harshly, he came to think afterwards. The theological ideas went hand in hand with a new and radical form of ethics. Dr Robinson submitted the view that 'in Christian ethics the only pure statement is the command to love; every other injunction depends on it and is an explication or application of it'. It seemed that a revolution in morals, particularly sexual morals, had come to stay and to do no small damage to the life of the nation.

Dr Welsby refers to the 1970s as a period of uneasiness, weariness, and pessimism in many quarters: 'It was against this background of growing disillusionment, the frantic search for material prosperity in face of inflation, the evidence of racial tension, and the canker of insularity, that the Church of England, along with the other Churches, attempted to respond to the problems facing the nation.' Dr Coggan, the new Archbishop of Canterbury, and Dr Stuart Blanch, the new Archbishop of York, launched a call to the nation with the goodwill of the leaders of the other Churches. As someone active in public life at that time, I felt immense respect for this initiative, but the response was not worthy of it.

Somewhat earlier, however, a moral revulsion had begun to reveal itself against some aspects of the new permissiveness. As early as 1964 Mary Whitehouse had started her national campaign to clean up the B.B.C. Her Viewers' and Listeners' Association is going strong as I write. In 1971 the Festival of Light set out to 'purify the land'. In the same year I initiated a debate in the Lords under the slogan 'Pornography has increased, is increasing, and ought to be diminished'. I received thousands of letters in support. A committee was set up with myself as chairman and Dr (now Sir) Norman Anderson as vice-chairman.

A number of leading Christians joined us, including Dr Coggan, then Archbishop of York, and Dr Williams, then Bishop of Leicester, Chairman of the General Synod Board for Social Responsibility. Among famous 'stars' were Cliff Richard and Jimmy Savile. The Archbishop of Canterbury, Dr Ramsey, went out of his way to show personal kindness to me at this time, but he admitted that he was not enthusiastic about our exercise. He could not help feeling that there were much more important issues. Speaking broadly, support for us was fervent among evangelicals such as Dr Coggan and Norman Anderson, cool among Anglo-Catholics, with Roman Catholics somewhere between.

Our particular target was pornography, but in the many debates I became involved in with students the real issue in their minds was the sexual revolution I have mentioned above. I left no one in any doubt that I was against it. The same would have been true, I should think, of all the Christians on our committee.

Throughout the 1970s there was a steady development of the synodical government introduced in 1969. The governing body of the Church now consists of three Houses: the Bishops, the Clergy, and the Laity. The precise relationship between these three elements remains indeterminate. A measure of popular influence has for good or for ill been introduced.

With 1979 we enter the era of Mrs Thatcher's government, of the archbishopric of Dr Runcie, and of various controversies – for example, women priests, the radicalism of the Bishop of Durham, and Anglo-Catholic unity. Mrs Thatcher's controversial social policies have coincided with, indeed collided with, the gradual emergence of the Church of England as a more and more caring force in society. In Robert Runcie's archbishopric (see page 17) I spell out two acts of great leadership: his insistence that the service after the 1982 Falklands war should be one of reconciliation rather than triumph, and his whole-hearted welcome to the Pope at Canterbury that same year. This went far beyond ordinary courtesy and made evident his own commitment to the cause of Christian unity.

In February 1983 there was a breakthrough. Not until the debate during that month on *The Church and the Bomb* had the proceedings of the Synod been televised and broadcast live. The new phenomenon was highly popular. Appreciations and congratulations flowed in to the Church authorities.

At the end of the debate in question, a compromise between unilateralism and multilateralism was accepted. It was agreed that there should be no 'first use' of nuclear weapons. The Synod was thus enabled to reflect its unease about the government's policies without having to go to a unilateralist extreme.

In July of that year, immediately after the general election, there was an emergency debate on capital punishment that also aroused considerable popular excitement. The overwhelming defeat of any attempt to restore the death penalty must surely have had no small influence on a similar decision (though with a much smaller majority) by the House of Commons, which followed immediately.

The Church of England Year Book for 1985, covering the year 1984, reported a continuance of public interest, but struck a grimmer note. The preface to the report is headed: '1984 in Retrospect. Theological Heat and Dust'. The final paragraph begins: 'For those who long for a quiet life in the Church, the prospect is bleak.'

The year was said to have been 'taken up with vigorous controversy'. The controversies were of two kinds, theological and quasi-political. The theological turbulence was compared in the report and elsewhere to the atmosphere of the 1960s, of Bishop Robinson and *Honest to God*. On the political side Mr John Gummer, Chairman of the Conservative Party and a prominent member of the Synod, took the bishops severely to task at the end of the year.

'Bishops', he said, 'can no more pontificate on economics than the Pope could correct Galileo on physics.' He attacked the archbishops, Anglican and Catholic, 'for their failure to get their facts right' about the Ethiopian famine. This, he said, was 'another of the continuing examples of bishops who have believed it is enough to get the sentiments right without bothering too much about the facts'.

Gummer was rebuked in his turn by Anglican and Catholic religious leaders. It must be remembered that this was during the coal-miners' strike and the unusual confrontation resulting. *The Church of England Year Book* refers to the view that has grown upon Conservatives over recent years of an unreliable and changing Church. The Church, however, had by this time come to see itself increasingly as the conscience of the nation.

The General Synod had been early in the field in February 1984 with a motion expressing concern about the British Nationality Act 1981. The bishops had opposed its passage through Parliament. Meanwhile, in Parliament, the Bishop of London and other urban bishops were in the thick of the fight against the bill that would pave the way for the abolition of the Greater London Council and the metropolitan authorities. They continued strenuous opposition until the bill was passed at the end of summer 1985.

Up and down the country during the summer and autumn of 1984 there were frequent references in bishops' sermons and addresses to the effects of unemployment and, as the year went on, to the miners' strike. As awareness mounted of the famine in Ethiopia, Church leaders demanded more aid to that country. At the November Synod it was strongly asserted that the government's policies and performance must be set in the larger context of human values. The Bishop of Durham, in his maiden speech to the Synod, gave an example of grinding poverty from his diocese that caught every headline.

The most significant set piece of the February 1985 sessions of the General Synod was that on the nature of Christian belief. It was given immense topicality by the remarks of the Bishop of Durham about the Virgin Birth of Jesus and aspects of the Resurrection story. He himself sat and listened, but did not speak. The Bishop was sharply attacked, but his right to express his opinion was strongly defended. In the end, the Synod invited the House of Bishops to reflect upon the debate and report back. Debates on embryo

8

research, following the publication of the Warnock Report, on the marriage of divorced people, and on Cruise missiles were impressive, if inconclusive.

I began work on this book in summer 1985. As regards the Church of England there seemed to be a kind of lull, with some expectation of a coming storm. There was much talk of a crisis. The elections to the Synod for the next five years were taking place shortly in October of that year. The number-one issue appeared to be the ordination of women. Prominent Anglo-Catholics and evangelists were coming together from opposite ends of the spectrum to organize resistance. The Bishop of Chichester, Chairman of the Anglo-Catholic Church Union, had expressed alarm at the number of defections to Rome. It was surmised that there would be many more if the ordination of women was confirmed.

There was no doubt about the alarm in the air. It extended, though in a less organized form, to many in all sections of the Church to whom the radical ideas of the Bishop of Durham were destructive of what they held most dear. There was a second call to resistance here. The third main issue to be settled during the next period was whether 'ARCIC' could be accepted. I am referring to the final report of the Anglican–Roman Catholic International Commission, which had been exploring possibilities of Christian union from 1968 onwards.

As regards relations with the government, there had been some relaxation of tension. The miners' strike had been settled. While unemployment remained at its present horrifying level and while confrontation appeared to be part of the government's philosophy, the Churches, Anglican and Catholic, were likely to be suspicious and critical.

Hopes were high at one time in the Church of England that there would be a resolution of the long-standing argument about the remarriage of divorced people. At present, however, there is deadlock. There is a free-for-all in the parishes in the sense that each clergyman can decide for himself whether to permit divorced people to remarry in his church. As regards the ordination of women referred to above, there has been movement – what I would call progress. Majorities for the ordination of women have now been obtained in the House of Bishops, the House of Clergy, and the

House of Laity. The legislation being prepared for the ordination of women requires a two-thirds majority in each house. At the moment this is forthcoming in the House of Bishops (41–6), but not in the other two houses.

*   *   *

Taking the post-war years as a whole and speaking as one who lapsed from the Church of England in 1940, I am far more aware of its influence in all parts of national life than I was in my Anglican days, although the decline in church attendance and a loosening of sexual morals might point to an opposite conclusion. The Church of England today acts in concert with the other Churches, in a fashion inconceivable thirty years ago. The development of the ecumenical movement has provided the great hope of these years.

No less a person, however, than the present Lord Chancellor, Lord Hailsham, has expressed himself in terms of vehement criticism in an interview that appeared in the *Sunday Times* on 25 August 1985. He was asked by his interviewer, John Mortimer, 'Don't you think the bishops are entitled to speak out if they think the government is behaving immorally?'

He replied:

> They totally misunderstand their role. The Church was told to be the leaven in the lump, the salt in the dish. It was not meant to make all people think in the same way. Don't they understand that the Holy Spirit directs some people to be Socialists and some to be Conservatives? The bishops treat everyone like patient peasants, waiting to be told which way to vote.

Lord Hailsham's brilliant mind and devout Christianity are recognized on all sides. Where the bishops are concerned, however, he seems to suffer from a strange obsession. He reveals himself, to use a phrase of John Mortimer's, as a 'moderately outrageous schoolboy'. He tells us that he is intensely bored on the Woolsack. 'I amuse myself by saying bollocks, *sotto voce*, to the bishops.'

There would, I think, be few members of the House of Lords to share Lord Hailsham's view that the bishops have thrown their weight about in that place too much. My own complaint would be that they have, if anything, asserted themselves insufficiently,

10

though in the last few years this is being corrected. There is a widespread view that there has been a real lack of leadership from the bishops. Dr Runcie has recently shown himself well aware of this criticism and (see page 20) is anxious to counter it. It remains to be seen how far episcopacy can be effectively combined with synodical judgement.

I agree with the view that the bishops today depend far more than they used to on their personal qualities, rather than on their splendid inheritance. Until 1954, for example, the Bishops of Bath and Wells occupied their historic palace. The present Bishop lives in a small part of it, his wife doing most of the housework. But the palace is used far more than ever it was by the whole community for exhibitions, conferences, and so on, and is visited from far and wide. Lambeth Palace provides a special case. Most of the palaces are used for public purposes. The standard of life of the typical bishop resembles that of the average professional man. (But see page 195.)

After 1542 no changes were made in the diocesan structure of the Church of England until the creation of the See of Ripon in 1836. Since then there has been a rapid expansion. There are now forty-four dioceses, and in addition to the diocesan bishops there are sixty-four suffragan bishops, and seven full-time stipendiary assistant bishops. The population and areas vary widely, and so inevitably do the structures. The diocese of London, with a population of nearly 4 million concentrated within 282 square miles, has been divided into five territorial areas. The rural diocese of Norwich has a population of only 635,000, but an area of 1,800 square miles. There are two suffragan bishoprics. There is controversy from time to time about the right size of a diocese and whether every diocese ought to be so small that there is just one bishop.

A few inadequate words must be said about the wider Anglican communion. The Anglican communion, we are told in *The Church of England Year Book*,

is a world-wide family of churches and dioceses which:

(1) trace their origins to the post-Reformation expansion of the Church of England in association with the other episcopalian or Anglican Churches of the British Isles;

(2) are in communion with the See of Canterbury and freely recognize the Archbishop of Canterbury as the principal Archbishop and the focus of unity within the communion;

(3) uphold and propagate the Catholic and apostolic faith based on the scriptures interpreted in the light of Christian tradition, scholarship and reason.

There are something like 500 Anglican bishops today and approximately thirty member Churches or Provinces, including the Church of Ireland and the Scottish Episcopal Church. They exist in all continents, very much including the Third World. The number of members in terms of those who describe themselves as Anglicans is about 70 million.

As regards episcopacy in the Church of England, the classic statement is to be found in the report of the Archbishops' Commission on Christian Doctrine (1938). The argument for episcopacy is there said to derive its strength from the convergence of many different considerations. Five were summarized as outstanding: (1) the episcopate symbolizes and ensures in an abiding form the apostolic mission and authority within the Church; (2) it has remained a function of the episcopacy to guard the Church against erroneous teaching; (3) the bishop represents the whole Church in and to his diocese and his diocese in and to the councils of the Church; he is thus a living representative of the unity and the universality of the Church; (4) the idea of pastoral care is inherent in his office; (5) he is the appropriate agent for carrying on through ordination the authority of the apostolic mission of the Church. These arguments for episcopacy provide a reasonable account of how the bishops today see their function.

Bishop Moorman, in his essay on 'The Anglican Bishop' (*Bishops, But What Kind?*, by Peter Moore), describes at some length the questions put to a bishop at his consecration. Great emphasis is laid upon a bishop as a teacher and expounder of God's word. After the first question, which asks him if he is sure of his vocation, the next three questions deal with the scriptures and his responsibility to 'instruct the people committed to his charge', to 'teach and exhort with wholesome doctrine', and to 'drive away all erroneous and strange doctrine contrary to God's word'.

But what is 'wholesome doctrine' in the Anglican Church? The Doctrine Commission of the Church of England (1981) devoted fifty-one pages to the question 'Where shall doctrine be found?' I will quote only two passages here. There is a reference to a sort of pyramid with the Bible at the top, then the Creeds, then the (Thirty-nine) Articles, with the rest in a less definite order underneath – 'the rest' including reports approved by Synod, and official pronouncements by bishops. It is thus characteristic of Anglicanism that it regards declared doctrine not in isolation, as it were in a test-tube under laboratory conditions, but rather as an essential part of a wider whole – namely, the worshipping, teaching, and witnessing ('confessing') life of the Church.

It would be impertinent of me to pronounce on the exact status of the Thirty-nine Articles in the Church of England today. They were mentioned to me in passing if at all and as providing no more than general guidance. The Bishop of Aberdeen, in a letter to *The Times* of 5 October 1985, wrote: 'Unlike the creeds and the great councils, the Thirty-nine Articles do not reflect the faith other than in a narrow part of Christendom and at a certain time.' I would suppose that most of the bishops would sympathize with that point of view.

The late Austin Farrer (1904–1968) was perhaps the most admired Anglican philosophical theologian of recent years. One sentence of his makes the whole matter as plain as any one sentence can: 'We are Anglicans not because of the psalms, or the poetry of George Herbert, or the cathedral, but because we can obey God here.'

How are the bishops appointed? In 1974 the then Archbishop of Canterbury and Sir Norman Anderson, the Chairman of the House of Laity, had discussions with the Prime Minister and the parliamentary leaders. Since 1977 there has been a committee called the Crown Appointments Commission, consisting of twelve members. These are the two archbishops, three members elected from the clergy of the General Synod, three elected from the laity of the General Synod, plus four members appointed by the vacancy-in-see committee of the diocese where there is a vacancy. The committee puts forward two names to the Prime Minister, who retains the right to recommend the second name or to ask the committee for a further name or names.

The system has recently been reviewed and approved by the Synod. I have dwelt at some length on the circumstances in which the present Bishop of London was appointed (see page 40). As far as I am concerned, the system was beyond criticism in that case. So long as the Church of England is the established Church of the country (and I am in no way suggesting a change), it seems ineluctable that a minimal degree of choice should be left to the Prime Minister of the day.

One cannot ignore the main divisions (some would call them parties) in the Church of England. Traditionally there are the Anglo-Catholics at one end of the spectrum (high church) and the evangelicals (low church) at the other. There remains a large central block, many of whom, though by no means all, could be called 'liberals'.

Of the bishops I have interviewed, the Bishop of London and the Bishop of Chichester are clearly Anglo-Catholic. The central Anglo-Catholic body is the Church Union. Archbishop Runcie resigned from the Church Union on becoming Archbishop of Canterbury. Dr Ramsey, a former archbishop, rejoined at the same time. Maurice Wood, the retiring Bishop of Norwich, and the Bishop of Bradford are recognized evangelicals. Bishop Montefiore and, in a different sense, the Bishop of Durham are often described as liberals. The others, I think, would not accept a label.

The elections for the Synod alike of the clergy and the laity are, to a considerable extent, fought on 'party' lines. An officer of the Church Union reckons that some 40 per cent of the clergy are Anglo-Catholic, 30 per cent evangelical, the rest somewhere in between. The laity, who are elected indirectly through the diocesan synod (the clergy are elected directly) are said to divide in the same kind of proportions. The estimates, however, are very rough and there is much overlapping and cross-voting. To take only one example: the ordination of women has received a majority, though not the two-thirds majority required for action, both in the House of Clergy and in that of the Laity. This, in spite of the fact that the Anglo-Catholics are strongly opposed and the evangelicals are split on the issue.

The Church Union was founded in 1859, an outcome of the Oxford Movement, even though by that time John Henry Newman had long since seceded from the Church of England. Members long for organic unity with the Church of Rome and, if possible, with the Eastern Church also. They believe that the Church of England with its episcopacy and its descent from the Apostles is truly part of the universal Church. They lay great stress on the Scriptures and on tradition. So do the evangelicals, but to a much greater extent than the Anglo-Catholics; they give priority to Scripture. The Anglo-Catholics agree with the evangelicals (and other Anglicans) that the Church of England is Catholic *and* Protestant, but with the Anglo-Catholics the first emphasis is on the Catholic, with the evangelicals it is on the Protestant aspect.

The Anglo-Catholics agree that at the time of the Reformation the Church was badly in need of reform. When they talk of the Church of England as reformed today, they look backward and forward: backward to its first beginnings, where its true nature can still be found; forward in the sense that they agree with the Roman Church that the idea of development under the guidance of the Holy Spirit is integral to Christianity. In such development it is for the bishops to give the lead, but not for the bishops in any one country acting alone. If all goes well, the bishops will be assisted by the *consensus fidelium*, the consent of the faithful throughout the world.

The distinctions indicated between the various groups or parties of the Church of England are by no means drawn as sharply by all my authorities. A distinguished leader of the laity, Sir Norman Anderson, is always referred to as an evangelical. He is happy to accept the title, but he considers that the real dividing line in the Church of England today is between those who accept traditional theology, as he does, and those who propound radical theories, such as the Bishop of Durham. Whatever the latter might have said when he was a professor, his remarks as a bishop or a bishop-to-be were equally unacceptable to many orthodox Christians, whether Anglo-Catholic or evangelical.

Sir Norman, an eminent lawyer, was happy to know that Archbishop Runcie hoped to give a firmer and clearer lead on doctrinal matters when the new document on doctrine under discussion by the bishops was published in 1986. At the moment, as a committed evangelical, he finds himself more in sympathy with traditional Anglo-Catholics than with clergy or bishops who are ready to be described as liberal.

15

In regard to women priests, Anderson is still open-minded. He has no *personal* objection to feminine leadership. 'I have had splendid colleagues whom I greatly respect. Nor do I doubt that God has called women to roles of leadership – even in Old Testament days.' He is ready to believe that the ordination of women will come about one day. I asked him crudely whether he would vote for or against the ordination of women if he were still a member of the Synod. He replied frankly, 'I don't know.' There are two New Testament texts (1 Tim. II: 12 and 1 Cor. XI: 3) that make him hesitate about whether it is God's normal plan to call women to posts of sole responsibility. The headship of man is there indicated plainly enough. 'I still do not know', he concluded, 'how far these verses (which seem perhaps to point to something more than cultural difference of age and social habits) apply to regular practice in the Church today.'

Somehow I don't think that if he were one of the leaders of the Synod he would, in 1986, really vote against the ordination of women. He is far too intelligent, high-minded, and realistic to take that line in the event. But he brought home to me how much St Paul means to the evangelical (far more than he does to me, incidentally). If we are talking about tradition we cannot neglect the significance of St Paul.

⌁ 1 ⌁

Robert Runcie,
Archbishop of Canterbury

'Robert Runcie', writes Margaret Duggan in her invaluable biography, 'is a very remarkable man and is well on the way to becoming a great archbishop.'

I fully concur. He is pre-eminently a *leader*. Not only because of his exceptional energy (which rivals that of his old Oxford contemporary, Margaret Thatcher); not only because of his fine analytical brain (he got a first in Greats). He has a special quality, indefinable though it is, which was exhibited by Churchill and Montgomery in wartime and by Attlee, very differently, during twenty years of leadership of the Labour Party.

I had met Robert Runcie on a number of occasions in the House of Lords. On 30 July 1985 he gave me lunch alone: a large, ruddy-faced man, athletic-looking in spite of his big horn-rimmed glasses. There was plenty of wine and more food than I could manage. Before lunch I had the pleasure of meeting Mrs Runcie. Mrs Runcie, not perhaps the orthodox idea of an archbishop's wife, won me over completely. She is a music perfectionist, teaching music, practising several hours a day, and passionately concerned to win the good approval of her own music guru. She is as dedicated to music as the Archbishop is to religion. A very happy partnership.

In a revealing interview published in the *Sunday Telegraph* of 12 December 1984, Graham Turner quotes the Archbishop as saying that from time to time he had to 'make pronouncements on political topics and he didn't really enjoy that. . . . It was a matter of temperament. He was not by nature a political animal. He had

17

never been involved in the school debating society or the Union at Oxford.'

His youthful involvement in politics seems, however, to have been rather more colourful than this suggests. His parents, we are told, had always been unwavering Conservatives. But at his school, Merchant Taylors', his classics master was a Communist. These were the Depression years. Robert seems to have been much influenced by this master. When he went to Oxford (autumn 1941) 'he still pursued his left-wing politics' (Margaret Duggan):

> The Labour Club at Oxford had been split, and the larger number of members had followed Anthony Crosland and Roy Jenkins into the Democratic Socialist Club, leaving a rump of an extreme Socialist Labour Club, which Robert joined. He also went occasionally to Communist Party meetings even though, since the Russian invasion of Finland, the Communists had been in embarrassed disarray.

Like innumerable undergraduates before and since, he was still sorting himself out. His church life, we are told, was 'rich and varied', which cannot have been true of many visitors to Communist Party meetings. And when the time came for him to be called up, he accepted with alacrity a commission in the Scots Guards. Three-quarters of his fellow recruits were Etonians. He had a bad time at first, but later, with the help of a brilliant gift of mimicry, he became popular. He does not seem to have objected to the 'deliberate inculcation of a consciousness of upper-class tradition'.

Under the command of Major (now Lord) Whitelaw, his performance in battle was altogether praiseworthy. He volunteered for paratroop service in the Far East, but the war came to an end too soon. He must be deemed to have enjoyed the life of a fighting man. He left behind many friendships, but absolutely no inkling that he had ever contemplated taking orders.

When he returned to Oxford he had, according to Margaret Duggan, matured in various ways. He had undoubtedly come under the influence of the friends he had been living with and fighting with. Most of them were traditionally Conservative, as his parents had

been. He was now convinced of the overriding importance of intellectual and cultural freedom.

He became college secretary of the Conservative Association – at a
time when young men like Anthony Crosland, Roy Jenkins, and
Denis Healey were inspired by the ideals of the Attlee government.
But Runcie was apparently not thought of as sufficiently dedicated
to the cause of the Conservative Party, a view that was shared by the
ex-president, Margaret Roberts, now Margaret Thatcher. Whatever
excited Conservatives may say, Dr Runcie, as he said in an interview
in the *Guardian* of 25 March 1985, sees the Church in 'critical
solidarity' with government, supporting politicians in their complicated management of power. 'That's not to think the Church can
provide a sacred coping to over-arch the social policies of the
government. I think we've had to probe some of the wounds of our
society at the present time and particularly those which seem to
harm whole groups of people.'

Before long he was dropped from the Conservative Association for
being too frivolous and not sufficiently single-minded in his allegiance.
From then on he seems to have washed his political slate clean and to
have been free of political leanings to allegiances.

During the miners' strike (1984–5) he pursued a middle way that
caused more annoyance to the government than to the left-wing
parties. More recently, in a speech about the inner cities, he has
caused considerable offence in Conservative quarters by calling
attention to many features of life in such places. One must bear in
mind that at present there is something of a moral vacuum on the
left-wing side in politics, which may or may not endure. In the meanwhile it has fallen to the established Church and the Archbishop
of Canterbury in particular to give effect to the conscience of the
nation.

Robert Runcie has thought hard about the peculiar requirements
of leading the Anglican Church. A few sentences may be quoted
from the interview, already referred to, with Graham Turner of the
Sunday Telegraph: 'Once you were set on high at Lambeth you were
isolated – yet somehow you had to represent the people from whom
you were cut off. . . . You were expected to be the voice of the
conscience of today on abortion and unemployment, but there
were so many views that it was all too easy to become an anodyne

spokesman.' When he was required to make an announcement, it had to be a subtle blend of loyalty to the institution and a readiness to lead it forward.

In the seven years since his enthronement, he has exhibited consistently leadership of a high order. On two occasions at least he has attained greatness. The visit of the Pope to England in 1982 was a triumph for Christians everywhere. The visit to Canterbury and the joint service were supremely an Anglican triumph. Robert Runcie displayed throughout a delicacy of feeling that may not up to that point have been associated with him in the public mind. For the insistence on making the service at the end of the Falklands war one of reconciliation rather than triumph, the main credit must also go to Robert Runcie. His support for the war and his own war record, which included the Military Cross, may have made his task somewhat easier. Be that as it may, these two displays of true Christian feeling – the Pope's visit and the Falklands service – gave the Church of England a significance that I do not think it has possessed since the death of Archbishop Temple.

In his closing speech to the Synod of 5 July 1985, he enunciated the need for a clearer and firmer leadership on the part of the bishops:

> I believe the General Synod and the House of Bishops have their mutual and distinctive parts to play. It is understandable that in the first fifteen years of synodical government the bishops have been reluctant to do anything which would have set them too far apart from priests and laity. Episcopal low profile as a House, if not as individuals, has been the order of the day. But ordination to the episcopate bestows a special responsibility as a teacher and guardian of the faith, both individual and collegial. Synod will know that the House of Bishops is now reflecting corporately on the matter of Christian belief with this in mind.

He elaborated the theme in talking to me; he saw the bishops as providing the leadership of the Church of England, and the Synod providing the government. I asked him whether there was an analogy here between the Cabinet and Parliament. He thought there was a loose analogy, but the bishops met only from four to six times a year, and the Synod only two or three times. He hoped that on doctrinal matters the bishops in 1986 would emerge with some clearer guide-lines. These would take the form of saying what kind of statement was or was not permissible within the Anglican framework, rather than of asserting any particular doctrine of the Virgin Birth or Incarnation or Resurrection. He hoped, however, that in practice this would preserve statements of the latter character within the traditional framework.

What lead, if any, has he given to doctrine? He told Graham Turner that his hackles were raised when people suggested that the Church of England 'did not believe anything'. He himself had no doubts about the Resurrection or the Virgin Birth. He spelt this out more fully in a much admired address to the Synod on 13 February 1985. The opening passages must be given in full:

To be a Christian is to worship and obey Jesus as Lord. Our historic conviction is that, in Christ, the Creator himself brought to our ravaged humanity a way of healing and salvation. We believe that Jesus Christ is a model to all humanity in his faithfulness to his calling and in embodying the very love of God.

Equally we believe that he is more than we are. We see not only humanity as God intended it to be, but the very presence of God in one who uniquely revealed the Father, and mediates to us His love and grace, the forgiveness of our sins, the recreation of our true humanity and eternal life.

What we say about birth, life, death, and resurrection of our Lord finds its grounds in the witness of the apostles and in the experience of all the people of God. But *our* resurrection depends upon his. To speak of the risen Lord is to speak of something that happened to Jesus Christ, not merely of something that happened to his disciples.

The above expands a short earlier statement that the doctrines of the Incarnation and Resurrection are not in doubt among the bishops.

Where does this leave Dr Runcie in regard to the Bishop of Durham, who in the popular mind has cast considerable doubt about the Virgin Birth, about the Resurrection, and, by an association of ideas, about the Incarnation? In the speech quoted from, Archbishop Runcie stressed the double role of bishops as *guardians* of tradition and also as *interpreters* of tradition. The latter role seems to leave a good deal of scope for pioneers.

The new Chairman of the Doctrine Commission, the Bishop of Salisbury, has spoken rather more clearly on the same problem. He has suggested that it is the business of the Church to define the limits of belief. Any bishop who passes outside those limits, e.g. by implication Durham, should make it clear that he is speaking for himself and not for the Church.

The same speech of Archbishop Runcie goes on:

A Church needs authority. It cannot do without authority. But if it became as tidy as the High Courts of Justice we should suspect it. The Church is not like a schoolteacher who must expel a boy from school lest he influence the others to wickedness. It is not like a king who must expel a troublesome subject. It is more like a mother with children, holding a lively family together. A Church cannot do without authority, but it ought to be gentle, tranquil, long-suffering, and therefore sometimes untidy. All ministerial authority is subject to the word of God and the Spirit who blows where it will.

I asked what the Bishop of Durham would do if he found himself unduly restricted. He shrugged his shoulders and remarked smiling-ly that the Bishop could always resign. The Archbishop obviously thought that he could be 'contained' without this crisis arising. He did not look upon himself as 'the servant of the Synod' but as one who was bound to pay much attention to its conclusions. The old tank commander is well aware that the heroic discipline of the Guards must be adapted to Anglican requirements, but the Bishop of Durham seems to be providing, whether consciously or not, the kind of test that every leader dreads, where his authority in the public mind appears to be under challenge. Dr Runcie has spoken up till now about the Bishop of Durham with a kind of humorous resignation. One cannot help detecting an underlying exasperation.

What of his spiritual and moral message? I have by now read many of his addresses, in and out of church, with admiration and envy. I could not have improved on any of them. They are always extraordinarily appropriate to the particular occasion. They do not, however, leave a very distinctive impression on my mind (I except such great efforts as those at the time of the Pope's visit and after the Falklands). The reason is not far to seek. Welsby tells us that Dr Runcie has taken steps to avoid some of the 'treadmill' by the establishment of an able and realistic secretariat at Lambeth and by the delegation of many of his diocesan responsibilities to his suffragans. Some price has had to be paid for the increased efficiency.

It seems that the first drafts of his speeches are usually prepared by others. Of course, he improves them a lot before he delivers them. But his practice here, one gathers, is far different from that of his predecessor, Archbishop Coggan, who felt that every utterance was a personal testimony. And one could think of earlier archbishops. Robert Runcie's practice is no doubt prevalent among political ministers. One could hardly imagine one man speaking on so many subjects without a great deal of help. But it leaves the student of his character a little uncertain as to what can be said to be his personal message. I imagine that he would not object to that comment. He is not in business to glorify Robert Runcie. In a personal letter, after his newspaper interview with Graham Turner, Dr Runcie added a postscript in his own hand: 'Spare a prayer for me, that I may speak with simplicity and wisdom at Christmas.' He is concerned with Jesus Christ and not with leaving a reputation for personal distinction.

On nuclear weapons he has taken a line that I happen to agree with and can admire all the more easily. He favours, as I do, multilateral, not unilateral disarmament. His personal tribute to the foreign policy of Lord Carrington during a crucial debate was rather more controversial. But two sentences from his speech should be taken together:

I speak as someone who has recently found himself at odds with the government in another place on the Nationality Bill and on a cluster of questions surrounding the Brandt Report, which seems in danger of promoting insular policies. But I believe at the moment we should welcome and support the statesmanlike way in which the Foreign Secretary wins respect as a genuine seeker for peace and international justice within the present political realities.

23

I have no doubt that he was speaking there for the vast majority, not only of the bishops but of the British people.

On the remarriage in church of divorced people, he seems to hold liberal views without as yet having found a way to bring about their success. On the subject of women priests, his position seems to be mobile. In his *History of the Church of England, 1945–1980*, Paul Welsby writes: 'Unlike his two predecessors, Dr Runcie has consistently opposed women's ordination, because he believes the arguments on both sides to be evenly balanced and because he does not regard the issue as being sufficiently high on the Anglican agenda.'

Dr Runcie's favourable foreword to Paul Welsby's book is dated 1983; but he had progressed considerably by the time he was interviewed by Michael Brown in January 1985. He said:

My own position is one of gradualism – if this thing is of God, it will prosper and develop. . . . Therefore I am inclined to think that if we move forward gradually – and we maintain our strong relations and dialogue with the Roman Catholic and Orthodox Churches – this may be an obstacle to immediate schemes of mutual recognition of ministries and sacraments, but in the long term may be more honest ecumenism.

This dialogue followed:

Q. 'How gradually would you like to see the Church of England move?'
A. 'Well I, of course, would like to see us have women deacons and women lawfully ordained abroad being able to operate in this country under the licence of the bishop in certain circumstances.'
Q. 'How?'
A. 'Now; immediate; as soon as possible; because I don't think that would create difficulties.'
Q. 'And the priesthood?'
A. 'And the priesthood after we had experienced that for a few years.'

24

Surely Margaret Duggan was right when she said: 'Judging from what he has recently said about all the best arguments about the ordination of women being in favour of women priests, it will be surprising if he ever votes against them.'

Dr Runcie considered that the Reformation had conferred a much wider role on the laity through their access to the Scriptures and the Book of Common Prayer. In this sense synodical government was thoroughly in keeping with the reformed position of the Church. I did not tell him that the Bishop of Bath and Wells had traced the part of the laity back to the first years of the Church.

The Archbishop, a man of powerful intellect, was obviously not dismayed by the intellectual balancing act that devolved on any leader of the Church of England. 'We recognize', he said, 'the Bible, the tradition of the Church, but also human reason (going back to Hooker).' And today, given the unique privileges of the Church of England, it must reflect in some measure the mainstream of the life of the country. He drew a distinction, admittedly over-simplified, between the way in which Roman Catholics and Anglicans approached new developments in the behavioural sciences. Catholics started with their tradition and asked how the behavioural sciences could be adapted to it. Anglicans started with the new developments and asked how their religious position could be fitted in.

Should Dr Runcie be described as ambitious? I have discussed this kind of point at some length in my book about the last eleven Prime Ministers. Robert Runcie has always been conscious of great powers and has felt a strong urge to seek the opportunity to develop them fully. But he declined the bishopric of Oxford, which was presumably a promotion, and the archbishopric of York, which was certainly one. When he was offered Canterbury, he seems to have found the responsibility and the exposure terrifying. His wife was aghast. She could see the move completely wrecking what family life they had left to them. I have no doubt that he accepted the colossal appointment out of a sense of duty.

Welsby describes him in 1983 as a committed ecumenist, evidenced by his diplomatic chairmanship of the Anglican–Orthodox Joint Doctrinal Commission. His long-term dedication to a closer relationship with the Roman Church bore fruit in the immense event of the Pope's visit. He has played a notable part on the world stage in securing the release of hostages in Iran and Libya. He has travelled thousands of miles to visit provinces of the Anglican communion and has shown himself alive in the fullest sense to the world responsibilities of his position. On the national stage he has laid stress time and time again on the special Christian duty towards the poor; witness his Commission on Urban Priority Areas (authors of the *Faith in the City* report). He has given the idea much wider reference in his approach to the Third World.

We talked in a general way about progress towards Christian unity. He is a strong supporter of ARCIC and delighted that the Catholic bishops in England have commented on its report favourably. He agreed with me that for the moment the most encouraging progress would take place at local level. The question of Anglican Orders would be a real obstacle until disposed of. The ordination of women in the Church of England would increase the difficulty in the short run. He himself had never met a Roman Catholic theologian who found a fundamental theological objection to the ordination of women. But tradition there was heavily against it. Hence his own objection for a long time to such a development in the Church of England. He was now favourable, in this matter a gradualist.

Dr Runcie agreed with me that it was wrong to talk of any kind of crisis in the Church of England. Admittedly, in his speech to the Synod, he had picked out four issues that he had called divisive questions of passionate importance. First, how ought the Church of England to deal both in charity and in faithfulness to Scripture and tradition with Christians who wish to remarry when a former spouse is still living? Secondly, can women be admitted to the presbyteries of the Church of England without our claiming an authority within the Catholic Church that we do not possess? Thirdly, are there limits to new interpretations of the Creed? Fourthly, granted that life is sacred and that no Christian is at liberty to dispense with respect for humanity actual and potential, are we morally free, even with the highest of motives, to carry out even very limited experiments on embryonic human beings?

These issues were not likely to 'go away', but Dr Runcie agreed with my impression that they were not disturbing the man or woman in the pew. I got the feeling that it was the kind of issue raised by the Bishop of Durham that was liable to cause real anxiety, unless countered by firm statements by the bishops in the future.

The Archbishop is filled, obsessed one might say, with a sense of the international significance of the Anglican Church. Whatever the total number of Anglicans, and it was very large, what was still more impressive was the wide distribution throughout the world, except in Eastern Europe. He agreed with my surmise that the Anglican Church might have closer contact with the Russian Orthodox Church than had the Pope at the present time. I asked him whether it was rather a pity that it was still called the Anglican Church. He agreed, but saw no way of altering the title. In view of its international character he was all the more anxious to see the achievement of unity with the largest international Church, the Church of Rome.

I put down here a few far-from-final impressions. I knew in varying degrees the Archbishop's four predecessors: Archbishops Temple, Fisher, Ramsey, and Coggan. Robert Runcie seems to me, for good or for ill, less clerical than any of them. No one could have mistaken any of the four mentioned, if encountered in mufti, for anything but a clergyman. Is that, or is that not, a compliment? Is one saying that there is or ought to be an invisible barrier between the laity and the clergy? Whether that is so or not, it does not exist with Robert Runcie. He has, on the face of things, more in common with former Guards officers, also holders of the Military Cross, like Lord Whitelaw and Lord Carrington, than with one's idea of an archbishop, though other clergymen have received the Military Cross.

Dr Runcie is a great communicator alike on the personal and the national scale. No archbishop has enjoyed the same facilities in reaching the multitude. I cannot think of one who, given his facilities, would have equalled his performance. But those who regretted his participation in a chat show with Michael Parkinson are entitled to argue that some atmosphere of mystery is lost by the multiplication of popular appearances. Robert Runcie is the most open and approachable of men – exceptionally so for an archbishop. He is correspondingly vulnerable.

He is said to be conscious of not having a theological degree, though, of course, he received a training in theology. There again, there may be gains and losses. He speaks today as a brilliant man convinced of the truths of Christianity in the way that they are understood by the mass of the population. He speaks as a devoted family man whose own life is based on traditional Christian values. He speaks at all times from a kindly heart.

❀ 2 ❀

John Habgood,
Archbishop of York

John Habgood, aged 58, married to a musician, father of four children, was appointed Archbishop of York at the end of 1983. He is widely known as the scientist Archbishop. The facts of his career are of more than usual interest. His father was a country doctor, his mother came from a well-known family. He was educated at Eton where his housemaster met most of his fees. He went to King's College, Cambridge, from school in 1945.

John Whale, 'An Argumentative Unbeliever', *Sunday Times*

Dr Habgood tells the story of how he went to a party given by evangelicals and was well and truly 'hooked'. The evangelicals 'picked him up and fed him into their machine' (as he has put it), but he pressed on with his science. He got a double first and later, as a young don, taught pharmacology. From 1952 to 1955 he was a Fellow of King's College, Cambridge; from 1954 to 1956 Curate of St Mary Abbots, Kensington. So the great leap was made. From then on the appointments were orthodox: Vice-Principal of Westcot House, Cambridge; Rector of St John's Church, Jedburgh; Principal of Queen's College, Birmingham.

In 1975 he was appointed Bishop of Durham, on the recommendation of Edward Heath. Durham is one of the five top appointments in the Church of England. The transition from being Principal of Queen's College, Birmingham, was, in a quiet way, sensational. After ten years at Durham, his appointment as Archbishop of York when a vacancy occurred was predictable. It is supposed that he was

one of two names submitted to the Prime Minister when the See
of London fell vacant a little earlier, when the present Bishop of
London was appointed.

By this time, to use his own expression, he was 'far from the
position of the evangelicals'. But it was not possible to place him
in any particular category of bishops. When he was appointed to
York, he was much written about – by John Whale, for example, in
the *Sunday Times*, and by Clifford Longley in *The Times* (10 November
1983), to mention two of the outstanding contributors. I will quote
from Clifford Longley later. For the purposes of this book I have paid
special attention to the personal postscript of Dr Habgood's book
A Working Faith, which was published in 1980. He has been described
as having 'a mind like a razor' and 'a heart of gold'. But the postscript
referred to has nothing cold and nothing particularly scientific about
it. A few sentences can be quoted here:

> Religion is about the unsayable, and the recognition that there is
> the unsayable is often the first and most important element in
> faith.

> I am a Christian because Christian language, symbolism and
> practice help me to express this sense of mystery, this awareness
> of extra dimensions of reality in a way that gives content to it,
> without seeming to falsify it. This is a large claim. It rests on the
> assumption that human beings are in some primary sense aware of
> the transcendent.

> The root of my religious awareness is thus summed up for me in
> words like aspiration, hope, longing, vision. For me the constant
> grappling with insoluble problems, the wrestling with words and
> symbols to express what has only been glimpsed in odd moments
> is one of the most satisfying of creative activities. . . . Beside
> such wrestlings much also can seem unbearably superficial and
> complacent.

Dr Habgood has written cogently about many matters where
ethics and science overlap, as they do in the whole area of so-called
medical ethics. I will take as an example his discussion of what he

calls 'the prolongation of life in the deformed new-born'. On utilitarian grounds, for 'the greatest happiness of the greatest number', he appears to conclude that there are likely to be cases where happiness for all those concerned is diminished if the baby is allowed to live. He points out, however, another approach to ethics. He brings before us 'the assertion of overriding moral principles, the example, the sanctity of human life or more generally the principle of respect for human personality'. Even allowing for this principle, he still seems to favour the extinction of life *in some circumstances*, at least for the new-born. But as usual he qualifies what might begin to appear as a dogmatic statement. 'We recognize that the criteria change' and should be subject to 'constant scrutiny' in the light of medical advance and the ethical conflict referred to above.

I have quoted from this essay at some length because it illustrates his general conviction that there are many situations where there is a conflict of principle. If one word seems to provide a clue to his own decisions in such matters, it is the word 'balance'. It may not be an inspiring war-cry. It is certainly a clue that will appeal to most of us who have had any responsibility in public life.

Dr Habgood himself is not satisfied with the word 'balance'. In his view, he told me, the word 'paradox' gets nearer the mark. 'It seems to me important to hold on to apparently conflicting truths, which is a much more dynamic thing than simply trying to find a happy mean. Engineers distinguish between static equilibrium and dynamic equilibrium, and I would hope to aim for the latter.'

Clifford Longley, in the article referred to above, makes the obvious submission that Dr Habgood's approach to religion is in some sense scientific. To be more precise, he calls it 'a pragmatic and sociological approach to the Church'. But scientists in my experience do not equate the sociological method with their own. Clifford Longley again tells us that Dr Habgood's invariable starting-point is factual and that his method is to assemble the facts in tidy order. But this could be said of all reputable thinkers in the humanistic disciplines. It certainly does not seem to me of overriding value in the search for God.

Let me acknowledge two points at once: first, that in spheres where scientific knowledge is necessary, e.g. the treatment of embryos, Dr Habgood would be making use of first-hand experience; non-scientists would be relying on the evidence of others. Secondly, in discussions (e.g. about the level of church attendance and the influence of secular developments in morality) I can well imagine that a first-class scientist such as the Archbishop of York is an invaluable contributor. But there are a number of bishops with first-class non-scientific degrees, and I would not expect to find that there are notable differences between their methods of work in the theological field and those of the natural scientists.

Clifford Longley's profile referred to carried the heading 'The Plain Man's Guide to God'. I have no idea whether Clifford Longley himself approves that headline, but it would be remarkably misleading to describe the thinking of Dr Habgood as that of any kind of plain man. A plain man is just what he is not. His combination of science and theology has produced a highly original standpoint, not just in the abstract but on every question that arises.

When in November 1983 Dr Habgood was enthroned as Archbishop of York, he preached a sermon that led to an extraordinarily vehement debate in the correspondence column of *The Times*. The leading article in that paper was positively vitriolic. As usual one distorts his meaning by quoting a small part of his address, but the risk must be taken: 'An archbishop', he said, 'is important, not for what he is in himself, but for what he represents. And what he represents, among many other things, is the public face of the Christian Church.'

The Times's leader, entitled 'The Way of the Cross', took him to task severely. 'Society', said *The Times*, 'is to be Dr Habgood's foundation for our faith. . . . To elevate community religion above man's individual struggle to know and love himself and, through that self-awareness, to know and love his neighbour' was quite disastrous. The article talked as though religion in Dr Habgood's view was *only* public faith and outward form. But this is to misunderstand his meaning. Any serious Christian must seek to maintain and improve his own personal religious life, but nine serious Christians out of ten, ninety-nine perhaps out of a hundred, will recognize the value of communal worship.

The Archbishop shows an amazing concern for the many varieties of Christian:

Some lean on ritual; others centre their faith on an intense personal relationship. Some find their main Christian experience in an ecclesiastical context; others outside it. Some wrestle with intellectual problems; others are activists, busily pursuing good causes. Six-sided Christians manage to have something of everything, but even the most balanced of them look lopsided to those who build their cube in a different way.

The Archbishop dealt with the Virgin Birth explicitly in a diocesan leaflet of July 1984. I am not sure whether the man or woman in the pew will be much wiser when he or she has studied the following passage:

As Christians we believe that God has done a new thing in Jesus Christ, revealing himself in a human life, subject to the ordinary conditions of humanity. The historical reality of this new thing is attested by the New Testament and by two thousand years of Christian experience. The doctrine of the Virgin Birth is a powerful symbol of this truth, but is not the only means by which the truth can be expressed or safeguarded.

There is no doubt about his belief in the Incarnation and the Resurrection. 'The doctrine of the Incarnation and the Resurrection are not in doubt among the leadership of the Church.' But as usual he will not let us off with a simple statement. 'There is', he says, 'a liberty of interpretation about the precise way in which they are historically grounded.' How much liberty in interpretation is to be permitted? Would it be possible, for example, for a good Anglican, let alone a good bishop, to believe that the tomb was not empty? (I am aware that Bishop Jenkins never said that he believed this, but he had appeared to treat it as a possibility.)

No one is more scornful than Dr Habgood of any steps to give simple replies to religious questions. I will risk his displeasure therefore by trying to sum up his central purpose. He is above all, it seems to me, trying to help people to think on Christian lines, to live their lives accordingly and so make their way to God.

The Archbishop has been playing an important part in the World Council of Churches. He has been much concerned with the production of the Alternative Prayer Book. Looking through a voluminous collection of Press cuttings, I cannot find him quoted in regard to women priests. Generally he must be described as being 'middle of the road'. His particular form of mental process with the overriding concept of balance or paradox will usually land him there.

Most prominent people and probably all bishops are liable to be misunderstood. John Habgood has been misinterpreted as frequently as many others. The reasons for his conclusions have to be given in full to be appreciated at their proper worth. A distinguished lady told me, when I said that I was going to call on the Archbishop, that she did not like his ideas. At about the time that she lost her only son he spoke about prayer in a way that led to headlines such as I now quote: 'Don't rely on prayer' (*Sunday Express*) and 'Don't count on prayer' (*Sunday Telegraph*).

He commented on these: 'My remarks on prayer have of course been grossly distorted. They arose out of a complex philosophical discussion and should be understood in that context. I subsequently expressed them more simply in a diocesan leaflet.'

I venture to express them more simply still. The Archbishop, if I understand him aright, is saying that no honest prayer is ever wasted. God is free to act in his own fashion, but he will normally respect the laws of nature.

The Archbishop has tangled more than once with Mr Enoch Powell. At the time of the miners' strike he expressed the view that 'there were clear reasons for caution about pit closures'. They might do irreversible damage to whole communities. Powell took him to task in his usual dogmatic fashion, the militant if independent politician rather than the amateur theologian. When the Warnock Report was published and Enoch Powell produced his bill to ban research on embryos, taking his stand on absolute values, the Archbishop pointed to the great dangers of such simplistic thinking. It is a fairly safe prediction that, always within the framework of Christianity, he will say the unpredictable.

One of the most thoughtful chapters of his very thoughtful book *Church and Nation in a Secular Age* is the one devoted to 'Establishment'. Balancing the pros and cons, he produced one argument that had not occurred to me, which I find convincing:

Only the Church of England could have insisted on counter-balancing the nationalistic thrust of the Falklands celebrations, precisely because of the relationship to the nation. And the fact that it did so was a direct consequence of its developing relationship with the Anglican communion and other world Christian bodies. It may seem bizarre to value a national Church as one of the antidotes to nationalism, but this is because a Church which is true to itself can never *just* be the Church of the nation.

Throughout *Church and Nation* one is conscious of the operation of a brilliant idiosyncratic mind. Its flavour can be given by a quotation from his diocesan leaflet dated June 1985:

The other day I was being quizzed by a television interviewer about a possible programme on the theme 'What is a Christian?' I launched into a long description of the six dimensions of religion – doctrine, ritual, myth, ethics, social institutions and personal experience – and was just about to explain how they applied to Christianity, when he interrupted me. 'What our viewers really want to know is whether you have to believe in the Virgin Birth.' 'I wonder what Gregory of Nyassa would have said to that,' I replied rather desperately.

Saint Gregory was a great fourth-century theologian who saw clearly the danger of trying to distil religious truth into precise propositions and turn faith into mere intellectual assent.

My visit with Dr Habgood at Bishopthorpe Palace revived far-off memories. I stayed there during the war with William Temple, then Archbishop of York. Suffering painfully from gout and a little sad to learn that I had become a Roman Catholic, he showed me his habitual kindness and escorted me to the bus when I departed. John Habgood, taller than I had expected, and very courteous in his reserved way, drove me back to York after the interview.

He had seen the foregoing pages, some of them revised after correspondence. A leading lay theologian of evangelical repute had told me recently that the real division in the Church of England today was between those who maintained traditional theology and those who had adopted radical positions. Not to my surprise, the

Archbishop said at once: 'That's far too simple.' As mentioned above, he believes that simple propositions are seldom valid about religious fundamentals. He himself, like perhaps a majority of Anglicans, could not be accorded either label.

He was not happy with my reference to his views as idiosyncratic. 'I should prefer to call them independent. I do not regard myself as out on a limb.' I apologized if 'idiosyncratic' was an unpleasant word. I myself had got used to being called eccentric, which was much less attractive. What I had tried to say was that he was an original thinker and his views were not precisely like those of anyone else.

I pressed on him the suggestion that the Bishop of Durham was a radical. The Archbishop said that David Jenkins was considerably less radical than many current theologians. He himself had consecrated him and would not conceivably have done so if he had not considered that his views could be accommodated within the ambit of the Church of England. This did not mean that he agreed with all of them, still less with everything that Dr Jenkins had said in presenting them, least of all with the way they had been interpreted or misinterpreted in certain quarters.

I quoted a booklet entitled *Easter in Durham: Bishop Jenkins and the Resurrection of Jesus* by Murray J. Harris. It took Dr Jenkins carefully and severely to task. It had a preface by the Bishop of London. He was remarkably frank about his brother bishop:

> As Dr Harris makes clear in his excellent study, the ultimate point at issue is the authority of the Bible as a source of divine revelation and the touchstone of Christian doctrine, the bar at which all belief which claims to be Christian must be tested. To reduce the Resurrection to nothing more than an experience in the minds of the disciples is not only to challenge the authority of the Scriptures. It is also to challenge what they reveal about God.

The Archbishop told me emphatically that the Bishop of London had misunderstood Dr Jenkins. The latter did not consider that the Resurrection was merely a subjective experience in the minds of the Apostles. He did *not* question its historical objectivity. But, I persisted, the Bishop of Durham had given the impression that the

36

tomb might not have been empty. He did not apparently think so himself, but he seemed to leave it an open question, the answer to which did not affect the fact of the Resurrection. Surely that was to reject in blatant fashion the testimony of all four Gospels.

At this point the Archbishop passed slightly out of my comprehension. He seemed to be saying that the Gospel accounts might have been symbolically or theologically true, but yet might not have described actual happenings. He himself believed that the tomb was empty. He seemed to be saying, however, that it was open to a good Christian to believe the opposite. I asked the obvious question. Was it open to a bishop? He emphasized the Church of England position of according the utmost freedom to theological exploration and free-ranging scholarship.

I asked him where the official answer could be found to the often raised question, 'What *does* the Church of England believe?' He said that the Church of Rome was a teaching Church. It laid down official doctrine in encyclicals and so on. The Church of England was different. If one wished to identify its doctrines, one could find them best in the Prayer Book. I was aware that he himself had been much concerned with producing the Alternative Prayer Book. Later in our discussion he remarked that he saw himself primarily as a teacher but not one, I gathered, whose teaching was mandatory on the taught.

We passed on to his unique role as a scientist archbishop. Yes, I was quite right in thinking that whilst still a science student at Cambridge he had undergone a conversion experience. Since then for forty years he had found a special vocation in interpreting Christians to scientists and scientists to Christians. Forty years ago scientists were much more self-satisfied, much readier to believe that they had, or would soon have, all the answers, much less interested in any religious contribution. Today they were much more aware of the limitations of their own form of wisdom, more open-minded to the possibility that they could learn a great deal from religious believers.

He had read with keen interest and indeed reviewed Hugh Montefiore's book, *The Probability of God*. His own approach, however, was different. He did not set out to bring together an accumulation of loose ends. He sympathized instead with a formulation of Einstein: 'The eternal mystery of the world is its comprehensibility.' Yes, in

37

reply to my question, it could be called a modern form of the classical teleological proof of God's existence.

We talked about Christian unity, much of course to be desired, and ARCIC, which he thought had made a very valuable contribution. The Catholic bishops had responded well, but so had the Church of England Synod. I said that Archbishop Runcie had told me that Anglican Orders would have to be recognized before there was major progress. He agreed, but thought that this was gradually coming about, as could be seen at the time of the Pope's visit. No one supposed that at Canterbury the Pope thought that he was praying alongside a layman. The Archbishop did not expect Rome to issue an official recantation. There would be a steady *de facto* recognition.

A more serious obstacle, he thought, was the centralizing tendency of the Church of Rome as compared with the decentralization of authority in the Church of England. Both tendencies could be carried to extreme. It would not be easy to bring them into harmony.

Towards the end of our talk I turned to social questions, for example the hideous unemployment in large parts of his diocese. I knew from my talk with the Catholic Bishop of Middlesbrough that he and the Archbishop had collaborated intensively in an attempt to mitigate the worst effects. They had joined in approaches to the relevant minister, Lord Young, for example. Dr Habgood acknowledged the fact of their joint effort, but he is not one to parade his exertions. When I asked him whether he had denounced government policies that, in my view at least, bore a heavy responsibility for the unemployment, he said: 'Denunciation is not my style; I try to do something constructive.' He believed that Mrs Thatcher is perfectly sincere in her feeling for the unemployed, but she failed to put that across to the nation. He himself had a pessimistic view of the long-term effect of the new technology on employment and unemployment.

I came away with the impression of a most unusual man delighting in the exercise of a highly rational mind, but inspired deep down by an unforgettable Christian encounter.

ᴄ 3 ᴄ

Graham Douglas Leonard,
Bishop of London

Those of us who have spent many years in politics are inclined to judge bishops, if we do not know them personally, according to political criteria. The crude test is applied: are they right wing or left wing? Are they favourable or unfavourable to Thatcherism? What have they been saying or doing about the unemployed? Have they spoken out about race relations?

In 1985 the Bishop of Durham hit the headlines not only on some of the issues mentioned, but on others strictly doctrinal. We are now asking about our bishops: Where do they stand on the Virgin Birth and the Resurrection? Are they radical or conservative on theology? This last distinction is by no means identical with another more familar division between Anglo-Catholics, evangelicals, and others.

The present Bishop of London is usually described as a Conservative, though he has always been at pains to insist that there is no reason why a good Christian should belong to any particular party. One thing is quite certain – he has not adopted any of his positions in pure or applied theology because they fitted in with those of some particular group. He is known to believe that one of the most urgent needs of the Church today is to recover the dimensions of eternity. This certainly does not mean ignoring this world or escaping from it. The eternal dimension should give freedom and the real reason for operating in the world we live in. He is the most coherent of thinkers; his starting-point is an unequivocal and orthodox Christianity.

Dr Leonard has received exceptional publicity on at least three occasions. At an earlier moment he came into the news with a sharp criticism of Princess Margaret's friends and, so it seems, of some aspects of her personal style of life. The storm blew over, leaving an impression that he had blotted his copy book in royal circles. Much more prolonged was the discussion, controversy indeed, that accompanied his selection as Bishop of London in 1980. He had previously served as Suffragan Bishop of Willesden (1964) and Bishop of Truro (1973). It was widely said that the relevant commission had not put forward his name to the Prime Minister as the first of the two submitted. This was not in fact correct. The two names are sent forward on a parity unless there is a two-to-one majority for one candidate, which was not the case on this occasion. The impression remains that a majority of the commission favoured the alternative, Dr Habgood. Mrs Thatcher, backed it seems by Michael Foot, then Leader of the Opposition, insisted that Dr Leonard should be appointed. Constitutionally she is entitled to prevail as she did. It is rumoured that she would have liked him to be appointed at an earlier moment Archbishop of Canterbury.

It should be mentioned that the clergy of his diocese (London) who knew him from his days at Willesden were strongly in favour of Dr Leonard. In that sense he was the choice of the grass roots but arguably not of the Church of England. What animated Mrs Thatcher in this strong personal preference? She herself was brought up in a devout Methodist household, attending church or Sunday school four times a day on Sundays, though now she is a regular worshipper in the Church of England. Dr Leonard is High Church by any standard. It may be that something old-fashioned about his theology appealed to her. It may be that she assumed that he would be sensible, i.e. Conservative on political and social issues. She would probably have found it impossible among the leading bishops to discover a true Thatcherite.

On one all-important issue, however, Dr Leonard has shown himself a doughty champion of her standpoint. He has spoken out more clearly than any other bishop about the Soviet menace. In the tense, highly edifying debate in the Synod in February 1983, he proposed the main motion rejecting unilateral in favour of multi-lateral nuclear disarmament:

We must not blind ourselves to the fact that Leninist control means the repudiation of natural as well as Christian morality. It means that the State, not God, determines what is right and wrong. I think the main reason why the working party [see below] does not give us the guidance we need is because it elevates its opinion that the possession and use of nuclear weapons is morally wrong to such a position as to override all other moral considerations.

In the circumstances the policy of nuclear deterrence, he said, was overwhelmingly justified.

Dr Leonard has attained an extremely high reputation as a pastoral bishop in all three of his dioceses. It has been said of him that, if he is hard in his views, he is soft towards people. He made a remarkable hit in Australia. We are told that the Australians called him a 'fair dinkum Pommy' and took him to their hearts. They had never previously encountered a leader of the Church of England who could match them face to face with their own type of homespun directness. Though he is quiet and, unless called upon, unobtrusive, he obviously likes meeting people and is widely liked in return. No doubt he benefited from his years in the Oxford and Bucks Light Infantry. His rank of captain gives me, a failed second lieutenant in the same regiment, an additional reason for looking up to him. Visiting him in his home in London, one is struck by his trim light-infantryman's figure. One can easily picture him leading his men on the march.

John Mortimer, in the *Sunday Times* of 22 December 1985, in one of his most intriguing profiles, sees him rather differently:

He sat in his study, in front of bookshelves full of theology, puffing at his pipe like a shy but determined headmaster. Like a headmaster he is very keen on authority, and his pronouncements are full of certainty.

Not for Leonard of London the tormented features of Bishop Jenkins of Durham, who will wriggle painfully in his chair groping for words to describe some elusive and indefinable Godhead. Leonard sits upright and gives it to you as clearly as next term's timetable.

For several years he was Chairman of the Church of England Board for Social Responsibility. A working party of that committee

41

under John Baker, Bishop of Salisbury, had brought forward a motion that seemed to go a long way towards unilateral nuclear disarmament. In the event their report, *The Church and the Bomb* (1982), was rejected. The end result was a qualified support for the Bishop of London. An amendment, moved by the Bishop of Birmingham, was carried opposing the first use of nuclear weapons. This amendment was opposed by Dr Leonard. The question was left very much in the air as to how the Atlantic powers, inferior in conventional weapons, would reply, for example, to a Soviet seizure of Berlin.

Since then Dr Leonard has played a prominent part (with which I am in total sympathy, as I am with his attitude to nuclear deterrence) in attempting to defeat or at least amend the bill to destroy the Greater London Council and the Inner London Education Authority as we know it. No one is better qualified to pass a dispassionate judgement on the government's proposals. He speaks with particular authority on education as Chairman of the Church of England Board for Education. He has shown himself the most incisive of all the government's many critics. A number of official Conservatives have spoken out with equal conviction.

Words like 'conservative' or 'hard-line', frequently applied to him, are altogether too crude, though not altogether meaningless. He has not shown himself opposed to all change, as he has made plain, for example, in connection with the Alternative Prayer Book. He has had plenty of friendly things to say about attempts to bring about reunion with Rome, though he has not been favourable to the proposals for Anglo-Methodist Union.

One gets him all wrong if one tries to label him according to his stand on this or that public issue. 'The fact is', he has said,

> that the problems of the world are not in the last resort simply caused by ignorance or bad administration. We face problems of violence, poverty, bad housing, and war because we human beings can be violent, grasping, unjust, greedy, and bitter. While as Christians we must take our part in remedying the situations that arise because of what is in man, that is, the symptoms, we must also proclaim boldly and without fear that the real solution is to deal with the root cause by the re-creation of men and women in Christ.

When I called on Dr Leonard, I began with a question that was based on something he himself had written in the *Sunday Mail*. 'Do you', I asked, 'agree that, unless the Church of England quickly returns to true faith and strong leadership, it will simply have no future as a national Church?' The Bishop did not withdraw anything that he had said. He was at pains to point out that, although we knew that the Church as a whole was immortal, there was no guarantee that any particular Church would last for all time. Turkey was an example of where the Christian Church had collapsed. Persecution was not the only reason. The Church of England could destroy itself if it lost its sense of identity.

There are of course issues on which the Synod is competent to make decisions and express opinions, as is clear from the Thirty-nine Articles. But the Synod still stands under the judgement of the Trust Deeds of the Church, which include the Scriptures and the Creeds. Certainly the Synod should not be allowed to continue to tamper, for example, with the Creeds. I failed to ask him whether the bishops were likely to prove any kind of bulwark at the present time on the crucial issues.

I raised with him the particular symptoms that I believed caused him social disquiet – women priests, for example. He is, as is well known, vehemently opposed to the ordination of women. He has written:

Is the fact that God was incarnate as a male significant or of no consequence in the debate? Is the distinction between men and women an inbuilt character of mankind as created by God, or is it a regrettable fact to be nullified as far as possible? If a priest is to be the sacramental expression in the Church of the headship of Christ over the Church, to which he and the whole Church must be obedient, should he, for psychological and symbolical reasons, be a male person?

He concluded a powerful article by attacking the whole conception of women priests: 'At a time when the Church should be looking for renewal in faith and life to commend the Gospel to a nation which so desperately needs it, should it commit itself to action which some would see as diverting the Church's energies from its true purpose and which all agree will be divisive?'

He repeated these views in conversation with me, saying:

In the first place, it is surely no accident that God incarnate took a male form. That is the deepest of all the reasons for opposition. But the movement for the ordination of women conducted unilaterally and without reference to the Church of Rome or the Orthodox Church contradicts the claim of the Church of England to become the Church Universal.

I asked him how any progress was possible at all if there was no machinery for reaching agreement with the Church of Rome. He said that informal discussions were increasingly taking place. The answer from Rome was that the ordination of women would be a grave obstacle to Christian unity. It was not quite inconceivable that women would one day be ordained in the Roman Catholic Church. But it would be most un-Catholic to proceed in that direction at the present time.

I asked him what was meant by saying that the Church of England was Catholic. He referred to the 'Lambeth Quadrilateral'. There were the Scriptures, the Creeds, the dominical sacraments, and the apostolic succession. Any alterations on that level would be disastrous, unless sanctioned by the Church Universal.

In January 1984 Clifford Longley, the religious affairs correspondent of *The Times*, called attention to a very important article written by Dr Leonard concerning the position of the Pope. Dr Leonard is quoted as saying: 'Much work has still to be done on how the Bishop of Rome exercises the providential role to which he is called.' Longley comments: 'This expresses both the growing acceptance in Anglicanism that Church unity must include the papacy, and the growing recognition that the Anglican terms for unity include a substantial reform of the papacy.'

I raised the question of the access of divorced people to the sacraments. I was already well aware of his views. Dr Leonard had ended an article under the heading: 'When a Partnership for Life should mean just that' with the trenchant statement: 'However much the Church may say it is committed to the idea of lifelong union, the remarriage of divorced persons in church will, in my judgment, inevitably be taken as change in the Church's teaching

44

and an endorsement of divorce as all right.' In discussion he acknowledged the pastoral requirements, the need for showing compassion to distressed people who found themselves in irregular situations. But nothing must be done to weaken the principle that marriage was a commitment for life. In other words, ways must be found of providing pastoral support to divorced people without marrying them in church.

On the ecumenical side, Dr Leonard thought, as have other bishops, that progress has now to be made at local level, rather than through dramatic doctrinal negotiations. He said that a lot was happening here. In his eyes, the great change had come about with the accession of Pope John XXIII. Until then it had hardly been possible for Anglicans to look on Roman Catholics as possible partners.

Just how inappropriate is the term 'hard-liner' applied to Dr Leonard in any pejorative sense could be seen when he preached to 2,000 people in the service for the murdered victims of the Harrods bombing. He spoke almost entirely of love; the love including even the assassins.

At my second visit to the Bishop of London, I told him that a friend who had seen my reports of my meetings with the bishops had said that I had been much too kind towards them. Why had I not asked the awkward questions: Do you believe in a personal devil? Do you believe in Hell? The Bishop answered these questions with complete urbanity and confidence. If he had to answer yes or no, his answer would be in the affirmative in each case. But he must explain what he meant. On the question of the devil, he quoted a formulation that had for a long time appealed to him. We will never take the measure of evil unless we think of it as personal and capable therefore of making its appeal to the deepest springs of personality in ourselves. The menace of evil would be vastly less if it were some impersonal force like a plague. There was of course no need to believe in a devil with horns. In fact such a devil is not presented in the New Testament.

I asked him whether we must believe in the stories told about the devil in the Old Testament. He said that the first two chapters of Genesis and the Apocalypse describe the situation of man in poetic language. As regards Hell, I told him that my main instruction for the Catholic Church had come from Father Martin d'Arcy, S.J. The Bishop greeted that name with enthusiasm. He spoke of the great influence that Father d'Arcy and Archbishop Temple had had upon his thinking – Father d'Arcy for the way in which he related all human thought and experience to the gospel, and Archbishop Temple for the way in which he showed the relationship of theology to devotion. I had asked Father d'Arcy whether I had to believe in Hell. He had replied: 'Yes, in the possibility of Hell, but you need not believe that anyone has ever gone there.' Dr Leonard said that this was just about his point of view.

The Bishop could not but believe that it was humanly possible to render oneself so incapable of loving that one cut oneself off permanently from God. But he did not presume to say that any human being had brought on himself such an unspeakable destiny. He was very emphatic that our redemption likewise on the Cross left us *free agents*. It was possible therefore for any of us to go completely wrong. He hoped and prayed that this had never happened and would never happen to any individual. This freedom of each of us obviously meant an enormous lot to the Bishop. He had recently been helping to prepare a friend for death, but always on the assumption that he would remain a free man to the end.

In connection with death, I raised the question of purgatory.

'Yes', he said, 'I believe in purgatory. I do not consider that now or when I die I shall be ready for Heaven. But purgatory has acquired a bad name through its association with indulgences.'

He did not have much time for indulgences. I told him that they had not figured prominently in the Catholic life I had known in England and Ireland. He said that they were more prominent on the Continent. Newman's *Dream of Gerontius* seemed to him to come close to the truth. In the afterlife, there would be the joy of seeing God. But also 'the plan of seeing ourselves as we really are'. This conflict would be linked through and transcended in purgatory.

As we drew to a close, he struck a note of guarded optimism about the future of the Church of England. What needed doing far more effectively than now was the teaching of Christian essentials. Sunday after Sunday through the pulpit. There was too much concentration on questions of the hour. There must be unremitting stress on the eternal Christian verities. The bad times, such as the 1960s had been, seemed to be over. The number of ordinands was increasing. Their quality was steadily improving.

To which I will add only a sentence from the last paragraph of Dr Leonard's book *God Alive*: 'Habitual awareness of God alive and active, the sense of mystery, discipline and sacrifice, a realization of the power of grace and a vision of our eternal destiny; these, I believe, are the qualities which are needed for an authentic way of Christian living today.'

I came away impressed by his conviction that this was a time of hope.

ᴐ 4 ᴐ

Eric Kemp,
Bishop of Chichester

Dr Eric Kemp, Bishop of Chichester, is very much an Oxford man. To me, whose life was for so many years based on Oxford, this is no small recommendation. His manner is pleasantly mild rather than acerbic, in contrast to the pungency of his speeches and writing. He was born in 1915. Going up to Oxford in the early 1930s, he returned after a short period as a curate to Pusey House in 1941, staying there until 1946. Then followed twenty-three years as Chaplain at Exeter College, before becoming Dean of Worcester and, five years later (1974), Bishop of Chichester. More than thirty of his years were spent in the city of the Oxford Movement, which figured so largely in his own intellectual and spiritual history. He has made, however, a deep impression as a pastoral bishop.

I told him that he was naturally looked upon as a leader of Anglo-Catholicism in England. He modestly conceded that he would appear to have achieved that position 'without really trying' (not his expression). Brought up as an ordinary Anglican, attending a county grammar school, his spiritual interests had been awakened when being prepared for confirmation. The Oxford Movement captured his imagination. Newman still appealed to him strongly. The *Life and Letters* of Dean Church continued to fascinate him. But it was almost chance that took him to Pusey House, the famous Anglo-Catholic Centre, when he went up to Oxford in 1933.

His first curacy possessed an Anglo-Catholic flavour; then came his return to Pusey House. The history of his religious life was inseparable from the Catholic aspects of the Church of England. I asked him what he meant by his references to Catholicism. 'I mean', he replied, 'the faith of the undivided Church.' He took his stand essentially on the teaching of the Primitive Church, on the first four Ecumenical Councils, on the period up to AD 451.

I should have liked to ask him a slightly different question relating to Anglicanism. I have since come across a passage in the journal of the Church Union called the *Church Observer* for winter 1984–5. 'Anglicanism', says Harry Smythe,

> is historic Catholicism reformed. It is no longer ethnic nor culturally confined and uniform. It is respectful of tradition marked in its pastoral dimension by a profound humaneness encouraging the growth of conscience and personal freedom. It needs however a much firmer hold on the fundamentals of the Gospel and a fresh, penitent and incisive commitment to the unity of the whole Church, one, holy, catholic and apostolic. Only thus may we hope to overcome the act and the sin of schism for which we are responsible in part, together with other Christians.

Would the Bishop accept this formulation? Is it in fact so wide that all or nearly all the bishops could accept it? In the 1920s and the 1930s, the Bishop told me, the Anglo-Catholic outlook dominated the Church of England. Then there came a sad decline. More recently there had been a considerable revival. He modestly refrained from telling me that he himself since 1977 had played an outstanding part in this recovery.

I have read many of his addresses and his diocesan messages issued over the last ten years. At no time has he concealed any of his beliefs; but, as with the Bishop of Norwich at the other end of the spectrum, it would be misrepresenting his pastoral achievement if one implied that he concentrated at all times on the distinctive features of his doctrine. You could read many of his addresses and messages (the same is true of the Bishop of Norwich) without becoming aware that he represented one party in the Church more than another. He has been concerned, like his brother bishops, to teach Christ crucified in season and out of season.

However, if one goes through the statements referred to one comes every now and then upon utterances that carry a personal stamp. Take this, for example, from his letter of July 1978:

> It seems to me sad, therefore, that just at a time when so much that is positive and hopeful is happening in the unity of our Church and the strengthening of its mission, the General Synod should be asked within a matter of months to make decisions about three issues of major controversy and to start legislative processes which could involve the Church in bitter controversy for the next five years. I refer to the issues of the Ten Propositions, the ordination of women to the priesthood and marriage and divorce. It seems almost as if the Synod had a death wish for the Church of England. We must all pray hard during these coming months that wise counsel will prevail and that the Synod will not embark upon the destruction of all that seems at the moment so promising and hopeful.

In order to understand the general position, we would do well to turn to a booklet, *Joy in Believing*, a collection of sermons preached by the Bishop on the occasion of the tenth anniversary of his consecration. Nine sermons are included, plus his presidential address at the 1984 meeting of the diocesan Synod, and the sermon that he preached at his consecration ten years earlier. 'I believe that what I said then is as applicable today.'

The theme of joy is struck repeatedly. A few extracts will give the flavour: 'Think of the opening words of the *Te Deum*: "We praise Thee, O God: All the earth doth worship Thee, the Father everlasting".' But the element of mystery is not neglected for long: 'There is so much more that we do not know and cannot conceive, and so it is with expectancy that we await the end of life here, not only to meet again those who have died before us, but to see them in all the unimaginable wonder of God's love, as it will then be disclosed to us.' Joy in the love of God runs hand in hand throughout his discourses with a sense of His unfathomable mystery.

Dr Kemp took for the text of his enthronement sermon, 25 October 1974: 'The joy of the Lord is your strength.' Another text of which he is obviously very fond is 2 Corinthians XIII: 14: 'The communion of the Holy Spirit be with you all.' After he had served for five years and later for ten, there was widespread recognition that the men and women of the diocese had, through him, received the Holy Spirit in no small measure.

But the joy that he disseminates so indomitably has been accompanied by certain developments in the Church of England about which he has not hesitated to speak his mind. In the sermon with which he commemorated his ten years as bishop, he laid much stress on the fact that the Church of England is part of the One Holy Catholic and Apostolic Church: 'It worships the one true God, Father, Son, and Holy Spirit. It professes the faith uniquely revealed in the holy Scriptures and set forth in the Catholic Creeds.' This passionate belief that the Church of England is part of the Church Universal led him on to emphasize the limitation so imposed on its freedom of action. 'The Church of England', he says, 'has no right to make changes in those things which belong to the whole Church without the evidence of some general agreement in the whole Church.' At first sight, this is a pretty stiff restriction.

Within a few weeks of the sermon just quoted from, Dr Kemp was delivering the annual presidential address to the Church Union (28 November 1984). Everything he said there was completely consistent with the message to his diocesan flock, but he was a good deal more untrammelled. He said:

> The meeting of the General Council today is overclouded by the decision of the General Synod two weeks ago to ask for legislation to permit the ordination of women to the priesthood. It is a decision which I know has caused great consternation, not only among many people, clerical and lay in this country, but also abroad where bishops, priests and people who have stood firm on the matter will now feel that the Church of England has let them down. The disastrous effects of this decision cannot be overestimated.

These are severe words, one could even call them harsh. The Bishop in the same address tried to put as bright a face as possible on a gloomy situation. He reminded his hearers that 'the decision of that black November day is only the beginning of a process which some

51

think may take as much as five years, and at the end of five years the two-thirds majority required for the ordination of women might still not have been secured'. But he made no secret of the grim prospect. 'We have no choice', he said, 'but to play our part in the battle, but I ask ourselves whether most of these other issues do not raise the same fundamental question as the ordination of women, namely the Church of England's adherence to the historic faith and order of the whole Church of which we profess to be only a part.'

The Synod. The General Council of the Church Union on 26 November 1984 passed a very stiff resolution, which should be given at length:

(a) The Council believes that the theological questions underlying the issue of the ordination of women to the priesthood and episcopate can only be answered conclusively by a consensus among those parts of Christendom which have retained the faith and order of the undivided Church. The Council holds that the Church of England, being and professing to be only a part of the Church, has no authority to act in this matter without a consensus.

(b) The Council regrets that the House of Bishops in its recent vote on Thursday, 15 November, appears to show so little concern about causing in England the kind of division and possibly even schism which has occurred in other provinces of the Anglican Communion. It further regrets that the House of Bishops is also prepared to place a major obstacle in the way of Christian unity.

(c) The Council believes that the handling of the marriage issue and the vote for the ordination of women indicates that the House of Bishops is unrepresentative of the Church of England and defective in the guardianship of its faith and unity.

By 1985 the Bishop was making a still more stark pronouncement about the crisis in the Church of England. In an emergency address to the summer meeting of the General Council of the Church Union, which is described as 'the largest Catholic body in the Church of England', he reminded his hearers that the pressures and events of the present time were very similar to those experienced by the contemporaries of Newman: 'In contrast to Newman, who joined the Church of Rome, Pusey and Keble remained and in spite of being isolated and vilified were the rocks of strength for many others. Such remains the situation today.'

Today Dr Kemp regrets the fact that for the moment the crisis over the ordination of women overshadows all else. On this issue he is not an extremist. There are various shades of opinion among the Anglo-Catholics. He himself takes a middle position. He neither affirms nor denies that as an isolated proposition the ordination of women priests is theologically defensible. It cannot in his opinion be considered apart from the ecumenical implications. In this matter 'truth and unity are inseparable'. I should have liked to have asked him whether he regarded this coincidence as directly brought about by the Holy Spirit. I rather imagine that he would have given an affirmative answer.

The Bishop implored all those who at the present time believed in the Catholicity of the Church of England to 'remain and fight'. He was speaking at a moment when there was, to use his own words, 'clear and increasing evidence that many members of the Church of England are contemplating joining the Roman Catholic Church'. Since then we have been assured by such a well-informed writer as Clifford Longley of *The Times* that more 'defections' of this kind are taking place than is generally known. Movements the other way are sometimes referred to, but the balance at the moment seems much in favour of Rome. Not that the Church of Rome in England seems to be exerting itself to win converts. It is even suggested that the Roman authorities would regret a movement of this kind if it weakened the forces making for Christian unity in the Church of England.

Not long ago I heard a young man of great gifts and a fine future ahead of him, a chaplain in a famous Oxford college, married with two children, explaining why he had decided to renounce his career and become a schoolmaster at Eton teaching English literature. He told me after the meeting that he had been thinking of this step for a considerable time. He is still only thirty-three. But it was the decision of the Church of England to move in the direction of women priests that clinched it for him and for another Oxford clergyman, the Vicar of St Mary's. It was not apparently that the whole idea of women as priests horrified him. It was the fact that the decision was reached in total disregard of attitudes in the Roman Catholic and Orthodox Churches.

There were many other questions that I should have liked to put to the Bishop of Chichester if time had permitted; particularly I would have wished to press him on the assertion that the Church of England is part of the universal Church. On his criterion, who passed the test? All the baptized, for instance? What of the Nonconformist? And so on. There is, however, no doubt about the strength of his own dedication to Christian unity. He was a member of the Anglican–Roman Catholic Joint Preparatory Commission, which led to the setting up of ARCIC I. He is the Archbishop of Canterbury's representative on the Council of the Anglican Centre in Rome. He is also co-Chairman of the Church of England's Faith and Order Advisory Group, which prepared the report on ARCIC I for the General Synod.

The present Catholic Chairman of ARCIC is his Sussex colleague and good friend, Bishop Murphy O'Connor. They work together closely on local matters. To give only one example: they paid a joint visit to Mrs Thatcher after she narrowly escaped a terrorist's bombing. I get the impression, as I move around from bishop to bishop, of a great deal of progress in terms of practical co-operation on the ground. But on the doctrinal level, is there a lull? Bishops Kemp and Murphy-O'Connor are not likely to allow it to turn into a stalemate.

☙ 5 ☙

David Sheppard,
Bishop of Liverpool

David Sheppard was captain of England at cricket in 1954. Meeting him today you can well believe it. He is tall and well proportioned. His shoulders are broad. There is no trace of superfluous fat on him. His eyes, though now usually bespectacled, are clear and penetrating. He is the friendliest and least self-conscious of well-known men. A few facts will be useful. Born in 1929, he was educated at Sherborne School (1942–7) and at Trinity Hall, Cambridge (1949–53). He trained at Ridley Hall Theological College, Cambridge (1953–5). He was ordained deacon in 1955, priest in 1956, and served as curate of St Mary's, Islington, from 1955 to 1957. In 1957 he was appointed Warden of the Mayflower Family Centre, Canning Town. In 1969 he was consecrated Bishop of Woolwich, and he was translated to Liverpool in 1975.

In 1978, in the presence of Her Majesty the Queen, the diocese celebrated the completion of Liverpool Cathedral after seventy-four years of continuous building. Pope John Paul II visited Liverpool Cathedral during his visit to England in 1982. According to an official Press release, 'The well-known ecumenical co-operation, sometimes called the "Mersey Miracle", has continued to develop between Church leaders on Merseyside over these years, and in May 1985 the Church leaders signed a covenant to "pray and work" together with all God's people for the visible unity of the Church'. This is no doubt strictly accurate. The new covenant and the new structures emerging are the product of all the Churches in Merseyside and not just of the Roman and Anglican communions.

The statement quoted, however, seems to play down the special relationship that has developed between Bishop Sheppard and the Catholic Archbishop Derek Worlock. A notable article in *The Times* of Monday 10 June 1985 referred to the Church leaders who worked in a unique partnership in what was potentially the most religiously divided city in England. 'Monsignor Derek Worlock, the Roman Catholic Archbishop , and the Right Reverend David Sheppard, the Anglican bishop, have many times acted together to support Merseyside's interests. They are household names, sometimes even the butt of wry Scouse humour. Their standing in the community has no parallel in any other part of Britain.'

Archbishop Worlock has told me how their partnership and friendship originated. They had known each other slightly in the East End, where Archbishop Worlock had served briefly and David Sheppard for twelve years. But when Derek Worlock became Archbishop of Liverpool, David Sheppard called on him within an hour of his arrival. From that moment nine years ago the friendship has deepened and made itself felt in every corner of Liverpool.

Asked what David Sheppard particularly stands for today, one turns naturally to his Dimbleby Lecture of 1984. The title, 'The Other Britain', and the content were equally arresting. So, for that matter, were the title and the content of his book published the same year, *Bias to the Poor*. A brief extract must be given from the lecture.

My first point is that there is real poverty in Britain. My second is that this is a priority subject for all of us, especially Christians. And, thirdly, I shall argue for some of the keys we should use to unlock the doors of that prison. There really are two Britains. There is what I call Comfortable Britain. I imagine that most of you see yourselves, as I do, as part of comfortable, fairly successful, middle Britain. I make no apology for attempting tonight to persuade you to stand in the shoes of people in the Other Britain, of whom I see a great deal.

In the summer of 1985 he spoke out sharply in the Lords against the destruction of the Merseyside Metropolitan Council. I have no doubt that in expressing these views he incurs a good deal of Conservative anger. I am not sure whether his glamorous sporting past reduces the animus. Possibly there is the opposite effect. At all times he has beside him a wife whose personality is a fine complement to his. The author of the *Church of England Year Book for 1985* pointed to the controversial role of the Church of England representing the conscience of the nation at a time of bitter social division. David Sheppard certainly stands in the front line in that battle – the very front.

When I interviewed him in his home in Liverpool and saw the beautiful garden, the special pride of himself and his wife now that he has given up playing cricket, I began by saying: 'You have been asked a thousand times whether it is right for the Church to "meddle" in politics. How do you reply?' I told him that I had interviewed the Bishop of Durham the previous week and a few days later had heard the Bishop delivering a withering attack on Conservative policies in the House of Lords. Conservative peers had not been slow to tell me that bishops should stick to their own business.

David Sheppard answered simply enough. He felt a personal responsibility for the welfare of *everyone* in his diocese. No power on earth would stop him calling attention to the distress inflicted on them by government policies. I asked him whether he saw any danger that he would be dividing his flock. Yes, he recognized the danger. It was never absent from his mind. But it was his right and duty to tell the truth as he saw it. He pointed out that he lived in a middle-class area of Liverpool. He was accessible to all – not to the working-class only. But it was the need of the poor that at the present time was much more evident.

At a later point in the discussion I asked him how he felt about the remarriage of divorced people. He told me that for a long time he had been reluctant to take any step that might weaken Christian support for lifelong marriage. He had felt that a church blessing after the civil ceremony was sufficient. 'But', he said, 'there are couples who feel very vulnerable as they start again after such a hurtful failure; they want the Church to stand with them in a marriage in church. I have changed my attitude. I am now ready for the remarriage of divorced people.' He went on:

The Church has always to walk a tightrope. On the one hand, there is the need to maintain high and strict standards of morality

57

– lifelong fidelity to marriage among them. On the other hand, there is the duty to hold out the hand of Christ to the fallen. If I ask which way our Lord seems to have leaned in the Gospels I believe it is in the direction of mending broken lives.

I asked him whether he could be placed in any of the recognized Christian categories. High Church, Low Church, Anglo-Catholic, evangelical, and so on. I had found him often referred to as an evangelical. He declined to accept any of these labels but agreed that his roots were evangelical. In a speech he delivered at Cambridge in conjunction with Archbishop Worlock he told of his conversion:

> I sat in this Church as a freshman thirty-five years ago: I had few connections with the Church: I believed in God in that unsatisfactory sense of agreeing to the Christian faith, faith in a God who seemed far distant from my everyday life. I didn't agree with several things the preacher said, who stood in this pulpit; yet somehow a whole tangle of loose threads started to come together. I went away with my friend who had invited me to come. We talked late. Alone in my room that night I prayed as I had never prayed before. I realized that faith was not just assenting to some historic beliefs or moral code. It was about opening the whole of me to this living Lord. I prayed and asked Christ to enter my life: I said in my prayer, 'Lord, I don't know where this is going to take me, but I'm willing to go with you.'
>
> As I look back on that turning-around – for me quite abrupt, for many others very gradual – I have a strong sense that it was God searching for me, choosing me, rather than my searching for Him, choosing Him.

At that time and for a long while afterwards he saw the main task of Christians, particularly clergy, as the personal redemption of their fellow men and women. This aspiration he had never lost. But as he laboured in the East End among so many who in the worldly sense 'had never had a chance' he became convinced that society could never look itself in the face until it did far more than at present to provide the social conditions in which personal salvation was made far more possible than at present. From then on he became what would usually be called a social reformer – motivated, however, to an extent unknown to humanists by a personal conviction that Christ can change both human hearts and social structures.

Where did this leave him in his efforts towards reunion with other Churches? He and Archbishop Worlock, as mentioned earlier, had worked out a special relationship in which personal friendship figured largely. But the affirmation also referred to above involved *all* the Churches of Liverpool – the Church of Rome, the Anglican Church, and the Free Churches – in a common statement that their objective was visible unity all round. He longed for unity with the Catholic Church but no less for unity with the Free Churches. He would never willingly consent to any step that led him towards unity with the one and diminish the prospect of unity with the other.

Where did he stand on women priests? Both he and his wife are strongly in favour of them. Was there an ecumenical argument against them? Not in the widest sense. He points out that the Greek word on which ecumenism is based means 'one inhabited earth'. In the narrower ecclesiastical sense it might at first sight seem to hold back the prospect of reunion with Rome. The cause of ecumenism is never served by holding back from actions that Christians deeply believe to be right. But, in fact, he believes, and here I agree with him, that a strong lead by the Anglican Church would make things easier rather than harder for those in the Roman Catholic Church already working for this eventual outcome. I put it to him that according to the religious newspapers the question of women priests was likely to be the most controversial in the Church of England in the immediate future. He agreed that it might seem at the moment to be so, but when the report was published at the beginning of December of the Archbishop of Canterbury's Commission on Urban Priority Areas (the 'inner cities'), of which he was a member, he believed that a major new agenda would be set.

It is hard to keep pace with David Sheppard. I shall be coming later to the report of the Archbishop's commission on the inner cities, in which David Sheppard played a leading part (*Faith in the City*; see page 201). No excuse, however, is needed for quoting at some length a joint document produced by Archbishop Derek Worlock and David Sheppard and appearing in *The Times* of 1 October 1985. For months, they said, people in Liverpool had been confused and helpless about the apparent collision course of the city council and central government.

'We are concerned', they said, 'that the case for Liverpool and other urban areas does not seem to have been adequately heard by Whitehall and we are increasingly anxious about the Council's policy of confrontation.' The article was all the more striking because up till then it would have appeared to most people that the Archbishop and the Bishop placed the main blame for the condition of Liverpool on government policies.

But now they wrote: 'as bishops and with the Free Church Moderator, the Reverend John Williamson, we wish to make it clear that we deplore the confrontation that has to a great extent been manufactured by the militant leadership of the City Council.' They pulled no punches in their criticism of government policy, where their record entitles them to exceptional attention. 'We believe', they said, 'that however much local confrontational tactics may exacerbate the situation, central government must recognize its share of responsibility.' Then came the crucial philosophical sting: 'Our Christian teaching is that we are members of one another. The dogmatic divisive policies of militant leadership reject this. Very significant resources are being ignored or damaged.'

At various points in this book I have suggested that Church leaders have been a shade timid in criticizing those responsible for policies that they themselves deplore. *The Times* article I have been quoting from was much discussed and criticized. It seems to me, however, to provide a noteworthy desperate attempt to point to the difference between Christian and anti-Christian approaches.

David Sheppard made, it would seem, the largest single contribution to the Church of England report on the inner cities. In the debate about it in the Synod (see page 205) he was generally considered to have made the most eloquent oration.

~ 6 ~

Maurice Wood,
ex-Bishop of Norwich (now retired)

No one who visited Maurice Wood a few weeks before he retired after fourteen years as Bishop of Norwich could doubt that he had been a great pastoral bishop. I knew something of this in advance. But I was hardly prepared for the flood of messages of esteem and affection that were pouring in from every quarter. Any long-serving bishop, I suppose, could expect a reasonable share of goodwill and gratitude. But there can have been few bishops who have received such overwhelming tributes as those accorded to Maurice Wood.

The atmosphere of mingled joy and sadness was enhanced by the almost miraculous return to health of his wife, Margaret. A former nurse and midwife, describing herself as Maurice's steward, she had participated in his unceasing mission at all times and in all areas.

It happened that, just as I was leaving, there began to arrive a multitude of retired diocesan clergy and their wives. The fact that they were a quarter of an hour early, but were perfectly happy to wait until I had been disposed of, was further evidence of their devotion to their retiring bishop, and also to his wife.

Maurice Wood and I discussed many topics, on some of which he and I are diametrically opposed. But as I ventured to say to his wife on passing: 'These differences are peripheral against a background of the immense pastoral achievement.' It was widely assumed that 'he had put Norwich on the map'. He was pleased at the somewhat extravagant compliment, but vastly more pleased at the suggestion that he had put Jesus Christ on the map in Norwich and the whole diocesan area.

Maurice Wood, now approaching seventy, former Naval and commando chaplain, decorated for valour, gives hockey and tennis as two of his hobbies in *Who's Who*. He still looks capable of putting up a good show in either sport. His eyes sparkle behind his gold-rimmed glasses. He exudes a benevolent interest in all his fellow human beings, especially those in his pastoral care. I have referred to him in a comprehensive article about the House of Lords as the most attractive speaker I had known there. In his book *Your Suffering*, a little classic and a fine contemporary presentation of the Christian approach to suffering, he says: 'The first stepping-stone across the river of suffering is the personal compassionate love of Jesus for those who suffer and for those who have to watch their loved ones suffer.'

I told Maurice Wood that he was sometimes referred to as the one surviving evangelical among the bishops. He repudiated his uniqueness; he mentioned three good evangelicals among the younger bishops. But yes, he was proud to be referred to as an evangelical.

The next question was obvious. What do you mean by saying that you are an evangelical? Speaking off the cuff, but articulating the thoughts and convictions of many years, he replied as follows:

As an evangelical, I am passionately concerned with the Christian gospel. I feel a continuing responsibility for proclaiming that gospel far and wide in Christ-centred terms. I insist on the unique atoning death of Jesus, not just as expressing his love, but in the sense that through him the sins of the guilty were washed away by the supremely innocent one. I have an unalterable belief in the historic fact of the spiritual and *bodily* Resurrection. I accept the authority of Scripture as the major authority determining Christian teaching. I lay great stress on the duty to promote and deepen Christian faith, through not only clerical but also lay witness. I believe intensely in personal conversion and in the miracle of regeneration.

The above statements are an admirable summary of what the Bishop has stood for and fought for for so long. If space permitted one would quote at length from his Islington Booklets, so-called because the first of the series was a broadcast from St Mary's

Church, Islington, where the writer was Vicar and Rural Dean from 1952 to 1961. Two quotations only can be given; this from No. 6, *How can I witness for Christ?*: 'A prayer: All through this day, Lord Jesus, let me touch as many lives as possible for thee; and every life I touch, do thou by thy Holy Spirit quicken, whether by the words I speak, the life I live, the letters I write, or the prayers I breathe. For thy name's sake. Amen.'

And this from No. 7, *How can I lead someone to Christ?*: 'Remember that you are not called upon to win an argument, but to lead a soul to Christ. This is supernatural work entrusted by God to human agencies. Therefore pray for the one who is seeking God, and God will work in his heart in response to that prayer. Pray also for the wisdom which you need (James I: 5).'

I took up the emphasis on the Gospels. What of the rest of the Bible? I, a Roman Catholic, would describe myself in my small way as a Gospel Christian. But in seeking ethical instruction I did not find myself consulting the Mosaic Law. I did not feel bound by everything said by St Paul, least of all when he is talking about the status of women. I reminded the Bishop of his speech at the Synod in June 1983 in favour of hanging. He was the only bishop who spoke on that side. His cause was overwhelmingly defeated. In that speech he had sought to argue that the doctrine of an eye for an eye was not only based on the Old Testament, but actually confirmed by Christ. Personally I could not accept that for a moment, in view of Matthew V: 38–9, where Christ clearly repudiated the older doctrine. More generally, I could not take Exodus and Leviticus very seriously as guides to contemporary penal policy.

How far did the Bishop take the Old Testament ethics as applicable to the present day (though, of course, the Ten Commandments are common ground)? I am not sure that I adequately grasped his answer. One or two points were clear; he regarded the Old Testament as verbally inspired by the Holy Spirit, which we neglected at our peril. Its ethical teaching was a big advance at the time it was issued. We must apply it today *mutatis mutandis*, though that was not an expression he used. I may be wrong, but I would expect to find most of the bishops sharing my difficulty in supporting him.

So with the question of women priests. Unlike the other Anglican bishops interviewed by that time, Maurice Wood is vehemently opposed to the ordination of women to the priesthood and the episcopate. But he is in strong support of their ordination to the diaconate. I am aware that the Church of England is deeply divided on this issue. This same division is one strong intelligible reason advanced by Maurice Wood for not proceeding with such a change. But in his eyes it is not the most profound objection. He refers back to texts such as those in the Epistle to the Ephesians and the Epistle of St Peter. Ephesians V: 23 reads: 'As Christ is head of the Church and saved the whole body, so is the husband the head of his wife, and as the Church submits to Christ, so should wives to their husbands in everything.' 1 Peter III: 1 reads: 'Wives should be obedient to their husbands.' He, Margaret Wood, and I had a pleasant argument as to what was meant in practice by saying that the husband should be the head of his wife. No more loving wife could be imagined, but I can't see her being bossed about by any man, even her husband. They were too polite to say so, but I think they were shocked by my readiness to ignore St Paul's guidance.

We talked about the ecumenical movement. Here again, he was more conservative than the bishops I had interviewed previously. None of them had seen an easy way forward towards Christian unity, but all of them had accepted organizational unity as a desirable, indeed an imperative, objective. Maurice Wood did not share this aspiration. He saw it as a sad day for Christian freedom if the Church of England came to owe an allegiance to Rome or in any way accepted the kind of universal primacy envisaged in the ARCIC report.

The way forward in his eyes was different. There was no limit to what could be achieved by local co-operation between the Church of England, the Church of Rome, and other Churches. He had struck up a close and harmonious relationship with his opposite number, the Roman Catholic Bishop Alan Clark – who was for some years the Roman Catholic Chairman of ARCIC. Their respective congregations had worked together fruitfully.

I asked him whether he was happy about the refusal of permission to Prince Charles to attend a Mass celebrated by the Pope. He did not consider that the affair had been well handled, but was satisfied with the outcome. If Prince Charles had attended a Mass at which the Eucharist was celebrated, it would have been a step towards his accepting Holy Communion in the Catholic Church. The Coronation Oath to preserve the Protestant succession might have been eventually imperilled.

On Thatcherism, as I call it, he did not have much to say compared with the bishops from unemployment areas like Durham, Liverpool, and Birmingham. He is certainly regarded among politicians as conservative in the political as in the theological sense. I am sure that he is genuinely determined not to be identified with any one party, but he seems quite happy to have saved the government on one occasion, in a cliff-hanger decision in the House of Lords on the Greater London Council.

He nevertheless came firmly against the government over the divorce bill (which subsequently became an Act), which cut down to a year the period of waiting before a divorce can be obtained. He tangled pleasantly with the Lord Chancellor and certainly did not come off worst.

Since I saw him, Maurice Wood has brought out a short but arresting book, entitled *This Is Our Faith*. I have not come across a stronger or clearer statement of traditional Christianity. It powerfully expresses the Christian doctrines in which I was brought up as a Protestant, but as a Roman Catholic for forty-six years I respond to it just as fervently today. No one could possibly suppose that the Bishop of Norwich and the Bishop of Durham view the Resurrection in the same light. He repeats unequivocally his statements in *The Times* and, incidentally, to myself: 'If the Bishop of Durham cannot unreservedly preach this Easter weekend that Jesus was raised on the third day, according to the Scriptures, then sadly I believe he should resign his bishopric and return to his academic work.'

Did he stand by this statement? Regretfully he did – entirely. Those who accepted the role of a Church of England clergyman and *a fortiori* those who accepted episcopal office did so on well-understood conditions. They were bound by a public Declaration of Assent, which included the Thirty-nine Articles. The commitment was not cast in legalistic terms, but an inescapable moral obligation was undertaken to be loyal to the full Anglican heritage. The Bishop of Durham had clearly failed to observe that obligation. A mistake had been made in making him a diocesan bishop on a very high level, without a trial period as a suffragan. Maurice Wood did not doubt that David Jenkins attached much significance to the historic fact of the Resurrection, but it was impossible to reconcile his view of the Resurrection with that traditionally understood in the Church of England.

In the course of our discussion, the Bishop acknowledged that he feared grave dangers to the Church of England from two disparate forces: first, the Romanizing tendency; second, radical theology such as that proclaimed by the Bishop of Durham. I suggested that there was a good deal of radical theology among academic Anglican theologians at the moment. Maurice Wood agreed that there was also a lot of it in the universities, but not much in the training and theological colleges. The peril was, however, acute.

I was already familiar with his opposition to the possibility of marriage in church of divorced people in the lifetime of a former partner. In a diocesan letter he had called attention to a resolution passed on 15 March 1980 by the diocesan Synod: 'This Synod would welcome in the event of civil marriage after divorce, during the lifetime of a former spouse . . . retention of a subsequent service of prayer and dedication authorized by the bishop on the advice of the incumbent.'

This issue brings out both sides of what has been called 'the Norwich way'. The Bishop has stood, on the one hand, for the fairest possible reassertion of the lifelong conception of marriage; on the other hand, for immense compassion for those who have not been able to comply with these standards and are yet sincerely anxious to lead a Christian life. A comment of the Bishop as to how this has worked out in practice is worth quoting. He writes of those who have been divorced and been through a civil remarriage, followed by a blessing:

These conscientious couples find the compromise helpful as, by not asking for a second marriage in church, they witness to the *ideal* of lifelong marriage. By sincerely desiring a service of prayer and blessing, they seek God's help and strength to establish as Christian a foundation for their new marriage as possible. If there is no danger of harming the parish eucharistic fellowship, I gladly assent to such a service, I formally renew them in their communicant status, and I send the couple a signed prayer card.

Right: Robert Runcie; pre-eminently a *leader*
Below: John Habgood, the scientific Archbishop.
They occupy two of the top five appointments in
the Church of England, that of Archbishop of
Canterbury and Archbishop of York respectively

David Jenkins is the Bishop of Durham who sees himself, and I certainly agree, as a 'questioning mind'

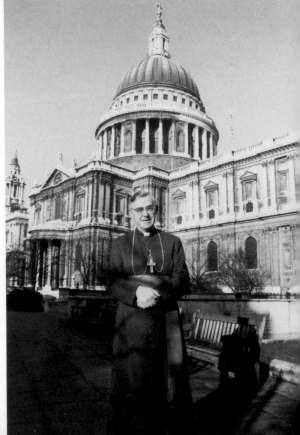

Graham Leonard, the Bishop of London, whose starting point is an unequivocal and orthodox Christianity

Michael George Bowen became Archbishop of Southwark in 1977. Southwark is a huge diocese which includes all of London south of the Thames and the county of Kent. He is a man so obviously devoid of vanity, and whose leadership reflects a higher guidance

The Bishop of Bradford, Robert Williamson, is unique because he has not got a University degree. Never before has such a man managed to reach the episcopal bench

David Sheppard, the Bishop of Liverpool, is what would usually be called a social reformer. He is accessible to all, not only the working class, but it is the need of the poor that at the present time is more in evidence

Derek Worlock, the Archbishop of Liverpool, holds the most important position in the Catholic hierarchy after Westminster

The above account of our discussions would seem to have emphasized our differences rather than our points of agreement. But it has not been so in the House of Lords. We have fought shoulder to shoulder in regard to the treatment of prisoners (hanging has not been an issue there), to pornography, and to all questions affecting the family. On the family he has been an outstanding Christian spokesman at all times. In regard to the Warnock Report, he had this to say:

> I have tried to see why, as I read slowly through the report, I began to find myself in a situation of dis-ease about the report. I think it was first of all because I did not find any clearly defined moral principles built upon the ancient Judeo-Christian traditions of moral principles of our nation. The light seemed to flicker back and forth.

Maurice Wood's light has never wavered. There is no one among the bishops who delivers more firmly the full and traditional message of Jesus Christ.

⌒ 7 ⌒

Robert (known as Roy) Williamson, Bishop of Bradford

'You simply must see the Bishop of Bradford, although he is quite new,' they all said to me. I was very glad that I had the chance of doing so. He is referred to repeatedly as a unique phenomenon. At the time of his appointment the Provost of Bradford said:

> He is quite unique because he has not got a university degree, and the appointment of a man from such humble beginnings is only rarely accepted for ordination in the Church of England, and never before has such a man managed to reach the episcopal bench. He is a superb personality with a real understanding of parish life, having ministered himself in the back streets and having been brought up himself in those selfsame backstreets of Belfast.

Meeting him in summer 1985, fifteen months after his appointment, I found a man thoroughly at home in his work, though still afflicted by the tragedy of the Bradford football ground fire. Now fifty-two, rather young for a bishop, burly, bespectacled, jolly, he is very friendly; so indeed are all the bishops I have met. The friendliness of most of them is closer to that of the senior common room; his to that of a football manager's office – Matt Busby's, for instance. The Bishop was himself a notable footballer. It is too soon for his achievements as a bishop to be picked out easily, though he has rapidly become accepted. There is the more excuse for concentrating on his unusual life story.

The youngest of fourteen children, he is always described as having a 'humble background' in the back streets of Belfast. His father, who worked in the Belfast shipyards, was a Protestant, and his mother a Roman Catholic. He came to London when he was twenty-three, working as a city missionary, and after six years went to Oakhill Theological College, London, to train for the ministry. He was ordained in 1963, and his first curacy was at Crowborough Parish Church from 1962 to 1966, moving to Nottingham in 1966 as Vicar of St Paul's, Hyson Green – a poor area of that city – and in 1971 to St Ann with Emmanuel. He served there for five years, going on to Bramcote, also in Nottingham, and in 1978 was appointed Archdeacon of Nottingham. For a year he served both as Vicar of Bramcote and as Archdeacon.

His most notable speech in the Synod was when he opposed the restoration of hanging. From his own sad knowledge of the animosities in Northern Ireland he insisted movingly that they would be exacerbated by the restoration of capital punishment. He is married with three sons and two daughters. His wife, Anne, whom he married in Ireland, was a magistrate in Nottingham. Although not usually thought of in a theological connection, he is Chairman of the Council of St John's Theological College, Nottingham.

Colin Slater, an ex-Bradford journalist who came to know him intimately in Nottingham, had this to say on his leaving that city: 'Roy Williamson will leave behind in Nottingham a countless number of friends and admirers who have recognized his putting into practice his favourite maxim: people matter more than things.' Colin Slater continued: 'He is undoubtedly very Irish and proud of his Belfast upbringing.'

His accent is unmistakable but not unpleasing, and he has a fine sense of humour. Congregations will find themselves laughing easily at his wit.

I told the Bishop that he was often referred to as the only working-class Anglican bishop. He hesitated to claim the title, but did not reject it. He had left school on his fourteenth birthday, which seems to confirm the description. We went over aspects of his life story. He recalled with fervour a profound religious experience he underwent at the age of nineteen. He was ready to be called a 'born-again Christian' – though he considered the expression tautological.

I asked him whether he was an evangelical, and he replied: 'An "open" evangelical.'

He is consumed with a great love of the Scriptures and, I should judge, a still greater love of Jesus Christ. He told me that the doctrine of justification by faith meant very much to him. I was aware of course of the immense part this doctrine had played in the Reformation. I told him, however, that even when I was an Anglican I had never really grasped the significance. To him it meant simply that we cannot be saved by our own exertions. We owe our salvation entirely to Christ.

Since talking to him, I have gone back to St John's Gospel, chapter XVII and St John's first Epistle. In John XVII, Christ said to his Father: 'I have loved these men [his disciples] as much as You have loved me.' Indeed he was about to undergo an agonizing death on their behalf. In St John's first Epistle, chapter III, we read: 'Let us love one another, since love comes from God . . . this is the love I mean, God's love for us when he sent his son to be a sacrifice to take our sins away. . . . We are to love them because he loved us first.' The Bishop agreed with me that our salvation by Christ does not rule out the necessity for good works; indeed it enhances it. After consulting St John's Gospel and Epistle, I think I understand a little better how a true evangelical proceeds from a consciousness of being saved by Christ to a fervent love for his fellow men. The Bishop laid great stress on an evangelical conversion such as he had had at the age of nineteen.

Was there, I asked, a crisis in the Church of England? No, he did not think so. The Church must be faithful to the past, but also relevant to the future. From this standpoint he was readier for change than a senior evangelical like my friend, the retiring Bishop of Norwich. Unlike the latter, the Bishop of Bradford was definitely in favour of women priests. Again, unlike the Bishop of Norwich, he considered that divorced people should not necessarily be precluded from remarriage in church. Each case should be considered on its merits. I did not ask him whether he was satisfied with the present 'free-for-all'.

He described himself as very enthusiastic about the ecumenical movement. He was doing all he could to extend the hand of friendship to non-Christians, including the 60,000 Muslims in

Bradford. Like Bishop Sheppard he would not favour any movement towards Rome that led the Church of England away from the Free Churches. The one bright spot in the horrible disaster at the football ground had been the close co-operation between all denominations and religious bodies.

I learnt from other sources that he had dashed to the scene after hearing of the blaze and was one of the first to visit some of the injured as they poured into Bradford Royal Infirmary's casuality unit. To quote his wife: 'He saw as many people as he could and offered encouragement. He felt everyone was very brave and was full of praise for the police, fire service, and all who were helping.'

On one or two controversial issues not unrelated to the Bishop of Durham, he had spoken with deliberate moderation. He was the first Church of England leader to warn that he would not submit to a 'heresy test'. 'I happen to believe that our Lord was born of a virgin and that he rose from the dead according to the Scriptures.' But he would not submit to examinations such as those suggested by a group of North-East priests who had demanded checks on bishops. He was equally firm in rejecting criticism of colleagues for their political pronouncements. 'In days when the social fabric of our nation is clearly under strain, the Church would be failing in its duty if it kept silent.' But the Bishop explained that he had not spoken out on the miners' strike because, 'having just come from Nottingham where the miners are working, it would have been the height of insensitivity to make pronouncements in a Yorkshire context'.

He was very anxious about the divisions in our society, which had recently been intensified. In that sense he was critical of present governmental policies. 'By their fruits ye shall know them' – though he did not quote these words. He summed up his own credo in the declaration: 'I believe that the Church needs to be motivated by its own gospel. It has got to embody its own gospel. People must look to the Church and its members as a society of love.'

No intention could be plainer. No man will try harder to carry it out.

⌐ 8 ⌐

Hugh Montefiore,
Bishop of Birmingham

Tolstoy and, following him, Sir Isaiah Berlin have divided men of distinction into foxes and hedgehogs. The fox knows many little things, but the hedgehog knows only one big thing. Bishop Montefiore might, at first sight, seem to be a prince of foxes (in the Tolstoyan sense). But no one could accuse him of being foxy; anyone who studies him with any care cannot fail to allow him the superior title of hedgehog. He is very tall, warm, voluble, and mobile. After a kindly welcome at his residence, he took me to lunch at Birmingham University. We skipped up two flights of stairs to reach the luncheon room. He could not disguise his pleasure at having reached the top before me but, fourteen years younger, he congratulated me on my relative agility. In the course of a working lunch and subsequent discussion, we covered every topic under the sun. He was still thirsting for more at the end.

Born, it is said, of one of the wealthiest and most prestigious of Jewish families, he underwent, when he was a boy of sixteen at Rugby, an experience that has affected him profoundly throughout the half-century that has passed since that time. He has not spoken a great deal about it. It is, though he does not use the word, too sacred to him. He is ready to describe it as visionary. He does not object if it is described as mystical. He saw, with absolute clarity, a figure in white who beckoned to him and said, 'Follow me.' He felt an irresistible call – in the first place to Christianity, in fact Anglican; in the second place to the life of a clergyman; and in the third to that of a missionary at home: someone mandated beyond question to disseminate the message and the personality of Christ.

72

To quote from an address he gave a few years ago:

> I have tried to work out my own beliefs about Jesus in a doctrinal system; but I must admit that it is only provisional. The mystery of Jesus is greater than any formulation about him. I find him as a person compelling and inescapable, and when he calls me to follow, I can but try to obey. I number myself among those who 'in the toils, the conflicts, the sufferings which they pass through in his fellowship can learn as an ineffable mystery who he is'. All our dogmas are partial and our doctrines provisional. It is not by these, but by my prayers and by my life, that, as a disciple of Christ, I make my ultimate affirmation about God, creator, redeemer, and sanctifier.

The Bishop has written a number of books; those on the Hebrews and St Paul have been of special interest to scholars. In a notable profile of him in *The Times*, which appeared when he was appointed to Birmingham, Professor Lampe, Regius Professor of Divinity at Cambridge at the time, is quoted as referring to his 'unrivalled ability to translate the teachings of the Church into language all can understand'. Professor Lampe added that he felt that Bishop Montefiore showed 'more human sympathy for others than intellectual sympathy with ideas not his own', a quality clearly more suited to a bishop than to an academic, and essential in a man who seeks to lead the Church.

I myself would venture to describe Hugh Montefiore as a creative factor in the religious life of our period. In his latest book, *The Probability of God*, he approaches the existence of the Christian God from the angle of natural religion and concludes: 'It is an enormous leap forward to be able to believe, on grounds of reason and after study of the evidence, that the existence of God is very, very probable. The existence of God can never be proved; but from this firm foundation we are fully justified in making the leap of faith.'

Cardinal Newman and, following him, Father Martin d'Arcy, S.J., from whom I learnt so much, used slightly different language in insisting that reason could prove the existence of God through the accumulation of evidence. I did not feel when I put this to the Bishop that there was much difference between their point of view and his.

Hugh Montefiore's career has been one of consistently creditable success. From Rugby, he obtained a scholarship at Oxford, but when the war came, though already thinking of a career in the Church, he served throughout in the forces. Like other bishops I have spoken to, he felt that he had gained a priceless experience through the comradeship under grim conditions of ordinary people. After the war he obtained a first-class degree in theology and, after a short period as a curate in Newcastle, he became Chaplain and Tutor at Westcott House and then Vice-Principal. A fellow and don at Gonville and Caius College, Cambridge, from 1954 to 1963, he was also a lecturer at the university between 1959 and 1963.

In 1963 he was appointed Vicar of St Mary the Great, Cambridge. He was consecrated Bishop of Kingston-upon-Thames in 1970 and Bishop of Birmingham in 1977, winning at all times a high reputation for pastoral zeal and understanding.

Today he occupies one of the key positions in the Church as Chairman of the Board for Social Responsibility. In that role he has already adopted a controversial stance in broad support of the Warnock Report. At the time the Church of England would seem to be as deeply divided on the question of embryo research as the rest of the nation is.

Does all this mean that Bishop Montefiore must be classed as a liberal? In the social area, the term seems not inappropriate. He has for some years been strongly in favour of women priests (he once edited a book in favour of them). He is just as firmly in favour of the remarriage in church of divorced people. He would have supported the 1967 Abortion Law Reform Act, though he is horrified at the way in which it has been abused. He expressed the opinion to me that it has been carried out in a manner never intended by its authors. There I demurred. I said publicly at the time that abortion on demand with euthanasia to follow was the real purpose of the reformers.

On most political issues I would expect to find him left of centre. While he has been Bishop of Birmingham, unemployment has risen from 3 or 4 per cent to over 20 per cent. He is unequivocal in his condemnation of the policies that have contributed to this result. He does not disguise his feeling that at the present time there is a lack of 'caring' in the highest circles.

To call Hugh Montefiore a liberal in the theological sense, however, would be to misrepresent him. As was pointed out in *The Times* profile referred to, he has given at times provocative sermons. Yet when examined none of his remarks depart from mainstream, orthodox, Anglican theology. There is no tampering from him with the divinity of Christ or the Resurrection. Admittedly he is, to use his own phrase, agnostic in regard to the Virgin Birth. He rather hopes that it is not true, though he recognizes that it might be, that God might have arranged matters that way. The issue in any case is rather low among his priorities.

I asked him a shade timidly how he felt about a widespread view that he had said that Christ was probably homosexual. He explained that he had pointed to certain features in the life of Christ – for example, his unmarried state and his special interest in outcasts – that were congruent (he laid stress on the word) with his having homosexual leanings. There was no question of his having indulged in homosexual practices. I think that he rather regrets the utterance now, though he did not say so. He considers that it was proper for a theologian to offer it as a speculative hypothesis, even if it would not have been right for a bishop, which he had not become at the time.

I ventured to compare the outcry this had aroused with that occasioned by the Bishop of Durham. He was quick to point out that the Bishop of Durham had delivered his most provocative utterance when he was already Bishop-Designate. He was well aware, of course, that the Bishop of Durham was in fact profoundly convinced of the historical fact of Christ's spiritual resurrection. He agreed that he himself, the Bishop of Durham, and I were all old university dons with a proper longing to stimulate thought. Bishops, however, must be more concerned to strengthen Christian devotion.

Was he, I asked him, High or Low Church, Anglo-Catholic for example, or evangelical? He refused, like one or two other bishops I have interviewed, to accept a label or pigeon-hole. I told him that Bishop Sheppard, an alleged evangelical but intimately associated with Archbishop Worlock of Liverpool, had told me that he would never support any movement by the Church of England towards Rome that would increase the distance from the Free Churches, and vice versa. Bishop Montefiore said precisely the same.

He was totally convinced that the unity of all the Churches was the will of God, that the present divisions were a scandal, that the ecumenical progress in present years was altogether to be welcomed.

But he did not, humanly speaking, take an optimistic view of further progress in the near future. The Bishop of Salisbury had told me that the Papacy in its present form and attitudes was the main obstacle. The Bishop of London was on record as saying that unity would involve some modification on the Roman side. Bishop Montefiore was admittedly somewhat alarmed at what appeared to be the conservative tendencies of the present Pope, due, it might be, to his Polish background. He was quick to add that it had been a memorable privilege to have embraced him and to have been embraced by him when the Pope visited Canterbury.

The Bishop was not altogether happy with the concept of the universal primacy of the Pope, as envisaged in the ARCIC report. But for him the difficulties lay deeper. How could Anglicans accept with a clear conscience existing Roman Catholic teaching on contraception and divorce? Or, for that matter, the Roman form of devotion to Mary? Yet, to repeat himself, he was happy to believe that the Holy Spirit would find a way to guide us all forward.

When the Bishop was asked, at the time of the profile referred to, what a bishop does, he replied: 'He supports the clergy, leads the Church, and serves the community in that order.' It can be surmised that he would give the same answer today. But there are no obvious limits to his activities in any of these directions. He is at work at all times, never ceasing to talk, to write, and to render pastoral aid.

Back then to the hedgehog. Hugh Montefiore has on more than one occasion talked of his theological positions as provisional. But there has been nothing provisional about his dedication to the various Christian tasks that have come his way. There is nothing provisional in the main assertions of his belief:

The divine intention in creation, redemption and sanctification embraces the whole world, not just mankind: it includes the fitting of human beings to share eternally in the divine life of love and joy; and for this the process of development continues after death. The Church therefore does not exist for itself, but to serve the true needs of all the world; to help to create a society where men and women can fully develop; and to help the individuals within it towards a ripeness of life and character to fit them for everlasting life.

76

✑ 9 ✑

David Jenkins,
Bishop of Durham

Before I interviewed the Bishop of Durham in the castle where he lives (modestly) at Bishop Auckland, I was in some impertinent doubt as to whether it was a good idea for him to be appointed Bishop of the Church of England. The dissatisfaction was expressed publicly and still more privately in Anglican circles (not to mention Conservative ones), though I think only two bishops called for his resignation. The general view among the bishops that I have met appeared to be that he had a perfect right to speak his mind, but it was a pity that he chose this particular way of doing it. After my visit to him and (here my political bias comes in) after a trenchant speech he made a few days later in the House of Lords, I was much clearer in my mind about his positive value to the Church of England.

He is one of the top three bishops after the Archbishop of London and Winchester, and as such he is immediately entitled to a seat in the Lords, instead of having to wait in the queue. His maiden speech there was a model of circumspection, if somewhat above the heads of the majority of his audience. I could see Lord Whitelaw, Leader of the House, enjoying its sheer dexterity. The Bishop's second speech, delivered soon after my visit to him, raised the blood pressure of Conservative peers very noticeably. It was greeted with surprised delight on the opposition side of the House. I cannot recall another such root-and-branch disparagement by a bishop of a government's ideology, which the Bishop of Durham described as idolatry (see page 187).

I had a long working lunch with the Bishop when I saw him over white wine, my favourite beverage, and sandwiches. I can think of no one to compare the Bishop with except the late R. H. S. Crossman. Both had been Oxford dons; like Crossman, the Bishop possesses a very active mind, hard to keep up with, and takes a positive pleasure in provoking thought – the Bishop with a twinkle in his eye, Dick with an occasional guffaw.

The Bishop is a short man, but could not be described as small. His head is large and impressive; his heavy shoulders would have qualified him to be a prop forward in Welsh rugby. I have heard a brother bishop attribute some of his idiosyncrasies to his Welshness. The Bishop does not see himself as Welsh, though his ancestors came from Wales. He is immensely articulate, but it would be misleading to call him a fluent talker. When asked a question he frequently pauses to search for the word that conveys his full meaning. And very often an unusual phrase emerges. He seems to feel that theological concepts require extraordinary care in definition, but the attempt to define them must be pursued relentlessly.

I told him that I had asked my wife what was the first question I should put to him. She had replied: 'Ask him whether his more sensational remarks are delivered off the cuff or after long thought.'

The Bishop commented: 'You can reassure her; there are usually forty years of thought behind them.'

He sees himself and I certainly see him as a 'questioning mind'. He has been accused of raising questions about Christian fundamentals – the Resurrection in particular – that are positively subversive in the sense of being damaging to the popular faith. I asked him how his questioning method, and frequently very original phraseology, impinged on ordinary parish congregations. (Incidentally, I heard from his chauffeur that he is very successful in such an atmosphere.)

He replied, as usual after careful thought: 'There is a time for criticism and inquiry and a time for simplicity and directness.'

He is by no means unaware of possessing a considerable mastery of the popular arts that open various avenues of communication. I gather that he uses plenty of gesture and other rhetorical devices. He slips in the vivid phrase to lighten an elaborate exposition, for example, 'Look at yourself in the glass, but don't look more than two minutes.' People who could make little of his or any theology have found this very inviting. But remove his presence and direct spiritual influence and is there not a risk that the public, relying on a not well-intentioned Press, will gain a false impression? I ventured to refer to my own experience in connection with pornography and my friendship with prisoners. We both agreed that the risk was there, but must not be shirked. We neither of us claimed any special quota of prudence.

Again, as a fellow sufferer, I asked him how he felt about the charge that he sought publicity. He insisted, and I accept it without question, that he never sought it; but if it came his way he welcomed it if it assisted the propagation of his message. Surely he must be right in this attitude. He may well have been saying most of the same things when he was Professor of Theology at Leeds. But, like Bishop Robinson of *Honest to God*, it was only when he became a bishop that the world took notice. I am told that he receives correspondence from all quarters of the globe.

This does not imply that I consider all his best-known dicta to be well advised. I still consider that it was a real mistake to refer to Mr Ian MacGregor, Chairman of the National Coal Board, as 'an elderly imported American'; but who can strike with confidence the ultimate balance sheet? (Winston Churchill asked in 1922 of the new Irish government: 'Will they die for it? Will they kill for it?') The fact that their bishop was ready to exhibit a certain ruthlessness in controversy may have helped to secure him his undoubted prestige in the North-East.

But it is time to go deeper. Can the present Bishop of Durham be considered a recognizable Christian, as the man or woman in the pew understands the term? In my view the answer must be 'yes', except perhaps in regard to the Virgin Birth, which is generally understood to be part of orthodox Christian doctrine. I find it difficult to discover any sense in which he can be said to believe in the Virgin Birth. I am ready to be corrected here, but on the face of it he is unorthodox on this issue. He is of course a professional theologian; he must be presumed to have arrived at certain insights beyond those possessed by most of us, having gone into these matters more deeply than all except a few of his fellow citizens. It would have been absurd to suppose that Clement Attlee, though a thoroughly orthodox socialist, had no deeper grasp of socialism than that of the ordinary comrade.

The Bishop of Durham draws a sharp distinction between accepting the Gospel stories as being 'for real', which we must do as Christians, and accepting them all as literally true, which he says is neither necessary nor rational. 'Many of the stories', he has said, 'are for real not by being literally true, but by being inspired symbols of a living faith about the real activity of God. . . . We worship, we believe, and we hope for the real God, who is to be found among the realities of this present day-to-day and down-to-earth world.' No one who has studied his teaching as a whole could doubt that the Bishop of Durham believes in the incarnation as he interprets it, and not only believes in it, but is inspired by it in a lifelong dedication.

He returns to the Resurrection at every opportunity. 'Our trust is in the God who raised Jesus,' he said,

> and our assurance comes through the apostolic witness, sealed to us by the working of the Holy Spirit in our own faith and in the faith of the Church. Hence the absolutely crucial importance of the Epistle for Easter Day: 'If ye then be risen with Christ, *seek* those things that are above.' If we want to know about the Resurrection we must live by the Resurrection, that is what the gift of the Spirit and the life of the Church is for.

Good. Very good. But as regards the empty tomb, I cannot pretend to go along with him. I ventured to say to the Bishop that I had no credentials – I am not sure who has – for placing a label, physical, material, or what you will, on the form assumed by the risen Christ before the Ascension. In a small book that I wrote about Jesus Christ some years ago, I followed in the footsteps of Norman Anderson, then Chairman of the House of Laity. Anderson pointed out that the form assumed by Christ, with his ability to come and go at will and move through doors, etc., was far from the form he assumed during his lifetime. The Bishop does seem to leave it an open question whether the tomb was or was not empty after the Resurrection. He has repudiated (though he has mentioned it as possible) the idea that the disciples stole the body. Setting this aside, how could the corpse of Christ have remained in the tomb while he was appearing continually to his disciples without the fact being brought up against him?

80

On a different plane of argument, how is it possible to reject the empty tomb and still accept the Gospels as substantially accurate? This brings one to the Bishop's whole approach to the Bible. The Bishop insists at all times on his right and duty to think for himself. To do otherwise he would regard as a betrayal, not only of our God-given reason, but in particular of the Protestant Reformation. He said in passing that we ought on no account to retreat from the Reformation. We ought always to think of moving forward from it. I asked him whether he regarded himself as a High, Low, or Middle Churchman. He replied that he was 'on the High side'. In his thinking and his conduct he would pay very great attention to the Bible as traditionally interpreted and to Church doctrine generally, but in the last resort he must decline to have his mind made up for him by any individual or group of individuals.

In the last resort it was for him as a Christian, most of all perhaps as a professional theologian, to make up his own mind. After all – though he did not quote him – John Henry Newman, long after becoming a Catholic, said: 'I will drink to conscience and the Pope, but to conscience first and the Pope afterwards.'

I must repeat that, fine intellectual though David Jenkins is, his lifelong devotion is to Christ, the Lord. He says of theology: 'It is a spiritual discipline rather than an intellectual exercise.' If one does not understand this about the Bishop, one understands nothing about him. It would be an affectation to pretend that his views on the empty tomb are the only cause of indignation among the bishops and Anglican critics. As mentioned earlier, the Warden of Tyndale House, for example, has taken him to task point by point in a short book entitled *Easter in Durham*. The Bishop of London warmly approves the booklet (see page 36) and writes: 'To reduce the Resurrection to nothing more than an experience in the minds of the Disciples is not only to challenge the authority of the Scriptures, it is also to challenge what they reveal about God.' Reacting in turn to those comments of the Bishop of London, the Archbishop of York has told me that the Bishop of London has misunderstood the Bishop of Durham. But with all respect to the Bishop of Durham, should it not be possible for him to avoid such a misunderstanding occurring?

I turn to his attitude to social questions. In the course of the miners' strike, he startled the country and infuriated the government by calling for reconciliation rather than victory for one side or the other, and insisting that the miners should not be defeated. This was hardly my attitude at the time, although I have been a member of the Labour Party for half a century and take strong exception to the social policies of the present government. I felt that Scargillism had at all costs to be defeated and was much relieved when this was more or less achieved in the outcome. But I was and remain happy that a third voice, a strong Christian voice, was raised. The words of W. B. Yeats came back to me repeatedly:

> The best lack all conviction, while the worst
> Are full of passionate intensity.
>
> 'The Second Coming', 1921

In the face of no little obloquy the Bishop of Durham stepped boldly into the moral vacuum. Not only in connection with the miners' strike, the Bishop has come to be looked upon as a potential saviour in the North-East – what Churchill might have called 'a rescuing genius'. He recognizes that without self-seeking he has raised the expectation that he is going to put the North-East right, an expectation that he is well aware no single man can fulfil. It is at least certain that he will not run away from the challenge.

I asked him whether what were understood to be his political views had led to widespread criticism of what was understood to be his theology. He said that, in view of the Tory character of the popular Press, something of the kind had occurred. His chauffeur told me that the Bishop had more than once been called a 'loony' in newspaper articles. Having enjoyed the same experience, I could readily sympathize. As Roy Jenkins once said, when asked how he liked being called 'Smoothy-chops': 'It is hardly the soubriquet I would have chosen, but it doesn't cut very deep.'

One or two additional points. I touched on his attitude to the Church of England – did he regard it as part of the universal Church? Yes, indeed, he said, there was one sense in which that was already true, although visible unity was still far off. He would certainly describe himself, all the more after his years on the World Council of Churches at Geneva, as thoroughly ecumenical in aspiration. But if the Church of England were to join with the Church of Rome, it must be a two-way movement, with modifications on both sides. A truly universal Church would be something still more comprehensive.

I asked him about the freedom to which a bishop was entitled. I quoted a passage from one of his addresses where he said: 'People have told me that questions that I can ask as a professor I cannot ask as a bishop, or at least I should not ask them openly. Such a suggestion appals me and in my view comes strikingly close to blasphemy.' Did he still look at matters that way? 'Yes', he said, 'broadly speaking. But some allowance must be made for prudence and for a spirit of collaboration with colleagues.' He liked people and being with people. At Oxford as a don, in Geneva as a functionary of the World Council of Churches, and as Professor of Theology at Leeds, he had not found it difficult to harmonize loyalty and independence.

I came away with two outstanding impressions: of a man of intense spiritual preoccupation; and of a man who at all times offered to all problems great or small what seemed to him a Christian answer.

✎ 10 ✎

John Baker,
Bishop of Salisbury, Chairman
of the Doctrine Commission

Before being invited to visit the Bishop of Salisbury in his home, I had made some study of his writings and addresses. Although in his own words he is still a 'junior bishop', he had been recently appointed Chairman of the Doctrine Commission, to whose work he has already made a powerful contribution as a member. I was aware that there was no more highly regarded theological thinker; he calls himself a biblical theologian. *The Foolishness of God*, published in 1970, is a profound book, at once original and traditional. Today John Baker would wish to improve on it. Since 1970 he has played a prominent and not uncontroversial part. But *The Foolishness of God* would still seem to represent his central message.

I need not recapitulate his colourful restatement of the main tenets of orthodox Christianity. I will quote only one key sentence: 'I am left to make a naked choice, the choice for or against love as the law of life.' John Baker comes down unequivocally on the side of love, alike in belief and in action. He is no sentimentalist. He brings instead a powerful intellect and strong humanitarian convictions to the task of applying the law of love to all things.

The Reverend John Meacham, the Bishop's chaplain, who had carefully prepared me for the encounter, met me at Salisbury station. As we drove past, we had a fine view of the cathedral, with plenty of young people disporting themselves on the sward in front. I murmured a recollection of Oscar Wilde: 'I shall go down to Salisbury', he wrote, 'and bathe myself in Gothic things.' John Meacham commented that Salisbury Cathedral was the only one in England that was entirely Gothic. Its spire was the highest in the country. We proceeded past a house about to be occupied by Ted Heath and another that had been the home of the late Arthur Bryant. We reached the Bishop's residence.

The official residence is a friendly, attractive period house of modest proportions, not built as a dwelling for bishops. The palace in which John Baker's distant predecessors led their lordly lives, a stone's throw away, is now the Cathedral School.

In South Canonry, as it is called, the Bishop has his personal staff. The chauffeur lives in a large independent wing with his wife, and the chaplain and the secretaries have their offices in rooms within range of the Bishop's study. At the back the garden reaches down to the Avon with its swans and ducks and other river-life in profusion.

The Bishop himself was on the doorstep to greet us, soon joined by his wife, Jill, equally hospitable. We were much assisted at lunch by Dr Sydney Evans, the Dean, his friend for twenty-eight years. The first impression made on me (apart from his unexpected height, accentuated by his leanness) was of his openness. Warm, yes. Friendly, yes. Many people are warm and friendly. But openness is not common in high places. He reminded me of the present Pope, with whom I had a short interview. John Baker sustained his openness through three hours of intensive discussion.

One felt one could say anything to him (I was not there to be offensive!). One felt that he would welcome the intellectual in addition to the human exchange. I asked him bluntly whether his opposition to blood sports and his alleged 'unilateralism' had caused him trouble in his diocese, much of it a hunting or military area. He replied frankly, 'To some extent, yes', in each case. But in regard to blood sports he had been at great pains not to make pronouncements in the pulpit.

As is well known, he was the chairman of the Church of England working party on nuclear weapons, whose report, *The Church and the Bomb* (1982), was debated at the Synod in 1983. The report was not 'unilateralist' but suggested so large a step in this direction that, in political terms, he and his committee were thought to have come out on that side. The report was not accepted by the Synod; the 'orthodox' attitude of the Archbishop of Canterbury, which I happen to share, prevailed. A resolution was passed, however, repudiating the 'first use' of nuclear weapons. So the Bishop's working party did not labour altogether in vain.

The Bishop spoke to me candidly about the fate of the proposals. They were widely misunderstood.

No doubt we failed to express them clearly enough. The key to our position was that we dealt with NATO as a single unit. We emphasized that NATO should not reduce its nuclear weapons unilaterally to a point which would endanger defence, but should make a reduction that would not imperil security, whether or not the Soviet Union responded in kind. The point of this action would be to try and change the international atmosphere and so improve the prospects of multilateral negotiations.

The really contentious point in the plan was in his view the proposal that NATO should make this reduction by discarding the U.K. independent nuclear deterrent. This would mean a total cut in NATO nuclear strength of some 5 per cent only. The point of making the cut in this way was to breathe some life into the 1968 Non-Proliferation Treaty by removing at least one nation from the nuclear weapons line-up. The working party did not believe, and the Bishop still does not believe, that the U.K. nuclear deterrent would be an adequate defence for this country were we to find ourselves standing alone; and as its contribution to total NATO strength is so marginal, it cannot be argued that it is essential for the Western Alliance.

The Bishop was by no means contented in retrospect with the way in which they had presented their case. They had failed to deal satisfactorily with the problem of consultation with the Allies, the timetable for phasing out U.K. nuclear weapons, the issue of other weapons on U.K. soil, and the pressures that U.K. nuclear disarmament might put on other NATO countries, West Germany in particular. He did not deal, however, with the conviction of most English people that they could not afford to be as completely dependent on the United States as they would be if they renounced their own deterrent.

The Bishop emphasized to me that he was still strongly committed on three points in particular. First, the use of nuclear weapons was morally indefensible. Secondly, pacifism was a valid Christian option in the light of the teaching of Jesus, and the Churches should stand up for the right of their members to follow that vocation if they so choose. Thirdly, the Churches, as corporate bodies, must devote themselves to the promotion of peace far more seriously. They must use their world-wide network to break down fear and tension and to foster reconciliation wherever possible. They must persuade governments and peoples to divert more and more resources to the urgent problems of health, food, population, and the global environment. They must question governments publicly about the assumptions behind their defence policies.

The Bishop sadly points out in conclusion that of the twenty-two recommendations in *The Church and the Bomb* nineteen were positive and non-controversial. They have been totally ignored.

What was said above about his personal openness applies also to his approach to ideas. He could be described as a seeker in all things. Today he is inclined to agree that the attempt in *The Church and the Bomb*, though arguably inevitable at the time, was claiming an expertise in foreign policy to which the Church was hardly entitled. I pointed out, what of course he was fully aware of, that his proposals for renouncing the British bomb in order to promote general disarmament were based on certain assumptions about Soviet reactions. Bearing this in mind, he seems today to consider that the pressure on the government by the Churches should take a more interrogative form. The government should be pressed at all times to answer the question of how far its policies could satisfy the requirements of Christian ethics. It would seem that a good many elderly people still write to him in a critical spirit under the impression that he is some kind of pacifist. But military authorities in the neighbourhood appear to understand his position perfectly.

I asked him what he considered to be the outstanding strength of the Church of England. Rather to my surprise he named its sense of responsibility for the whole people of Britain (we did not pursue the issue overseas). He recognized that this aspiration could not be fulfilled. But a sense of community between the Church and the people as a whole had always inspired and would always inspire the Church of England.

He said that from the time of the final break with Rome onwards, the role of the Church of England has been understood by Anglicans as the pastoral care of the whole nation. The vision was of the people of England at worship in one Church. Hence the insistence on being both Catholic and Reformed. I asked him whether in practice this vision had ever been realized. 'A modified version of it still means a lot to many of us.' Roman Catholics and Free Churchmen were not, thank God, penalized as they once were in the supposed interests of this vision. 'Today there is friendship and co-operation beyond anything ever dreamed of in the past.' Clearly the pastoral care of the nation was shared by all the Churches, which was right. Equally clearly in our pluralist society many people had nothing to do with the Churches, nor any wish to do so either because they were of other faiths or none.

The crucial point, however, is this. Most Churches see their task as caring for their members only, those with a definite affiliation to them in some way or other. The Church of England traditionally sees its responsibility as extending to all the people who live within the geographical area of the parish, whether members or not. Today, one would not interfere with those who are provided for in other ways, be it church, mosque, synagogue, or whatever. But the Anglican parish is there for everyone, if needed, in the way appropriate to their need. It also accepts a responsibility for permanent mission, again in all appropriate ways. This is one reason why with an active membership no larger, perhaps smaller (disregarding baptized Church of England people who have little or no contact with their Church) than the Roman Catholics, we still have almost three times as many clergy and believe we need them.

I pressed him about the relation of the Church of England to the universal Church. In reply he stressed two points in particular. First, the Church of England has always insisted that it shares the faith of the great Catholic Communions, because it holds to the Scriptures, the Apostles' and Nicene Creeds, and the decrees of the first four

Ecumenical Councils, as well as having preserved the threefold Catholic order and the apostolic succession. Secondly, the Church of England recognizes a duty to give only such teaching and to take only such actions as are compatible with this common inheritance which it shares with the universal Church. In this sense it seeks to act, in conjunction of course with the other Provinces of the Anglican Communion, not in the isolation of independence, but as a member of the universal Church.

He seemed to feel that the main weakness of the Church of England today was an unchecked tendency for individual congregations to behave according to their own likes with too little respect for authority.

At some point I touched lightly on the activities of the Bishop of Durham. I had not yet interviewed him (though I had met him in the House of Lords and listened to his maiden speech). John Baker and the other two present at lunch were agreed that, unlike the Reverend Don Cupitt, whose television programmes had aroused violent controversy, the Bishop of Durham was basically a sound Christian. Cupitt's own defence of his remaining in Holy Orders was a conviction that his views would become orthodox in time to come. I ventured to offer my opinion that the suggestion by the Bishop of Durham that the disciples might have stolen the body of Jesus was inconsistent with even the most liberal understanding of the Gospel texts. The Bishop of Salisbury sought to tell me that the Bishop of Durham was not trying to say that he personally believed that this might have occurred. He was only indicating it as a plausible hypothesis. All of us, however, at lunch agreed that the presentation was unfortunate.

Since my interview I have looked up again the Bishop's speech on the nature of Christian belief, prepared for the Synod on 13 February 1985, though not in fact delivered. I will quote a few sentences:

We cling to the comforting thought that, though we as individuals may get things muddled or wrong, the Church, if faithful to the Scriptures, will have at least the essentials permanently defined. If we guard these formularies, and teach them, then we hope the faith will be secure.

And then, later in the speech:

God is continually revealing new aspects of His work in our expanding knowledge of His universe and of ourselves, and thus deepening our understanding of the revelation we already have in scripture and tradition. 'The faith once delivered to the saints' was true. But where we are obedient to the spirit of Christ in prayer, life, and thought, the faith we preach today is more completely true, because it unfolds yet more of the treasures of wisdom and knowledge hidden in Christ.

In helping us to this creative obedience, we need two kinds of teacher: those who refuse to let us ignore the unique primal revelation of Scripture and the insights of the Creeds; and those also who refuse to let us ignore the unanswered questions and the gifts of new truth.

I do not myself see why a bishop should not be one of the second kind. But he ought always to make clear when what he says is not the teaching of the Church, and what that teaching is. For only the Church as a whole can define with authority the limits of belief.

These remarks, one hopes, have been studied by the Bishop of Durham. But the Bishop of Salisbury seems to imply that the teaching of the Church of England today has been, and is, readily available. He says that only the Church as a whole can define with authority the limits of belief. I asked him where such definition was to be found. In reply he handed me to take away a document presented to ordinands.

I asked him about the task confronting the Doctrine Commission of which he has become Chairman. He thought it was essential that they should deal with every crucial issue referred to them. He hoped this reference would be made more effectively than in the past. He was also hopeful that the work of the Doctrine Commission (under his chairmanship) would do something to break down the insularity of British theological thinking. He himself has done major work in the translation of European texts.

The Bishop is rightly described as a liberal in most respects, but on marriage he is firmly traditional. He has always opposed the use of the marriage service in church for anyone whose previous marriage to a partner still living ended in divorce. 'In my view', he told me,

> a further marriage of this kind cannot witness to the ideal Christ set before us for marriage, and should not therefore be solemnized with a rite designed for those who are in a position to live out such a witness. On the other hand, marriage breakdown is a human pain and sadness which calls for the utmost the Church can do to give help and support; to encourage penitence (where appropriate) and to bring God's forgiveness; to foster reconciliation, healing, and hope for the future.

There would be cases where two people believed that a further marriage was right and sincerely wished to bring it to God for the help of His grace. In such cases, after a civil ceremony, there should be available for them a positive service of prayer and dedication in church, which their family and friends could attend. He told me that he was one of the 'ten bishops' who pressed this point of view during the debates in the General Synod. 'We have such a service', he went on, 'in this diocese on which the Church of England Liturgical Commission drew very substantially for their official form. Experience shows that this service, when combined with good pastoral care, is deeply appreciated by couples and in the great majority of cases meets their needs.'

The Bishop laid immense stress on the need to base all Christian doctrine on the Bible. As already mentioned, he is a biblical theologian. He is certainly no fundamentalist. In a contribution to the Doctrine Report of 1981, he set out at length the manner in which doctrine has been and should be developed. He acknowledges a large debt to Newman. But John Baker, a restless intellect, to whom fresh thinking is attractive, will always possess a firm anchor in the Bible as his ultimate authority.

He can be unhesitatingly described as an ecumenical man. He has done splendid work of an ecumenical character in Northern Ireland, with his wife as always beside him. But he had no hesitation in answering the question, What is the main obstacle in the way of reunion between Rome and Canterbury? 'The position of the Pope.' He had been profoundly moved by the Pope's visit and by the Pope's personality. He had been embraced by him in Canterbury Cathedral and had gone to Coventry to hear from him further. He did not doubt that a formula would be discovered that would satisfy Anglican leaders and many Catholics. But he did not think it likely to be acceptable at the present time to the Papacy. For the moment he did not seem to expect much further ecumenical progress. He continued to hope and pray for it.

Had his beliefs been much affected by the course of his life? He was educated at Marlborough with its strong Anglican tradition. While there, the idea of a religious vocation had begun to take shape. He benefited much in retrospect from his two years in the army. He rubbed shoulders with all sorts of people. (The Bishop of Birmingham told me the same story about himself.) But one part of his army experience was traumatic. For one year of his national service he had served in a hospital for those still suffering from dreadful war injuries. Some had faces so badly burned as to be barely recognizable. His inclination to be ordained was confirmed. From then on, I should judge, he was drawn especially to those in desperate need of rescue.

I could not help expressing mild surprise at the statement he made early in 1983 that he had always voted Conservative. I think that today he slightly regrets not the way he cast his vote but the public revelation. He doubts whether a bishop ought to indicate his party preferences. We discussed at some length the extent to which the Church should, as the saying goes, intervene in politics. We both recognize the old dilemma that if the Church remains silent it is accused of not giving a lead, and if it pronounces on issues with which the political parties are concerned it is accused of helping one party or another. We did not arrive at any new conclusions. I would guess that the Bishop would never find it possible to suppress strong convictions on any matters, political or otherwise, but that the duty of holding his flock together would never leave his mind for a moment.

To return to his party allegiance: the Labour Party, it would seem, had never satisfied him that it would possess the practical capacity to perfect his ideals. I told him that I myself spent four years (1932–6) moving from the Conservative to the Labour Party and agonizing over just this issue. I could not help reflecting that his bomb working party must have brought him much closer on those matters to the Labour Party. I am left to speculate how he voted in 1983 and how he will vote next time round.

The Bishop, after three hours of courteous and stylish exposition, escorted me to the door. I noticed that he was limping and could not help wondering if he was in pain. I learned afterwards that though still only fifty-seven he has had a replacement hip operation. I feel confident that this will not prevent him from assuming heavier and heavier responsibilities. The gospel of love in high places has need of such a champion.

❧ 11 ❧

John Bickersteth,
Bishop of Bath and Wells,
bishop by tradition

It is not, I hope, paradoxical to describe the present Bishop of Bath and Wells as energetically serene or, if the phrasing is preferred, serenely energetic. Both qualities are exhibited in his present life-style and in his attitude towards it. He now lives in simple style with his family in the north wing of the historic Bishop's Palace, Wells. For more than 1,000 years the site of the palace has belonged to the Church. The centre of the present palace dates from the thirteenth century.

Until 1937 there were five gardeners, two chauffeurs, and eight indoor staff. Now only two gardeners remain; the Bishop's wife does most of the housework. Until 1954 the main building was occupied by the Bishop of the day. Now the 'plant', as the Bishop calls it, is fully used in the service of the community – more so, he likes to think, than in any other diocese. It is made much use of for conferences, exhibitions and social events. When I visited the Bishop in July 1985, 10,000 visitors were expected during the following fortnight. The Bishop and his wife are untiringly involved in all these activities. But here the serenity comes in. He would move out tomorrow to modest quarters without the slightest hesitation, if that were the wish of the community; but manifestly it is not.

The Bishop's own evaluation of his dedication to his 'plant' is worth quoting:

My wife's and my own commitment to this house and grounds [we see] as a real sacrament of the job of being a bishop of this

94

particular diocese. We spend hundreds of hours a year on this part of my episcopal life! Working out and carrying through a wide variety of entertaining, welcoming the thousands of casual visitors, planning the house or the garden's refurbishment. I am sure there are those in the diocese who feel we give too great attention to all this detail; but you have to be yourselves, and this is our approach, given the astonishing plant of which we are temporary custodians.

Some of his serenity as a bishop, his sense of being at home in the job, may well come from his background. There are a good many family networks in the Church of England, but the most remarkable is that of the Bickersteths. We are told in Tim Heald's *Networks*:

John Bickersteth, Bishop of Bath and Wells, is the fourth Bickersteth bishop in the last hundred years. Other Bickersteths have been Head of the Community of the Resurrection at Mirfield, Dean of Lithfield, Chaplain to the King and Chairman of the Mission to Seamen. Even those who did not become clergymen were strong churchmen and Christians. Henry Bickersteth, who was a doctor in Kirkby Lonsdale at the beginning of the eighteenth century, wrote a useful volume called *Medical Hints to Clergymen*. In the long family tree of the Bickersteths, I counted sixteen Bickersteth priests. Eight of the Bickersteth women married clergy. And rummaging through the Bickersteth family tree, I completely lost count of the male Bickersteths who married the daughters of clergymen.

The present Bishop insists that he originally wanted to be a farmer. In some notes that I sent to him after my visit, he felt that I did not bring out sufficiently his

countryman's approach to life . . . my garden (and my dogs!) loom large in my life. If I had not been a priest I would have been somewhere in the farming world (while waiting to join the Army I worked in a Kentish wood for the Forestry Commission, learned to swing an axe there, and thereafter have had a great interest in trees, culminating in the planting of the Jubilee arboretum here).

The man who changed his mind was his wartime *padre* (he was commissioned in the Buffs), who said to him towards the end of the war: 'Why don't you stop fighting against what you really want to do?' He was forced to admit that the *padre* was right. Surely the subconscious force of heredity can be detected here. In the Church he says that the various strands of thought were so well represented among his ancestors that he is not likely to be committed to any one of them.

His serenity, not to be mistaken for complacency, extends to the religious situation in his essentially rural diocese. A report on *Rural Anglicanism* that painted a depressing picture annoyed him as it annoyed many others. He could not dispute its facts. Attendance at church was admittedly low. What the report totally failed to appreciate was the ever-increasing vitality of the Christian life among those who did attend church. There were something like 250 lay readers who had taken a three-year course. Altogether there were 450 or 500 men and women now qualified to administer the sacrament. In his ten years as Bishop, this represented real evidence of spiritual growth. He did not, of course, claim that all was perfect or nearly perfect in the Church of England at the moment. He regretted for example the non-adoption of the bishops' proposals for dealing with the remarriage of divorced people.

Now it had become a most unsatisfactory 'free-for-all'. Whether you could or could not get remarried in church depended on the particular view of your particular clergyman. Naturally there were wide variations. But even here the Bishop refused to be discouraged. It was sensible that some divorced people should be allowed to be remarried in church and that others should not. The question is: how do you make the selection? How do you separate, so to speak, the sheep from the goats? (The Bishop did not himself use this expression.) No doubt, in time, a reasonable solution would be arrived at.

Still less was he worried about the development of synodical government. I told him that two days earlier I had interviewed the Bishop of London, who expressed grave anxieties on that score. The Bishop of London did not consider that the laity should be allowed to play a large part in determining doctrine. They might be permitted to raise the question whether a particular proposal was in accordance with Anglican traditions. The Bishop of Bath and Wells took

the precisely opposite view. He considered that the involvement of
the laity in so-called synodical government was a most welcome step
forward. He gave various examples from his own diocese where lay
opinions were most valuable. In administrative matters such as
boundaries and even on doctrine it was entirely right that they
should have their say. I mentioned the recent approach of the
Archbishop of Canterbury, which announced a more positive
leadership of the bishops. Bishop Bickersteth had heard the speech
and entirely agreed with it. The Archbishop was saying that in the
fifty years of synodical government the bishops had bent over
backwards to give the Synod freedom of action. The time had come
for a stronger assertiveness by the bishops in order to bring about the
intended form of synodical government.

I asked how synodical government with a strong lay element fitted
in with the apostolic succession on which I thought the Church of
England based a large part of its credentials. He replied that in the
early days of the Church an important part was played by what
would now be called the lay element.

His attitude to synodical government – after all a very recent
development – showed that he was anything but hidebound. He has,
however, said publicly on more than one occasion that he is a
Conservative voter. I did not ask whether it was wise for a bishop to
favour one party openly, though it is not, of course, unprecedented.
He answered the unspoken question by pointing out that his diocese
was overwhelmingly rural and Conservative.

He thought that Conservatism was truer to the English way of
looking at things. But he would like to think of himself as a *progressive*
Conservative. He was horrified by the fantastic increases in top
salaries just announced when I saw him. He had written in protest
to an old friend much involved. A much more fundamental defect
in our society at the present time was unemployment. It was very
small in his diocese compared with some others. He had done what
he could to join in local efforts to offset the corroding effect on the
young.

Inevitably we got on to women priests. Here again he declined to
talk in terms of crisis. He was definitely in favour of women priests,
but nothing must be done to disturb the underlying unity of the
Church of England. Sweden provided an awful example of how it

could all go wrong. He was confident that Archbishop Runcie would handle the issue with skilled diplomacy.

Did he not think that the ordination of women in the Church of England created a new obstacle in the way of unity with Rome? Not at all. He understood that Cardinal Hume had stated that there was no fundamental theological objection to women priests. I told him that a good many of my Catholic friends favoured women priests.

On the prospects for Christian unity he was optimistic, taking a reasonably long view. Inter-Church relations in his own diocese were excellent. Something like eighty of his Anglican churches were now used for Catholic Masses – inconceivable before Vatican II. There was no doubt a residual Anglican suspicion of Rome, but far less than of old. 'Provided that a reasonable independence was retained for the Church of England, he did not foresee an ultimate Anglican objection to an allegiance to Rome.' This was clearer language than I had met elsewhere. It would be an absolute requirement for Anglicans that the *central focus* of Canterbury should be maintained. He laid great emphasis on the need for this central focus. Personally he was entirely favourable to ARCIC, though few men and women in the pew would know much about it. I told him that one or two Anglican bishops had given me the impression that the attitude of the present Pope was somewhat disappointing. He declined to comment, though he admitted that John Paul II was a traditionalist. One of his bishops had recently come back from Rome enthusiastic after meeting the Pope and, of course, the great occasion of Canterbury 1982, when the Pope and the Archbishop of Canterbury came together, would never be forgotten.

On international affairs, more particularly nuclear warfare and East–West relations, he has come recently to speak with a special authority. In the spring of 1985 he represented the Archbishop of Canterbury at a conference arranged by the Russian Orthodox Church. He was the only Englishman present, but for some time previously he had spoken out on the nuclear issue with extreme urgency. In April 1983 he delivered a presidential address at his diocesan Synod in Minehead. In that speech he expressed his conviction under ten headings summarized below:

(1) Pacifism is an honourable Christian way forward, but today it must remain an ideal.

(2) Nuclear war is in a different category from all other wars (the Bishop fought in the last one).

(3) Nuclear weapons cannot be disinvented.

(4) The unilateralist hope is a non-starter; there is real mileage in a freeze and in banning all nuclear weapon tests.

(5) All people of goodwill in the West must back the idea of negotiating with the Soviets.

(6) All inflammatory remarks about evil Soviet intentions are not acceptable.

(7) Churchmen should give time to going to peace meetings.

(8) C.N.D. has become too labelled politically as left-wing; the leaders should consider disbanding it and joining the struggling world disarmament campaign.

(9) We must all learn to be pre-active rather than reactive.

(10) Have we not a unique opportunity as a Church to unite our country in peacemaking?

I asked him whether his views had been much or at all changed as a result of the conference in Russia. 'Not appreciably,' he replied. It had been hard to assess the sincerity of their Orthodox hosts. Their status, indeed their survival, depended so obviously on the Communist rulers, their overwhelming love of Russia was patent. His already expressed convictions seemed valid.

Soon after his return, he addressed a vast Campaign for Nuclear Disarmament gathering at Easter. He had made it plain that he was not speaking as a member or supporter of C.N.D., simply as a lover of peace and one who respected their motives. He repeated to one of the C.N.D. notables his view that C.N.D. was now so identified with the Left in British politics that it would do well to disband and reform under non-party or all-party auspices. The notable replied: 'I hear what you say', which was sufficiently cryptic.

As with women priests, so with the Bishop of Durham a question had inevitably to be asked. John Bickersteth expressed agreement with my reference to David Jenkins's charm and his donnish pleasure in provoking thought. I called it 'teasing'. He himself had been a great friend of Bishop John Robinson, generally considered David Jenkins's predecessor as a stimulator of controversy. Looking back, he believed that what had been new and good in John

Robinson's message had survived – to the benefit of the Church. The rest had been forgotten. So it would be with David Jenkins.

When I visited the Bishop of Durham I learned that in less than two years he had already aroused devotion in his diocese. In ten years the Bishop of Bath and Wells had done that and more 'with knobs on'. The Bishop finds in the Church of England the Holy Spirit perennially at work sustaining, renewing, guiding forward. He retains the wider vision of Christian unity. To convey his full message, another passage from a recent speech must be quoted: 'The famine in Africa must be at the heart of Christian concern, as the escalating arms race must also; because neither can be according to the will of a loving creator God.'

$\backsim$ 12 $\backsim$

John Armstrong,
Archbishop of Armagh,
Church of Ireland Primate of All Ireland

Dr Armstrong, whom I visited in August 1985, is a man of medium height, of strong squarish build and dark countenance, young-looking for his sixty-nine years, firm and direct of gaze, with a slight suggestion of a Northern Irish accent. A true son of Ulster, one might say, and one would not be too far wrong. He was born in Belfast in 1915 and educated at Belfast Royal Academy and Trinity College, Dublin.

No one hearing him speak in poignant terms of, for example, youth unemployment in Northern Ireland could doubt his deep commitment to the province of his birth. He and the leaders of the Catholic, Methodist, and Presbyterian Churches called on Mrs Thatcher when she visited the North and gave her a piece of their collective mind about the training of young people in particular. 'She listened very patiently and promised to do what she could. Little has happened since.' I suggested that her free market philosophy would always limit her readiness to interfere with the free play of market forces. He did not appear to dissent.

He confessed to a love of gossip and in that and more fundamental ways he bore many traces of his long and distinguished sojourn in the Republic, where he will go to live when he retires. He was for ten years Dean of St Patrick's Cathedral, Dublin, and for twelve years Bishop of the diocese that became Cashel and Ossory. He was then chosen as Primate of All Ireland by the other eleven bishops (half the Irish bishops are from Northern and half from Southern dioceses.)

He spoke warmly of the good treatment that he personally and the Church of Ireland generally had received from successive Irish governments. He had a particular admiration for Mr de Valera. 'Dev. once said to me: "I have always longed to visit St Patrick's." I received him at the cathedral; there was much cordiality on both sides.'

He formally dispelled any loose talk about discrimination against Protestants in Southern Ireland. This was confirmed to me by the Reverend Norman Ruddock, parish priest of Castle Pollard, County Westmeath, the small town close to Tullynally Castle, my family home now in the possession of my son Thomas. As a boy, I used to attend what is now Norman Ruddock's church in Castle Pollard. I was thirty-four when I became a Catholic. In those days we children used to snuggle down in our family box in the gallery where none of the congregation could see us. I told the Archbishop that, when writing the life of Mr de Valera in conjunction with Dr Thomas O'Neill, I interviewed one of his former chaplains about his religious life. The chaplain (by that time a bishop), while stressing Mr de Valera's exceptional devotion to the Catholic Church, remarked additionally: 'He would have made an excellent Protestant.' The Archbishop recalled that a Protestant girls' school in Dublin used to perform a play every Christmas. 'It was always written for them by Mrs de Valera.'

I mentioned the synodical elections about to take place in England. In the Church of Ireland a Synod had been elected in 1984 to run for three years. I suggested that in England the main issues would appear to be women priests (most prominently), the movement to Christian unity in the light of ARCIC, and the doctrinal controversies sparked off afresh by the Bishop of Durham. Dr Armstrong told me that the last problem had not arisen at all acutely in Ireland. 'The Bishop of Durham affair has made practically no impact.'

On women priests he was in the forefront. He was chairman of the committee formed to promote their ordination. As regards women deacons, Ireland was keeping in step with England, but in Ireland, unlike England, the Synod had not yet passed a general resolution in favour of women priests.

Much of our talk was devoted naturally enough to one aspect

or another of Christian unity. The Bishop himself was strongly in favour of ARCIC. In fact, all the bishops, with one doubtful exception, were in favour of it. But it would be a hard struggle, to which the Bishop looked forward with some relish, to get the proposals accepted by the Synod.

The Orange Order, inveterate foes of unity with the Catholic Church, were still powerful in Northern Ireland. They had been on the decline, but the violence of recent years had somewhat revived them. They were especially strong in County Antrim, a key area. I must realize that two-thirds of the elected members of the Synod – that is, excluding the bishops – were laymen. They would provide a large element in the resistance. Ian Paisley was not a member of the official Orange Order. He had been extruded some time ago; but his political followers were all too influential in the Order and therefore a significant force in the politics of the Church of Ireland.

Norman Ruddock has told me what the Archbishop did not mention – that Paisley had led a protest meeting close to the cathedral when Dr Armstrong was being consecrated Primate. The alleged excuse on that occasion was the presence of Charles Haughey. Generally speaking, the Paisleyite and Orange influences were the main cross that the Archbishop had to bear, though he did not use that expression.

The Archbishop left me in no doubt that, politics apart, he was a heart-and-soul believer in the aspirations expressed in ARCIC. But reconciliation between the Anglican and Roman communions would probably bring greater political and social blessings in Northern Ireland than in any other part of the world.

I mentioned that Archbishop Runcie had told me that the question of Anglican Orders would have to be settled before there was much further progress. I had been told by more than one Catholic bishop that *this* problem should be by no means insoluble. Dr Armstrong agreed with both statements. He added the subtle thought that, if read carefully, the ARCIC documents accepted Anglican Orders by implication.

I told him that some Anglican bishops had expressed anxieties about some of the attitudes of the present Pope. Dr Armstrong understood very well what they meant. The present Pope was undoubtedly a conservative, but theologically the Protestants of

103

Northern Ireland were conservative. There was not a fundamental difference on abortion and contraception, for example, between the attitudes of the Pope and his own, though he felt that what the Pope had said about contraception could well have been put differently. If he were asked to criticize the Pope, it would be on the grounds that he seemed to have retreated on occasion from statements that had given encouragement to Anglicans in search of unity.

When the Pope visited Dublin, he made a deep impression on the Protestant leaders, not least in regard to mixed marriages. Later, however, a far less helpful reply was received from the Vatican. We agreed that in British political terms it might be the case of a charismatic leader going back to the office and being told by the permanent secretary: 'No, Minister.'

The Archbishop can fairly be described as a progressive thinker. The foundations of Anglicanism are said to be found in Scripture, tradition, and human reason. This formulation seemed to be acceptable to him. I failed to ask him, as I should have done, whether the working of the Holy Spirit introduced a fourth element. This way of looking at things seems to fit in well with the Catholic development of doctrine, well accredited since the days of Cardinal Newman. The Archbishop considered that we would be failing in the use of our God-given reason if we did not deepen our interpretation of the Christian message as the years and centuries passed by.

I asked him about the Thirty-nine Articles. 'I assent to them', he said, 'but this does not mean that I take every one of them literally.'

He promised to send me some of his sermons. In the meantime he laid his final emphasis on spiritual renewal. So many of us suppose that we can 'do it all ourselves'; this is obviously impossible.

In due course some of his sermons arrived. There is space here to quote from only two of them. On the face of it, two more conflicting occasions could not be imagined. The first was given at the Royal Ulster Constabulary sixtieth anniversary Diamond Jubilee Service; the second on St Patrick's Day, in each case in 1982. The R.U.C. is a controversial element in Northern Ireland politics. A number of Roman Catholics have always joined, but it has been regarded widely in nationalist circles as a British rather than an Irish force. Dr Armstrong was unequivocal in his praise of the R.U.C.:

We give thanks to God today for the magnificent way in which that task has been carried out. We remember especially those pioneers sixty years ago who took over from the Royal Irish Constabulary and falteringly began to lay the foundations of a police force which has continued to do its duty in preserving law and order in this province, despite at times great difficulties.

So much, taken on its own, would bring joy and encouragement to every Unionist heart. But Dr Armstrong, speaking there and elsewhere, on a level beyond and above politics, said this at Downpatrick, on St Patrick's Day 1982:

We who gather in this cathedral today have come on a pilgrimage, because this is St Patrick's Day and we are come to this state in honour of *our* [emphasis added] national saint. . . . It was Patrick who became the real bishop, the first one of the Irish people, and our primary purpose today is to offer our praise to God that he separated Patrick who had been a slave boy in Ireland to be the chief shepherd in this island.

There speaks the true voice of Christian Ireland, irrespective of whether a political border separates six counties from the other twenty-six.

❧ 13 ❧

Michael Hare Duke,
Bishop of Saint Andrews

Michael Hare Duke, Bishop of Saint Andrews since 1969, has had a closer connection with psychiatric thought and practice than any of the other bishops interviewed. This is not to assert that his understanding of the human psyche is more profound than theirs; but it gives his utterances a distinctive underlying flavour, though he does not make use of psychiatric jargon. The impression he creates is one of active concern.

Can one distinguish any special influence of psychiatry on his thinking? I would suggest that he is inflexibly resolved to appreciate the standpoint of 'the other fellow' as an essential step towards reconciliation.

But first a few words about the Episcopal Church of Scotland and the Bishop's own background:

To be an episcopalian in Scotland is to belong to the world-wide Anglican communion. That is not the same as being a member of the Church of England. Our offices are similar, and our liturgical year shares the same pattern as other Anglican worship, but we are an independent Church. The Scottish Episcopal Church is not to be confused with the Church of Scotland. The Presbyterian Church of Scotland is the national Church, as the Church of England is established in England.

The roots, the Bishop told me, of the Episcopal Church 'are deep in the country's history'. After various 'ups and downs', with the restoration of Charles II the bishops and the Prayer Book came back to Scotland; from the time of William and Mary they were 'outed' again. From 1690 the established Church of Scotland has been Presbyterian.

Today, the Episcopal Church takes its place with the Kirk and the Roman Catholics in ecumenical explorations and activities. Most of our churches are small and built in the nineteenth century. They serve about 45,000 communicant members in the whole of Scotland. We have seven bishops, whom we elect ourselves, and they elect their Primus who is *primus inter pares*, first among equals and not an archbishop. We are a small, independent, democratic, and Anglican Church in Scotland.

The bishop added that 'even though the Episcopal Church is very much a Non-conformist body, its bishops have a kind of "establishment" '.

This is a book about bishops. For our purposes, the Episcopal Church of Scotland qualifies. The Presbyterian Church of Scotland, the national Church, does not.

The Bishop's involvement with mental health began when he was a student at Westcott House.

Having read theology at Oxford, I had a spare academic year and used this to join with the medical students in their clinical lectures on psychiatry and do some wide-ranging reading in the analytic field. As a curate in London, I found opportunities for further learning and a welcome from the medical world of even a junior clergyman's interest.

When Dr Frank Lake first appeared on the scene in the late 1950s, Hare Duke was an incumbent in Lancashire, and joined one of his clinical theological seminars.

He was exercising a peripatetic ministry to the clergy, teaching them a particular amalgam of theology and psychiatry. After a while he invited me to join the staff of a small centre he was setting up in Nottingham, and I went there as its 'pastoral director'. This

107

job involved me not only in teaching pastoral care to clergy and laity in seminars which were set up all over the United Kingdom, but also in doing a considerable amount of counselling of the clergy.

After about eighteen months full time, Hare Duke began to recognize that he was not cut out to operate on a medical model, with consulting rooms, appointments, and so on. 'I returned to the parish and stayed alongside the clinical theology centre, doing the teaching and the counselling from a parochial base.' He remained on the staff of the centre until he came to Scotland. There he has been actively involved with a variety of organizations. He took over the chairman-ship of the Scottish Association for Mental Health, a post he has just relinquished after seven years.

His earlier background was very much Oxford.

I was taught both Greats and Theology by Austin Farrer and owe a very great deal to him. I first went up to Trinity in the summer of 1944 for what was then called a university naval short course. I was matriculated in the bizarre combination of bell-bottom trousers and a scholar's gown! I then spent two years in the Navy and returned in 1947 to Oxford. I then went on from there to Westcott House and was ordained in the London diocese as curate of St John's Wood with Noel Perry-Gore as my rector.

Perhaps his psychiatric approach emerges most clearly in an article that he wrote to the *Scotsman* in 1984 about the ordination of women. 'The answer', he said, 'we give as to whether or not women should be ordained goes to the heart of our Christian belief.' The public debate was 'the tip of the iceberg'. He said that there were four major concerns beneath this iceberg's tip. The first was theological and affected the way that we understood the meaning of the humanity of Jesus. How significant was it that he was a male Jew of the first century? The second large underlying issue concerned the nature of authority in the Church. If some change was to be made, like allowing women to be priests, on whose authority could it be done? A third part of the iceberg was concerned with another question closely related to the one of authority: How do we read the signs of the times?

The Bishop is at his most characteristic when he deals with the final section of the iceberg, however, which he labels 'the understanding of sexuality':

Every individual, whether a man or a woman, has a masculine and a feminine dimension which need to be reconciled within an integrated personality. Where this goes unacknowledged, man and woman are seen as opposing stereotypes; he powerful, decisive, unemotional, she delicate, yielding, all heart and no head. In this way the two aspects are split and set over against each other as though they were mutually exclusive. This results in one half of each personality being denied. It is part of the liberation of the masculine in women that has led them to claim a vital and creative role in society. In this process they have set free the man to explore the feminine gifts that have too often been concealed under a male exterior.

He maintained the interrogative form to the end of an intricate argument. 'If Jesus', he wrote, 'is totally human, did he have a feminine part to his personality? And, if so, in what sense is that also healed?' Hare Duke leaves us in no doubt by the end that the whole matter should be discussed on a much more profound level than hitherto. But equally, when it is so discussed, there will be no resisting the ordination of women.

The Bishop has delivered a number of arresting addresses in the last few years. I will concentrate mainly on one that was given at Kilkenny in October 1985, as part of the 700th anniversary celebrations of the cathedral. His Irish credentials were excellent:

My mother's father left Kilrae in County Derry to become a young subaltern in the Indian Army in 1843 when he was only eighteen years old. My paternal grandfather stayed in his native land as a clergyman of the Church of Ireland, but his sons dispersed far and wide, which is how I came to be born in Calcutta and to end up as a bishop in Scotland.

He refers with feeling and some sense of family responsibility for 'the tragic split in Ulster'. 'I am aware', he says, 'of how the

Churches of my grandfather's day poured theological petrol on to the fires of social division, and we still suffer from some of those attitudes that they mistakenly taught.'

In November 1985 news reached us of the most promising developments in Northern Ireland for many years: the consultation agreement between Westminster and Dublin. The news also reached us of the hostile reception accorded the new settlement by the Unionist leaders. The attitude of Dr Hare Duke is badly needed at present in Northern Ireland.

Dr Hare Duke's search for reconciliation carries him far beyond these islands. He played a notable part at a conference in 1985 in Prague. His basic philosophy in the search for reconciliation between East and West has been expressed on a number of occasions.

> The collaboration upon which peace could be built is increasingly frustrated. There is an urgent task for Christians in this generation to find a way through the new barriers that are being created. Yet part of the uncomfortable truth is that those barriers actually use the language of Christian belief as a way of heightening the opposition between the opposing factions. It is disheartening to see the way in which the Churches of East and West quickly become chaplains to the warring tribes instead of holding fast to the fundamental unity which they have in Christ.

I mildly reproached him for his readiness, so it seemed to me, to place on equal terms the forces at work in the East and the West. He is certainly not unaware of the horrors of Communist ideology, nor of the evil that may be present in man. In reply to a question of mine, he said clearly that he did not believe in a personal devil; the evil lay in human sinfulness. I feel myself that he is so conscious of this factor that he is reluctant to see Christians climbing on to their high horse – in other words, to see the West treating itself as the 'goodies' and the East as 'baddies'. I understand this feeling very well from my own prolonged, if not very successful, exertions on behalf of criminals. But I myself cling to the ancient slogan: 'We must hate the sin and love the sinner.' I therefore side with those who feel that Soviet expansionism must be resisted like German Nazism by force or by the threat of force.

I recognize that, on issues such as these, Christians will differ from one another to the end of time. Meanwhile the Bishop of St Andrews and many like him will preach a message of reconciliation and find plenty of support in Matthew V: 'Love your enemies and pray for those who persecute you.' Modern psychiatry cannot add to this message except to deepen it.

Interlude:
The Bishops in the House of Lords

A research thesis could be written about the contribution of the twenty-six bishops to the House of Lords since the war – the period during which I have myself been a member of the House. The years of Mrs Thatcher's government alone provide plenty of material. However, the influence exerted would, in the last analysis, be as difficult to quantify as that of any other group in the House.

The bill that later became an Act (in 1984) reforming the divorce laws caused deep anxiety among the bishops, of which they made no secret. The period after marriage that must elapse before a petition can be lodged was reduced from two years to one. There were other aspects of the bill that enabled the Lord Chancellor, Lord Hailsham – himself a strong Christian – to persuade himself that divorce would not be made easier. But the bishops collectively thought it would. The Bishops of Rochester and Norwich expressed grave doubts with much eloquence. A passage from one of the latter's speeches illustrates the tone adopted:

> In no way can we call a one-year period a Christian marriage. I would not use the word 'laughable' – if I can think of a better word to use I will use it – but it is totally opposite to the Christian view of marriage. Your Lordships will remember that we are not simply concerned with Christian marriage in our nation, because marriage is a creation ordained from the early dawn of time. We are concerned, therefore, with marriage as an institution, whether for Christians or for people who feel towards the stability, happiness and joy of Christian marriage. Therefore though we strike but a very small blow for the idealism of marriage, let us at least vote not to wit but to conscience on the matter of at least a two-year period.

113

But in the crucial division the two-year proposal was defeated by 66 to 32. Only five bishops recorded their votes in the lobby.

It is well understood that it is almost impossible for bishops to preserve a high record of voting, and for most of the time they are a very small group indeed. In the event, therefore, they remain a minor factor in the politics of the House. This is as regards the short run; in the long run their moral influence is incalculable, but in my view far-reaching.

In a rapid survey it is tempting to pick out speeches delivered by the Archbishop of Canterbury. If only from his position they count more than those of other individual bishops, and Robert Runcie has not needed his rank to make him carefully listened to. The British Nationality Bill which was introduced in 1981 was sharply criticized by the leaders of all the Churches. An extract from one of the Archbishop's speeches gives the flavour of them all:

The present bill, even though it has no preamble declaring a theory of national identity, cannot avoid establishing by its provisions a picture of British national identity. The fact is that many feel that it gives a picture of first- and second-class citizens. It is no help to an individual Jamaican or Barbadian to say to him: 'Don't worry about this bill, because you've been registered here and your children were born here. So you will be all right', or, 'You still have five years in which you can register as a British citizen and get full rights here.' The bill does not seem to spell out the securities of citizenship within the multi-racial society that this country has now become.

The forces of Christianity did not prevail on this occasion but it was not for want of trying, or due to any lack of candour.

The much-admired speech with which the Archbishop of Canterbury initiated a debate on crimes of violence at the end of 1983 illustrates the strength and weakness of Christian leadership in the Lords. A better survey of the whole subject could not be looked for. No penal reformer could have improved on this passage:

We must never forget that the Christian belief in God on which the ethical framework of our country has been built combines a

114

realism about the fundamental corruption of human nature with a determination not to despair about the potential in everyone for redemption. It is an ethic which draws its inspiration from a unique marriage of discipline and compassion. That is the face of God in Jesus Christ.

The debate took place soon after the Home Secretary had announced the policy of inflicting more severe penalties on certain classes of criminals and for interfering, lamentably in many eyes, with the working of the parole system. The Church of England had the opportunity through its leaders of speaking out against these new and harsh developments in penal policy. The most the Archbishop would permit himself to say was: 'I hope that it may be possible to review these policies in due course.' No doubt the members of his Church and the other Churches were, and are, sharply divided about the new government policies, but this writer at least must offer the opinion that the passage quoted above is incompatible with even a tentative acceptance of them.

On the Falklands issue, the Archbishop was at his strongest, fortified no doubt by his own fine war record. He was generally understood to be supporting the Falklands war, and this is no doubt true; but on re-reading his speech to the House one is almost more struck by the emphasis laid on the need to achieve a peace in accordance with Christian principles:

My Lords: If a greater degree of force now has to be needed – and this seems likely – let us remember that its purpose must always be to achieve a just political settlement and not a military victory. We need to be very clear that our objective is not to punish or to avenge hurt pride. It must be to achieve a settlement which is based on justice and which upholds the two principles which I have mentioned – and, ultimately, that can be achieved only by negotiation.

This was in keeping with the fine stand made by the Church of England when the war was over in its insistence that the service of celebration should be one of reconciliation rather than of triumph.

On unemployment the bishops have never hesitated to speak out eloquently in the House of Lords and elsewhere. No one has put the matter in a Christian perspective better than the Bishop of Birmingham in his maiden speech, inhibited though he was by the non-controversial rule restraining maiden speakers. Here is a passage from the speech of the Bishop of Derby in the same debate on 23 January 1985:

> Among people of all ages, including the young unemployed, there is a mood of helplessness, an awareness of inability to change what appears to be a deteriorating situation in almost every area of our national life. Ordinary folk feel that their views do not count and their votes do not count. The wife of a man once on strike but now working said to me, among a small group of people, that they do not know what the powers are which now control their lives. They are just weak and find themselves incapable of doing anything to bring about change.

Is the government much affected by these and other similar cries from the heart? Much less than it might be for one simple reason: the bishops seldom see it as their function to say what ought to be done in any concrete terms. The government goes on its way, if not rejoicing, at any rate relatively unscathed. I am talking nationally. Within each diocese the bishop can and does exert all kinds of pressure for a more humane and constructive application of national policies.

Many individual bishops, most prominently the Bishop of London and the Bishop of Liverpool, protested in the strongest terms against the government's bill, which became law in July 1985, to abolish the Greater London Council and the metropolitan councils. It would be impossible to do justice to those speeches here nor to those with which the bishops in December 1985 denounced the bill to remove restrictions on Sunday trading. The government was bound to win, unless it allowed its own party majority to collapse. I venture only one criticism, which may not even be valid. A friend of mine, the former Lord Hinchingbrooke, M.P., who renounced his title as Earl of Sandwich to become Mr Victor Montague, once told me that among his reasons for leaving the House of Lords was the fact that in this place 'there is no intrigue'. He was deploring the absence of the hectic lobbying and manoeuvring behind the scenes that apparently are such a feature of life in the House of Commons. Had the bishops held a little bit too much aloof from these perfectly respectable features of political life, which are a good deal more pronounced in the House of Lords than when Lord Sandwich renounced his peerage? I hardly like to say it, but there is no doubt that if they were rather less reluctant to stoop, they might find it easier to conquer.

If it is a criticism of the bishops that they are reluctant to speak out strongly enough in the House of Lords, this criticism would certainly not apply to the second speech, made on 11 November 1985, by the Bishop of Durham. His first speech was in duty bound uncontroversial and left most of the peers uncertain about his meaning. There was no such uncertainty about the second occasion. He was nominally speaking on transport, but his remarks were in effect an indictment of the whole Thatcherite philosophy. He showed himself aware of the criticism that bishops should stick to theology, and starting from that position he courteously but scathingly disparaged the whole Thatcherite point of view as a false idolatry. He said that he felt that the bill was based on faith – 'a faith about the nature of our society and the forces at work in it'. He went on to say that this faith 'is very probably a false one and quite possibly verging on idolatry'. He spoke of the 'quaintly archaic air of romantic unreality' which pervaded the bill and accused the Government of wearing 'ideological blinkers'; if they would only set them aside 'they might very well see that there are very considerable arguments on a number of sides and on a number of issues'.

As he spoke, the Labour and Liberal benches could hardly prevent themselves from breaking into applause. The Conservatives could scarcely repress their indignation.

This emotion was rapidly expressed by the Conservative speaker who followed the bishops. Later, I congratulated the Bishop of Durham on the delightful *jeu d'esprit*. He hoped that he had not lost any possible votes by his controversial speaking. I begged him not to worry, but to continue to speak his mind. I feel sure that he will always do so (see page 77).

As I remark elsewhere, the influence of the bishops has expanded considerably in recent years and on present indications is likely to expand still further. From what has been said about the line taken over the Divorce Bill, the Nationality Bill, the bill abolishing the GLC and other metropolitan councils and the Bill facilitating Sunday trading, it will be clear that the bishops are certainly not government 'poodles'. In the chapter of Conclusions we deal at some length with their radical criticisms of government attitudes towards the inner cities.

As this book goes to press, the government bill to throw open Sunday trading has been dramatically defeated on a second reading in the House of Commons and killed stone dead. I cannot recall an occasion when the Churches combined so effectively in the secular sphere. The Anglican bishops in the House of Lords took full advantage of their presence there. Apart from bishops already mentioned, the Bishop of Southwark is the first to come into my mind. I shall get myself into further trouble if I try to apportion merit.

PART II

THE ROMAN CATHOLIC BISHOPS

Introduction to Part II

The Catholic Hierarchy, the collectivity of bishops, was officially restored in 1850 after nearly 400 years' exclusion from Britain. Throughout those centuries the flag had been kept flying by a gallant minority, infinitesimal at the beginning but swelling steadily with the Irish immigration in the nineteenth century. Indeed after several hundred years of isolation, in the first half of the century, immediately after Catholic Emancipation (1829), there were four striking happenings: first, the Irish immigration already mentioned; second, the slow emergence of the old Catholic families into a fuller participation in the life of the country; third, the Oxford Movement, bringing into the Church some of the choicest minds in the country, such as Newman, Manning, Ward, and Faber; fourth, the return of the old religious orders with their monasteries and colleges, and the arrival of the newer religious orders, mostly Italian in origin, like the Passionists, including Dominic Barbieri, the Redemptorists, the Rosminians, and the Oratorians.

In the following 100 years the Catholics in England and Wales increased continuously in sheer numbers and in success in the professions and business. When the Vatican Council was called in 1859 they still had, in worldly terms, the point of view of a beleaguered minority.

The Reverend Edward Norman, a very illuminating Anglican writer, has dramatized effectively the situation: 'As the English bishops left for the Second Vatican Council, the centralized, clericalized, disciplined Church fashioned under Ultramontane influence in the nineteenth century lasted until well into the middle of the succeeding one.' By 1962 most of the bishops were aware, says Norman, of new attitudes in relations with the non-Catholic Churches, but none of them was conscious that the whole pattern of authority within the Church itself was about to be altered.

121

Cardinal Heenan, recalling his own unpreparedness for the change – which he came to welcome – declared that, as Bishop of Leeds from 1951, 'I was to do my duty by giving orders and the priests theirs by carrying them out.' Since then there has been an immense change, both actual and potential. We can place the developments under various headings: decentralization, collegiality of the bishops, free discussion of everything under the sun, a new assertion of the rule of conscience, the changes in the Mass (notably the translation into the vernacular), an altogether new emphasis on the participation of the laity in the Mass and otherwise. The real point, Archbishop Worlock has told me, is that the revision of the rite of the Mass now reflects the ecclesiology of the Church as seen in Vatican II. The changes in the Mass and the increased participation of the laity would seem to many rank-and-file Catholics the most significant changes, though the new assertion of conscience may hold out still more far-reaching possibilities.

There are at the moment twenty-four Catholic bishops and sixteen auxiliaries. With the exception of Cardinal Hume and, in the north of England, Archbishop Worlock, they are less likely to hit the headlines than their Anglican counterparts. An expert judge, Clifford Longley of *The Times*, considers that the Catholic bishops have not as yet developed a sense of their need to justify themselves to their following. Another way of putting it is to refer to their overriding determination to present a united front, to their sense of collegial inter-responsibility.

They are not yet represented in the House of Lords, where they would be more or less bound to deliver individual opinions. Nor is there any forum like the Anglican Synod where individual contributions are called for. A Catholic bishop, as Archbishop Bowen remarked to me, is always supposed to be speaking for the Church as a whole. It is expected, moreover, that to a greater or lesser extent his commandments will be obeyed. This is hardly the case in the Anglican communion, with its stronger accent on freedom.

These factors add up to an influence making for individual caution among the Catholic bishops. Collectively, however, it is rather the other way round. Whatever emerges in the near future, the Anglican bishops have not been notable in recent years for combined pronouncements. There is some idea in the minds of Anglican bishops, for example, that under the present Pope the Vatican has assumed a more commanding role. If true, this would be an obstacle to further progress towards unity. It is admitted by well-placed Catholic friends that in certain disciplinary matters – for example, the laicization of priests enabling them to marry – the Pope has stiffened up the rules. But the secretary of the hierarchy in Britain assures me that there is an increasing independence among the conference of bishops. Not only in this country but throughout the world the contributions of national and indeed continental conferences are becoming increasingly significant.

The most substantial of the documents to flow from the Catholic bishops was issued in 1980 in time for the Papal Synod to be held at the end of the year. It was called *The Easter People* and was published 'in the light of the National Pastoral Congress' held at Liverpool earlier in the year. It begins with a glowing reference to the National Pastoral Congress: 'Rich in sign and symbol, the National Pastoral Congress was for those who took part in it an extraordinary experience of what the Church is and a foretaste of what it can grow to be.'

All the bishops were there, together with those clergy, religious and lay people chosen to represent every section of the Catholic community, and also observers from other Churches. It seemed that almost all walks of life were present, and from every age group. 'As the delegates assembled in the Metropolitan Cathedral in the evening of Friday, 2 May 1985, there was a strong sense that here was a gathering together of the People of God.' (I myself was invited, but would have been unable to attend the whole congress, which was a prerequisite of attending any part of it.) The bishops wished to declare 'our belief that the National Pastoral Congress of England and Wales was a great Grace of God to our Church. We believed that the presence of the Holy Spirit could be detected in the sense of living unity which we felt with the whole Church and with our Catholic heritage and in our common purpose.'

The role of the bishop indicated caused surprise to some people, but it was consistent with all the preliminary consultations. There was no mistaking the emphasis laid on baptism and on its implications. The continuing task of the teaching Church is to open the eyes of all Catholics to the treasures they have in their baptism.

123

At the same time we commit ourselves to work for unity with our fellow Christians. We accept in faith our baptismal mission to every human being.

We can only touch here on four other documents that have emanated from the Bishops' Conference. Two of them, which deal with abortion and the Warnock Report, are not difficult to summarize. The bishops are 100 per cent against abortion. They point out that Christian teaching has always regarded the unborn at all stages of pregnancy as possessed of a personal quality, which no one could rightly seek to destroy. The Christian teaching is adamant about the right of the innocent to live. Even admitting of a right of self-defence in some cases, 'We are never entitled directly to kill the innocent.' The word 'directly' must be noted here. The bishops admit that action leading to the death of an unborn child may in some cases be permitted. 'We are speaking of cases where the interference with the unborn child is in fact an unintended, though foreseen, side-effect of procedures necessary to save the mother from some underlying or supervening condition that threatens her life.' For example, a treatment for cancer of the uterus can be justified even if it also causes a miscarriage.

The late Archbishop Heenan told me that he regretted the failure of the Catholic Church in England to come out fighting more fiercely when the Abortion Law Reform Bill was being passed. There was a calculation, which he afterwards considered mistaken, that it was better to let the Anglicans take the lead. But, in fact, they were much divided on the issue. For a number of years the Catholic Church, led by its bishops, has left no one in any doubt as to where it stands.'

The Warnock Report was roughly handled by the Catholic bishops' Joint Committee on Bio-ethical Issues: 'The Inquiry's formal recommendations afford quite inadequate protection to the human embryo. In more ways than one they seriously compromise human rights. They offer no reasoned basis for these compromises.' Unabashed by the fact that the chairman of the committee, Baroness Warnock, is herself a professional moral philosopher, they speak with disdain of the Warnock Committee's idea of morality.

In the Warnock view, 'Moral questions, such as those with which we have been concerned, are, by definition, questions that involve not only a calculation of consequences, but also strong sentiments with regard to the nature of the proposed activities themselves.' In the view of the bishops, this is all wrong. It totally neglects the rights that each member of the community possesses by virtue of being a human individual. The embryo represents human life at its earliest stage. The bishops' report spells out the steps it considers necessary for adequate protection of the embryo.

The bishops' response to the final report of ARCIC I can be said to accept that report in principle. The Archbishop of Canterbury has spoken about it to me in those terms. In their conclusions the bishops specifically identified themselves with the common declaration signed by the Pope and the Archbishop of Canterbury in 1982. In particular, they say, 'we support their hope and expectation for ARCIC II and we accept their call to us all'. However, the Catholic bishops did not merely say 'ditto' to ARCIC I. Most of their comments might be described as refinement, but they made one or two unequivocal criticisms. In regard to the Eucharist they are glad that the Real Presence of Christ is clearly stated; but 'What needs to be said more forcibly is that the Eucharist is offered to the Father by the whole Christ, head and members, in the power of the Spirit.' The present text, by concentrating on the Eucharist as gift to the Church, gives an emphasis that is too passive in tone. In this treatment of the Eucharist there is also insufficient reference to the Resurrection of Christ.

They recognize that the question of Anglican Orders is 'unresolved'. But they consider that 'The development of the thinking in our two communions regarding the nature of the Church and of the ordained ministry has . . . put those issues in a new context.' The bishops appear to be hopeful that a solution can be arrived at.

Authority is generally considered to be the hardest nut to crack. When my wife was moving towards the Catholic Church, there came a moment when she could accept anything except the Pope. Finally this difficulty was overcome. More than one Anglican bishop has told me that the main obstacle to union at the moment appears to be the way in which Papal power is employed. The Catholic bishops, however, say emphatically: 'One of the most outstanding achievements of the Commission is the progress made in tackling the question of authority in the Church, through patient and exacting dialogue.'

It may be that there is some misunderstanding in Anglican circles about the degree of Papal interference with the local hierarchies. As mentioned earlier, I am assured on the Catholic side that local independence is steadily maturing, not only here but throughout the world.

The Archbishop of Canterbury was justified in saying that the Catholic bishops had accepted the ARCIC report. The Anglican response, by reason of their more democratic machinery, is taking longer to emerge. But the Synod has already shown good will. On 4 February 1985 a very elaborate process of consultation was set up between the Anglican, Catholic, and Free Churches.

On 10 and 11 July 1985 the Conference of Catholic Bishops held an extraordinary meeting to prepare their submission to the Extraordinary Synod of Bishops to be held in Rome in November of that year. In the last few years, following a promise given at the National Pastoral Congress in 1980, the bishops had comprehensively reorganized their machinery of consultation. The most elaborate consultation of the laity had taken place before this extraordinary meeting of July 1985.

Responses had been received from fifteen dioceses, eleven conference bodies, four national organizations, five seminaries, and half a dozen entities described as 'other', including a number of individuals. On the face of it, the substantial document resulting might seem rather tame, but those with eyes to see have attached to it considerable significance. *The Tablet* applauded the bishops for 'giving a lead'. They certainly threw their weight unequivocally behind Vatican II and expressed the fervent hope that it would be put into practice with more and more zeal and determination.

Why was it necessary to labour this conclusion? The answer is plain enough. There were considerable fears, not altogether without reason, that reactionary forces would try to use the Synod to undo as far as it could the achievements of the Council. The bishops of England and Wales and also those of Scotland and Ireland certainly did all in their power to ensure an ever fuller implementation of Vatican II.

☞ 14 ☜

Basil Hume,
Cardinal Archbishop of Westminster

Cardinal Hume's two books, *Searching for God* and *To Be a Pilgrim*, are spiritual classics. In my eyes – though he would regard this as a preposterous comparison – they are the nearest things that our period has produced to *The Imitation of Christ*. But the thought of Thomas à Kempis as a cardinal or even a bishop is, to say the least, unreal. The question being considered here is the performance of Cardinal Hume as leader of the Catholic Church in England and (for eight years) of the European bishops. Essentially a monk, Abbot of Ampleforth by the time he was forty, admired then and now by all – how does he 'make out' in the role of cardinal?

Someone who has worked closely with him singles out three aspects of the Cardinal: his rare spirituality, his European culture, and his sense of community and community leadership. What strikes one above all in reading his spiritual books is his consciousness of the persisting difficulties of belief, though with him, to use the old phrase, a hundred difficulties do not make a doubt. He lays tremendous emphasis on prayer, but there again he is perpetually aware of the problems involved. To take only one example, in *To Be a Pilgrim* he teaches us, not for the first time, about the 'prayer of incompetence':

Most of us know this type of prayer only too well. It occurs when thoughts about God or anything spiritual are quite impossible and when our desiring is confused and unclear. . . . When this is the mood, we have to make a deliberate decision to pray, set times

127

aside, survive through all the difficulties, *stay there* just to show God we want to please him. There is much merit in that prayer, if little in terms of immediate rewarding joy.

At all times, so to speak, he sits down beside the struggling Christian. He is a profound believer in helping from shared weakness, rather than exhibited strength. No doubt his years as a housemaster at Ampleforth (he was the confessor of one of my sons) have revealed to him areas of the human heart out of the reach of most of us.

Again and again in his book *To Be a Pilgrim* he returns to the idea of the Cross and through the Cross the Resurrection. To take one passage almost at random:

'Into thy hands I commend my spirit.' That was Jesus Christ's prayer at the last moment, repeated down the ages by men and women, tortured and killed for their beliefs, the martyrs. That prayer has been said by countless men and women lying sick in hospital, martyrs too, in their way; by parents mourning a child; by lovers broken through their parting from each other; by people tortured by anxiety and worry; by men and women of great courage and endless patience, each of them masters of their pain and sorrow, because disciples of their suffering Lord. These are the people who have discovered in the carrying of their cross the secret of the resurrection – that new life comes from the dying seed.

Cardinal Hume is much more European than any previous Archbishop of Westminster, in spite of his many years at a great public school in Yorkshire. His mother came of a fine old French military family. She met his father, later an eminent physician, during the First World War. French was always spoken in the home. Not surprisingly, Basil Hume is bilingual; he studied at Fribourg in French-speaking Switzerland. He is also excellent in German. Soon after he became Cardinal he was accepted by the European bishops as their leader.

The third strand in his make-up, his sense of community and community leadership, is at least equally important. Every monk knows more about community life than a non-monk. But an abbot for fourteen years knows more than anyone about community leadership. Cardinal Hume has said that, of the three most difficult jobs known to him, the most difficult was that of Abbot of Ampleforth, the next most difficult was that of Archbishop of Liverpool, and the least difficult that of Archbishop of Westminster. An abbot must at all times unite his community; he must never on any account press some idea of his own if it is in any degree disruptive. Fellowship and fraternity are all. This background throws light on what may be regarded as the strength and weakness of the Cardinal's national leadership. He is not and never will be a crusader. A crusader has to go out in front and hope that the flock will follow after. A successful abbot will remain at all times at the centre of his community.

On special issues, the Cardinal has not been identified with many personal initiatives. On nuclear weapons and the Warnock Report, he has spoken out with extreme clarity. Behind the scenes he may well have had to coax along dissident colleagues. In penal affairs, however, where I acknowledge a special interest, he has pursued a conservative course, well aware no doubt that on such matters Catholics, like other citizens, are sharply divided. He has, nevertheless, carried out the biblical instructions, 'I was in prison and you came to me', with singular fidelity and success. Individual prisoners have told me that he comes into their cell, says simply, 'I'm Basil Hume', and asks permission to sit down on their bed. The visit is never forgotten.

No one, it is well understood, derives more strength from solitude, from being alone with God, than Cardinal Hume. His life in what he calls 'the desert' is essential for his great achievements in the 'market-place'. But he is readier than most bishops or other public figures to discuss his life and difficulties with the utmost candour. During a television programme on 24 February 1981 it was pointed out that a Benedictine takes three vows: to obey his abbot; to stay a member of his community; and to devote his whole life to his religion – a vow that includes celibacy. Cardinal Hume commented modestly but firmly as always:

At times it has been very difficult. I have always thought that at the heart of celibacy there is always pain. It is a sacrifice, the sacrifice of a close relationship with a woman and also the loss of that intimate companionship which anybody embarking on marriage presumably expects to have, and then not having your own family. I don't regret it, because although it's very easy to say that if you are celibate then you . . . you acquire a greater freedom to relate to a lot of other people. It never sounds quite convincing, that argument, but I think it's true.

He is remembered by his contemporaries at Ampleforth as an excellent all-round athlete, finishing up as an extremely successful captain of the first rugby fifteen. In 1941 he took a decision that certainly affected his whole life and, in the event, the lives of countless others. It was a dark period of the war. The young Hume, aged eighteen, had to make the crucial decision of whether to join the Army or join the monastery community at Ampleforth as a novice monk. The Cardinal comments on his decision to become a monk with characteristic frankness: 'I always, certainly in that year, had the kind of boyish idea that we would be invaded and that all priests and people like me would be strung up on lamp-posts, and there was another kind of heroism which seemed to be round the corner. And looking back on it now, if I had to make the decision again, I would have gone to the war.'

In due course he became a housemaster. His first head of house was Hugo Young, later political editor of the *Sunday Times*. Young wraps up a criticism in a compliment: 'He probably wasn't organized. He certainly wasn't a disciplinarian and, indeed, I should think in so far as I was aware of that, one would say he probably was disorganized. And we liked that, that he just was – he reflected our own disorganization and didn't impose a kind of artificial excessive hour-by-hour order on boys who really were not at the age to take to it.'

Did this very relaxed form of leadership foreshadow the methods he would adopt later on? One thing is certain, that he was looked upon as a most successful housemaster, and in 1962 he was elected Abbot at the incredibly early age of forty. He himself has referred to mistakes he made when Abbot. No one else seems to have noticed them. His appointment as Archbishop of Westminster and a little later Cardinal was accepted with acclamation by all who knew him and by all, except a few malcontents, who did not.

130

The familiar face of Cardinal Hume, Archbishop of Westminster, radiates his rare spirituality, his European culture and sense of community and community leadership

John Bickersteth, the Bishop of Bath and Wells, whose lifestyle and attitude can be described as serenely energetic

John Ward, the Archbishop of
Cardiff, whose welcome was warm
and unselfconscious, strikes me as a
very happy man

Maurice Couve de Murville, Archbishop of Birmingham, riding with
the Pope on his tour of England in
May 1982. The Archbishop has
always displayed an exceptional
fidelity to Papal attitudes

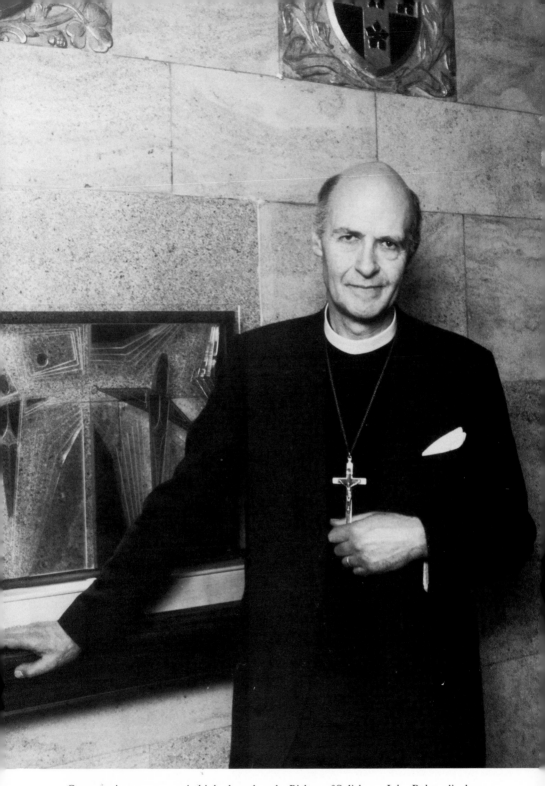

Openness is not common in high places but the Bishop of Salisbury, John Baker, displays this virtue

Cardinal Hume, for all his spiritual stature, enjoys a good laugh. As already mentioned, he captained the rugger fifteen at Ampleforth. In later years as a monk and master in the school, he was a very successful rugger coach. Later again, he suffered from severe arthritis, causing him at one point to limp heavily. When I called on him for my interview at the gloomy Archbishop's House, he was moving freely. I asked after his mobility. 'First class,' he replied. 'I can do everything except cut my toenails.' I told him that, curiously enough, I was visiting a chiropodist for the first time that afternoon. I could reach my toes all right, but with advancing years (I am eighteen years older than the Cardinal) I could not cut them. I have referred above to his readiness to share incompetence. The ice was broken; we laughed together.

I began with a question that he must have been asked many times. By now it may rather bore him. 'Do you think that the life of a monk, and indeed that of an abbot, is a good preparation for the life of a bishop and indeed a cardinal?'

He had read my notes about him quoted above. He was quick to resist the implication that his alleged sanctity might interfere with his effectiveness on the national scene. Immediately he spelled out the names of a number of monks who had become bishops in the Middle Ages, Lanfranc among them. 'Monk into bishop is an excellent tradition of the Church', he told me. 'I am sure you did not expect that answer', he said gleefully.

He rejected any implication that his knowledge of politics and politicians when he took office was inferior to that of other archbishops in recent times. He repudiated the idea of himself as a man far removed from the world suddenly being transported into an alien environment. As Abbot of Ampleforth, he had presided over the lives of 900 boys and 150 monks. A great friend of his, who was present at the interview, told me afterwards that any implied reference to his holiness, sanctity, or humility always produced a jokey answer to cover embarrassment. We agreed that if you say to a holy man, 'Is it true that you are holy?' no serious answer is feasible.

I ploughed on. Did he agree that, having spent so many years at Ampleforth, he had been subjected, boy and man, to powerful conservative influences?

131

'What do you mean by conservative?' he asked me. 'Do you mean politically Conservative?'

'That', I replied, 'is certainly included in the question.' All great public schools are conservative institutions, not least Eton, where I myself was educated, or Ampleforth, where four of my sons were. I had taken part in many debates at Ampleforth. My side always lost until on my last visit it was decided to give me a walk-over.

The Cardinal did not deny that there was an element of truth in what I said. He could not know how far the influence in question had affected his outlook. He told me, to my surprise, that in his day the monks tended to divide equally between the parties at election time.

I submitted that the Catholic leaders had been remarkably mild in any criticisms they had made of government policies in connection with the 4 million unemployed. As a Labour supporter myself I might be expected to feel that way. But various Church of England bishops, not only the Bishop of Durham, had been a good deal franker in criticizing the government. Of course, the Church of England has the advantage of twenty-six bishops in the Lords, where the Catholic Church has none. But that is another story.

Could the Catholic Hierarchy point to any national influence that it had exerted recently on government policy? I am not belittling what individual bishops achieved within their own dioceses. Inevitably I raised the question of penal reform with which I had been connected for half a century. The Cardinal told me in his own terms that we sent far too many people to prison and kept them there far too long. But when has he said that publicly? He replied that he was resolved not to make pronouncements on matters where he was insufficiently informed. Penal reform was in this category, in spite of his many visits to individual prisoners.

I recognized the force of his argument that everyone wanted him to come out in favour of their particular nostrum. No one man could possess or acquire the amount of knowledge necessary. Nevertheless, he had spoken out with great authority on at least three social questions: abortion, embryos, and nuclear weapons. I suggested that he found it easy enough to gather experts round him in these connections. Why could it not be done in penal reform, or delegated to an expert bishop, such as Bishop Harris? I told him what he probably knew already, that Bishop Harris, for so many years a prison chaplain, was thoroughly dissatisfied with the penal policies of the government. Yet not a bleat came from the bishops, or at any rate none came that reached me.

The explanation lies, I suppose, that in penal matters Catholics are just as much divided as the rest of the country. On abortion and embryos, a Catholic unity is readily available. It is, therefore, much easier to give a lead in those cases. I will quote at some length on Cardinal Hume's article on Warnock, which appeared in *The Times* of 7 June 1985. He had taken steps to ensure that he was speaking for the Catholic bishops as a whole:

It is not intolerant fanaticism but common sense which insists on the relevance of moral principles in the face of what is a difficulty of the imagination.

In making the leap between a collection of cells, and a baby, and a mature person capable of fully personal relationships, it is the imagination which baulks. The intellect is readily able to grasp what recent scientific knowledge has illustrated, the continuum which stretches from the moment of fertilisation up to birth and beyond, which is radically different from the state of affairs prior to fertilisation. There is a new principle of organisation, a new subject, a human subject with interests and rights because of its humanity.

He concludes in sombre fashion that the abandoning of objective moral principles and the dogmatism of permissiveness have combined in our day to undermine society.

On nuclear weapons, the conflict of opinion found almost everywhere is reflected among Catholic priests. There would be many to look on Monsignor Bruce Kent as a hero. The Cardinal agreed that the decision to let Bruce Kent continue to act as the very efficient director of C.N.D. (from which he has now retired, while remaining active in the movement) was highly controversial. But at least Bruce Kent had made it certain that the moral dilemma was appreciated throughout the nation and beyond. The Cardinal's article in *The Times* (17 November 1983) gave full expression to his hatred of nuclear weapons, but at the time declined to abandon the principle of self-defence. He called on the Western powers, and particularly Britain, to press on towards multilateral disarmament:

> My nightmare is that man will undo at the end of time what God had created in the beginning. I fear that the human story which began in Genesis may end with a fearful chapter given over to Nemesis. . . . Intellectually I can accept that the policy of deterrence is morally defensible, but only on the understanding that it must be no more than a stage towards multilateral and total disarmament. Nonetheless, everything Christian and human within me cries out in protest against the sheer horror of a world where these weapons are allowed to exist at all.

In this case, the pressures for a statement of some kind could not be resisted. Speaking generally about social issues, he told me that in the last resort they tended to be relative and secondary against the background of the overwhelming task falling to the lot of the bishops. This was nothing less than to promote in every home a worshipping relationship with God and a love of Jesus Christ and his Church. For that supreme purpose, the maximum possible degree of Catholic unity, ideally Christian unity, was indispensable. He presided today over a Catholic community split and likely to remain split on certain issues. But unity, he insisted, is possible on the religious plane. 'It is surprising,' he remarked, 'how much unity can be secured among those who are ready to pray together.'

I was hopeful that the Cardinal would throw fresh light on the comprehensive submission of the bishops to the special Synod which would take place in November 1985. The Catholic bishops had been congratulated, for example in *The Tablet*, for giving on this occasion at least a firm lead. What lay behind it? Was there a fear that there were forces at work in Rome, personified in Cardinal Ratzinger, that were determined to put the clock back and nullify the progress made since Vatican II? At this point the Cardinal was naturally somewhat guarded. He knew Ratzinger well and liked him. It might be better if he did not issue so many pronouncements. But Ratzinger or no Ratzinger, the bishops of England and Wales were determined to press for ever fuller implementation of Vatican II.

The Cardinal did not know why the special Synod had been

called. The Pope loved anniversaries. The twentieth anniversary of
the ending of Vatican II seemed to him and indeed to many others a
good moment to celebrate. Possibly it was felt that in a celebration of
this kind one recaptured something of the divine guidance and the
Holy Spirit at work in Vatican II. The Synod would last for only
three days. Nothing sensational must be expected. No harm could
come of it, and much good might result in the long rather than the
short term.

I asked whether at the last Synod the liberal ideas of the English
hierarchy in regard to birth control and the access of divorced
and remarried people to the sacraments had not been 'slapped
down'.

The Cardinal did not accept this language at all nor this version of
what happened. The Synod on the family took place shortly after the
National Pastoral Congress in Liverpool. Archbishop Worlock and
himself had conveyed to the Synod some of the points that had been
made at the Congress. As far as his own intervention was concerned,
he had attempted to point out that the whole Church ought to listen
to the experience and Christian insights of those who were the
ministers of the sacrament of matrimony, namely married couples
themselves.

The Cardinal has not devoted much space in his two books to
questions of sexual morality. Nor does he make much reference to
them on other occasions. The only major exceptions have been on
the publication of the Warnock Report and when the controversy
over Mrs Victoria Gillick – who sought to limit young teenage girls'
right to birth-control advice without their parents' consent – was at
its height.

When I asked the Cardinal why, he was clear about his reasons.
Society today seems to be obsessed with sex, which all too often
becomes identified with the pursuit of pleasure at almost any cost.
He is convinced that constant moralizing on such issues at this time
is not only ineffective but tends to reinforce the idea that sex is the
only real concern in life. In point of fact, attitudes to relationships
and to human love can be healthy and positive only if they are part of
a wider and deeper commitment of an individual to God and to the
person and teachings of Jesus Christ. Sex must never be isolated
from other human, religious, and moral values. It must always be

seen in the context of a human being's relationship to God and to other people. Then there is a chance of getting it right.

We spoke about the encyclical letter of Pope Paul VI on these issues, *Humanae Vitae*. The Cardinal recalled that at the time of the 1980 Synod on the family he had described that encyclical as prophetic – not in the sense of foretelling the future, but as commenting on the present from a religious standpoint. Given the contemporary attitude to sexual morality, the Pope and the Church had taken a stand against permissiveness, the commercial exploitation of sex, and a basically selfish attitude towards relationships. The encyclical continues to arouse controversy. It is often criticized for severity and absolutism in its condemnation of artificial means of contraception.

The Cardinal emphasizes the constant tradition of the Church, which condemns sexual activity outside marriage, and Catholic moral teaching on contraception. The conclusions, he believes, are absolutely right and offer the only way to achieve human maturity and healthy relationships. Individuals must, of course, always be helped with sensitive pastoral counselling and encouragement, especially when they find the going hard; but the ideal has to be vigorously upheld and shown to be within reach. The Church as a whole must continue to reflect on all aspects of human relationships and sexual morality. Deeper and more convincing explanations and reasons should always be sought to support the conclusions of traditional Catholic morality.

Cardinal Hume has delivered a number of memorable addresses. It is difficult to select one passage that is more representative than another, but this one must serve:

When I say that I have this terrific need for solitude and silence – putting it in more poetic terms, it is the need for the desert . . . walking through life and between myself and God, there is the cloud, the 'Cloud of Unknowing', and from time to time the cloud parts and a ray of light comes down through it. And that ray of light is something which will help the mind, lighten the mind and warm the heart . . .

– and through Basil Hume, the minds and hearts of many others.

More than once during our talk, Cardinal Hume returned to the

136

theme that a priest, still more a bishop, and most of all a Cardinal, must see himself as a servant and act instinctively as a servant. Some years ago, greatly daring, I wrote a small book on *Humility*. I distinguished there several forms or aspects of humility: seeing oneself as one really is; the suppression of pride (Cardinal Hume clearly qualifies for a first class there); another form was meekness (I am not quite so sure about his meekness; it is not a quality generated by dashing prowess on the rugby field); but under the last heading of mine, humility as service, Cardinal Hume emerges as a true champion, alike in theory and practice. This is as true today when he is a world figure as when the monks of Ampleforth selected him, at the age of forty, to be their Abbot.

He was very kind to me as I left. In reply, I said that I hoped to do justice to him and the other bishops. I had taken copious notes during my interview; unfortunately I could not always read my own writing – 'I must fall back on the prayer of incompetence'. He laughed without inhibition.

137

◇ 15 ◇

Derek Worlock,
Archbishop of Liverpool

Archbishop Worlock holds, after Westminster, the most important position in the hierarchy. He is a welcoming man, slim, with heavy glasses, a typical priest it might be thought, but in fact he is in no way typical. To begin with he played rugby football for Rosslyn Park, and in other ways his background is unusual. He is a man who has been described as having changed more during his lifetime than any other Catholic. He himself sees a thread of continuity and the palpable hand of Providence. His father and mother were both Catholic converts; he was the only Catholic at his preparatory school. He stresses his political background. His father was an agent for the Conservative Party. (Today Derek Worlock is accused of progressive leanings.) His mother was an ardent worker for women's suffrage.

He was born in 1920. Within a few months of becoming a priest, he was appointed secretary to Cardinal Griffin and for nearly twenty years (1945–64) he served a 'red hat trick' of cardinals: Griffin, Godfrey, and Heenan. He emphasizes the value of his own political and sociological education during the period of the Attlee government and the construction of the Welfare State. He was in regular contact with ministers. The abstractions of Catholic social principles acquired a new human reality. He was of the utmost value to Catholic peers and M.P.s during this period, as I know full well. Then and always, he was a brilliant draftsman, a rare talent, if not without dangers.

For many years he cherished the desire to become involved in parish work. Resisting all pressures to serve in the West End, he made a bee-line for East London. He is very grateful for the experience, but it lasted only eighteen months. In 1965 he was appointed Bishop of Portsmouth, where he served for ten happy and successful years. He was held in affection by many of his clergy and respected by all.

By 1976 he was very well known at Rome and very knowledgeable about events and personalities at the headquarters of the Church. He had been appointed one of the experts attached to the Vatican Council, his area of study being the laity. During his long period at Westminster, he had shown much imagination behind the scenes in helping to prepare Catholics, particularly working-class Catholics, for public life. A new role for the laity and its apostolate was perhaps the greatest of all the changes brought about by Vatican II. If so, Derek Worlock, working as so often behind the scenes, deserves a good deal of the credit.

Before the end of the Vatican Council meetings, he had become a bishop and was a personal friend of the bishop who is the present Pope. The friendship has continued and expanded ever since. One reference to what he learned during the period of the Vatican Council throws light on his immense subsequent concern with the ecumenical issue. 'We were discovering the nature of the Church; the relationship between Christians who were as yet divided in faith but, marvel of marvels, united by the bond of baptism into Christ's life and mission.'

Speaking directly of his subsequent partnership with David Sheppard, he says: 'That day of recognition of each other's baptism was probably the most important day of my life. It transformed our relationship with one another, and gave a new dimension and direction to our work together in the service of others – now no longer just "our own".' When vacancies occurred at Westminster and Liverpool, I remember speculation as to whether Derek Worlock would obtain a senior position. In fact, Basil Hume was chosen for Westminster. Derek went to Liverpool. Looking back, he sees the hand of Providence here. His political background, of which he never fails to be conscious, his up-to-date knowledge of the whole philosophy of Vatican II, especially in its ecumenical aspect, made Liverpool exactly the right place for him. Liverpool, traditionally cursed with sectarianism, even fanaticism, presented a great challenge and test of his spiritual and mundane talents.

All the bishops referred to in this book are, I am sure, revered by their staff. In the case of Derek Worlock some of the testimony has been especially striking. A gifted young woman with two theological degrees described him to me at some length at my invitation. 'He is a holy man. He helps you to understand what the Catholic Church is about – how to love the Church. . . . It is his manifest love of the Church and the way he shows it which has carried us in Liverpool away.' She goes further. 'In recent years his vision has grown much wider. Now it embodies the way the Church must serve the world.' Which brings us back to the so-called 'Mersey miracle' referred to in the essay on David Sheppard.

On the ground the joint approach has been very concrete. I interviewed Derek Worlock on a Thursday evening and David Sheppard on a Friday morning. David Sheppard kept me waiting a few minutes while he and Derek Worlock tackled a rather desperate situation concerning the black community in Liverpool – typical experience in their lives. When I visited Liverpool on this occasion, the tragedy of the Brussels Cup Final lay heavy on the city. David Sheppard and Derek Worlock had both held services attended by the other, in which the grief and horror of the whole community was expressed by those whom the community has come to look to as its national leaders.

And yet today it would not be possible for Archbishop Worlock to allow his priests to administer communion to non-Catholics, or for his flock to receive communion at non-Catholic hands. I do not get the impression that he thinks of inter-communion as the next step towards the much desired unity. He seems to see it flowing naturally from a further advance in understanding. This advance will come as part of an all-round process of *sharing*: sharing in talk, in work, and above all in prayer. Along these lines we must hope and believe that full unity will eventually be achieved. Meanwhile, though he did not mention this, the rest of the country could reasonably be expected to emulate the spirit of Liverpool.

Anyone interested in Archbishop Worlock (and by this time there are many such inside and outside Liverpool) should make sure to study his book, *Give Me Your Hand*. If asked to pick on one essay,

I would choose the one entitled 'Humility in Christian Unity'. He lays the utmost stress on Christ's teaching and example, on humility expressed in service: 'And he got up from the table, removed his outer garment and, taking a towel, wrapped it round his waist; and he then poured water into a basin and began to wash the disciples' feet and to wipe them with the towel he was wearing.' (John XIII: 4, 5). Derek Worlock admits that then and now this kind of humble service could be embarrassing. It was not just the humble nature of the task that humiliated the disciples, it was the utterly unselfish love 'with which he tended them which brought all their jealousy to an end'.

Having myself written a small book on humility (see page 137) – 'a very elusive subject', as a bishop remarked to me at the time – I take I suppose a special interest in what is said about it by our spiritual leaders. Humility, writes Worlock,

> is not really a human quality. It comes from the Creator. The little man who bows in reverence before the great may be acting prudently or obsequiously, but he is not necessarily acting in humility. Truly humble is the great man who bows before a lesser because he recognises in him a mysterious dignity from the very fact of his creation. Humility is not an inferiority complex. It is voluntary self-abasement. In Christ and in the foot-washing it is overwhelming.

I am not sure whether everyone recognizes the Archbishop's humility. Religious leaders, like eminent politicians, are seldom credited with it. But in the course of our long friendship, I have found him inflexibly seeking to practise this same humility in service.

He finds the divisions among Christians an obstacle to the belief of many people today and he says boldly: 'We know that we cannot rest in our common pursuit of a full Christian unity. . . . What came into existence so many years ago as the result of the life, death, and resurrection of Christ was a visible community of people, the people of God of the New Testament.' No day dawns, I would guess, without him asking himself what he can do to further the realization of this ideal.

Archbishop Worlock has been attacked a good deal and he is a

141

man by no means insensitive to criticism. Old-fashioned Catholics were distinctly suspicious of his determination to carry out Vatican II to the letter, and in particular of his ecumenical passion. This opposition has, I gather, grown less amid the general enthusiasm for his leadership, but another kind of criticism is not likely to evaporate in his case or in that of David Sheppard.

One attack on 'meddling bishops' in general and on Archbishop Worlock in particular came from Paul Johnson, as brilliant a journalist as can be found in Britain, a Roman Catholic, and an admired friend of mine. The tone of his article can be illustrated by the opening sentences:

> One of the curious things about our very verbal political bishops is that they appear to have absolutely no sense of Christian priorities. That is, they pronounce constantly on matters which are not really of immediate concern to the episcopate, such as the details of economic policy, while remaining totally silent on issues which are, or certainly ought to be, their particular province.

Paul Johnson concedes that bishops, if they would only stick to their fundamental and traditional role as custodians of morality, have an important part to play in reducing economic hardship. His argument can be put in this way: sexual immorality leads to broken homes; broken homes create delinquents in the next generation. The damage is done throughout society. Poor economic performance is one of the products. 'It is a long time since I have heard any clergyman, let alone a bishop, preach a sermon on the evils of fornication. . . . The deadly sins of the flesh, the sins that lie at the root of our problem of poverty, remain uncastigated.' He notices that Archbishop Worlock has joined the new body set up to bring pressure on the government to spend more on reflating the economy. 'I wonder', he concludes, 'how long it is since His Grace preached a sermon on the virtue of chastity.'

A sharp reply was not long in coming from the Archbishop's Press secretary. Mr Johnson has insinuated that the Archbishop had nothing to say about marital problems, the rising number of illegitimate children, or sexual morality. He pointed out that Archbishop Worlock had issued a pastoral letter on those very issues on 30 December 1984. The Archbishop, he added, always preaches on the virtues of Christian family life when making a visitation in a parish. He insisted that the Christian gospel applied to current social and moral standards with equal force. A Christian leader must deliver that message wherever it is needed – which is what Archbishop Worlock has done. He had preached a sermon on chastity in Liverpool's Metropolitan Cathedral only a few weeks earlier (11 February 1985).

The answer was a fair reply. I cannot help thinking, however, that Paul Johnson has a point that could be made against not just Archbishop Worlock but all of our Church leaders. When have we last heard any clergyman preach a sermon on the evils of fornication? I have a suspicion that it is done very seldom explicitly, though I suppose that most clergymen of all denominations believe that they preach the lesson of chastity in whatever fashion seems likely to be effective to their congregations.

I will leave that issue to try to give some impression of the Archbishop's approach to social questions. I will select for consideration a lecture he gave to the social and industrial ministry of the diocese of Bristol in Bristol Cathedral on 7 March 1985. He began his address by describing at some length a particular personal experience. He had received advanced notice of far-reaching redundancies in a tobacco factory for a major part of the workforce. It was tantamount to closure. 'Customarily Bishop Sheppard and I receive such advance information – either from the management, anxious for our services as consolers if not conciliators, or from the shop stewards' committees, anxious for our voice.' So it was on this occasion. Following these local discussions, 'Bishop Sheppard and I bounced up and down like yo-yos between Liverpool and London, to talk to politicians, kings of industry and commerce, and others about what was happening in the North, about mutual responsibility and the danger of two nations, about specific proposals to try to generate new industry or new investment for new forms of employment in Merseyside.'

I have already mentioned that in 1984 Archbishop Worlock and Bishop Sheppard met the Prime Minister three times at her invitation. The first question is to ask ourselves whether hectic activity of this kind is or is not seemly in two leading ecclesiastics.

143

I unhesitatingly answer 'yes'. But one is bound to observe that the two Liverpool notables have carried partnership much further than any other religious leaders. It is hardly possible that they could have done anything like as much if they had gone to work separately. Other bishops please take note!

In this same address Archbishop Worlock dwelt on what he calls certain moral consequences of the development of information technology:

> I have much sympathy with the visionary in a severely deprived area with massive unemployment, who said how marvellous it would be if men, freed from the drudgery of the grinding work they had always known, might in the future have the freedom to enjoy some of the wonder and beauty of God's creation. But before we can reach such heights, we have to do something to remove the stigma of unemployment and the indignity of the dole.

He faces the possibility that the introduction of new techniques will not create new jobs on the scale of those they have displaced. Hence it is vitally important that we recognize that full employment of the conventional kind will not return in the foreseeable future. At this point he comes into conflict with the philosophy of the Thatcher government and lays himself open to the criticism already mentioned of Paul Johnson. 'I personally would favour the introduction of a vast programme of public works, believing that unemployment figures have reached an unacceptable level in an attempt to keep down inflation.' More broadly he demands that we should give our minds not just to job-sharing and early retirement, but to a renewed understanding of what a real job can be.

I cannot spell out here his policy for dealing with unemployment. At all times he and David Sheppard have been acting in concert with those who seemed to them to be the responsible leaders of the community. Meanwhile under their leadership the Churches have set up their own unemployment unit. Bishop Sheppard has just completed seven years as chairman of the area board for special programmes. Archbishop Worlock is actively engaged in the Merseyside Enterprise Forum. I cannot begin to list the many aspects of their involvement in the struggle for a more prosperous

Merseyside. The only serious objection that could be raised against such phenomenal activity is that it tends to work against the Conservative government. The explanation may be partly the fact that the government of the day happens to be Conservative, but one is bound to mention the possibility that the Conservative 'wets' are right and the present government is not sufficiently caring.

The Archbishop always claims that if he generalizes about social issues he is accused of no worse than moralizing. If he is specific he is accused of political intervention. He says that he prefers not to sit on the fence, but to be understood where it matters.

Archbishop Worlock has spoken out with unrelenting clarity about the horror of unemployment and deprivation in Merseyside and about the abolition of the Merseyside Metropolitan Council. Is that interfering in politics? It certainly comes close to it, but few in Liverpool would regret the intervention.

It is not surprising that he was asked to deliver the 1985 Gore Lecture in Westminster Abbey on *Faith in the City*, the Church of England report on the inner cities. It is just as unsurprising that he endorsed the report warmly. But the lecture he gave on that occasion reveals that at all times his mind has been very much his own. His intimate co-operation with David Sheppard has been far more than an expression of personal friendship. It has illustrated a profoundly ecumenical approach. His recommendation of *Faith in the City* leaves one with the impression that the ecumenical message could have been, and must be in future, more emphatically delivered.

As in the case of other bishops, I must end by repeating that these are men of God and not politicians. I would say of Derek Worlock what was said in a very different context: 'He was a priest. It was his mission to hold the Host aloft, to look neither to the right nor to the left, and to hear his Saviour through the world.'

❦ 16 ❦

Michael George Bowen, Archbishop of Southwark

The first thing one notices about Archbishop Bowen is his height, accentuated by his erect carriage and leanness. I myself am over six feet, but he is considerably taller, as indeed is Bishop Murphy-O'Connor, his old companion from their days of study in Rome. His friendly smile comes next; then as you get down to business his simplicity makes the dominant impression. A passage from an otherwise forgotten book comes back to me: ' "Truth makes life so simple!" she sighed. "Honour makes it so lovely," she thought.' I am ready to credit all our bishops, Anglican and Catholic, with truth and honour. But simplicity seems a word especially designed for Archbishop Bowen.

Not naïveté by any means. His life has been too varied and unusual to make that likely. The beginning was conventional enough for a Catholic of good family. He was educated at Downside. He did his national service in the Irish Guards where he obtained a commission. Resisting the temptation to pursue a military career in a regiment where he had connections, he went up to Cambridge studying English. Rather surprisingly for a future archbishop, he left after a year to enter the wine trade.

Why wine? it may be asked. The answer is simple. The firm had been founded by his great-great-grandfather and it was still to some extent a family concern, though it has long since been taken over. He had every chance of becoming a director and, it might well be, chairman. His mother was anxious, as he was, for him to get started in life.

146

Looking back, he considers that he had had up to that time a sheltered, socially élitist existence. Now he had to rub shoulders on equal terms with all sorts of ordinary people. He was plunged into every aspect of the trade, buying, selling, importing, tasting, and so on. He travelled extensively; he won a scholarship in Port! I expressed the hope that the wine we were drinking was not of special quality, as it would have been wasted on me. He gave me a cryptic smile.

Though he mixed with so many people in the course of business he lived internally a lonely life. At Cambridge he had read a great deal of poetry. His devotion to it persisted.

'I had been seriously considering the priesthood for over a year before making the final decision in Gibraltar to offer myself as a candidate for ordination.' The call to follow Christ (these were not his words) and abandon all worldly prospects came to him as clearly as to the rich young man in the Gospel. Seven years of study in Rome followed. Particular friendships were forbidden, but an intense community of spirit flourished. The students were allowed home only once in the seven years. They seem to have preferred it that way.

Ordained in Rome at the age of twenty-eight, he was curate at Earlsfield (1959 to 1960) and Walworth (1960 to 1963) before returning to Rome as lecturer in theology at the Beda College. From 1966 to 1971 he served on the personal staff of the first Bishop of Arundel and Brighton, Bishop David Cashman, as secretary, chancellor and, briefly, coadjutor Bishop. This close involvement with the establishment and running of a new diocese, at the time when many changes were being introduced in the wake of Vatican II, was a totally different and highly useful experience for him. By the time he was forty-one, he became Bishop of Arundel, his diocese covering my own village in Sussex. I owe to him and to our parish priest at that time, Father Docherty, the great honour of becoming a Knight Grand Cross of St Gregory.

In 1977, on his forty-seventh birthday, he became Archbishop of Southwark. For someone manifestly devoid of ambition or obtrusiveness of any kind, his progress had been remarkably rapid. 'I became a bishop too young,' he now suggests with his habitual modesty. But his varied experience was equal at least to that of the great majority of bishops.

Southwark is a huge diocese, including all London south of the

Thames and the county of Kent. A slight complication arises from the fact that Archbishop Bowen has not one but three opposite numbers in the Anglican Church: the Archbishop of Canterbury, the Bishop of Rochester and the Bishop of Southwark. Ecumenical partnership is somewhat easier for Archbishop Worlock in Liverpool.

Why do I refer to his simplicity? To begin with, I think of him as doing the obvious things, but doing them extremely well. The Archbishop's first concern was to get to know the diocese. 'You have to put in a good deal of shoe leather,' he said. 'You have to go and see places. It is not enough to know about them.' In fact, within a year he had 'done the rounds' of 173 parishes and 120 convents, and had talked to priests, religious and groups of lay people in every parish.

He set about consulting his priests and lay people about the question of whether the diocese should be split up. In the end it was decided to create 'pastoral areas'. The existing auxiliary bishop in Southwark was joined by two more auxiliaries, each one dealing with one of the three areas. This is beginning to make him sound rather matter of fact, but more than one of those best qualified to judge have described him to me as among the most caring of men, sensitive to people's needs and problems.

He was naturally much concerned with the unforgettable service in St George's Cathedral, Southwark, for the handicapped that the Pope addressed in 1982. He has spoken about the disabled with special insistence:

Through the sacrament of baptism we each receive one and the same spirit; we are reborn with the same new life, we become members of one family, children of God, brothers and sisters in the risen Christ. Every member therefore has an equal place and equal rights within that family. This means that the disabled must be given their rightful share in the sacramental and liturgical life of the Church; and everything should be done to provide them with suitable instruction in the faith. We remember that the disabled in the Gospels were brought to Jesus; they heard his words and enjoyed an important place in his teaching.

And he adds this poignant footnote: 'The miracles, the teaching, in fact the whole of the life of our Lord contributed to the work of

148

our redemption. But in that work the moments of greatest value occurred when our Saviour was unable to move hand or foot on the Cross.'

The ethnic composition of South London makes it inevitable that racial questions should confront him all his waking hours. In one infant school in his diocese some twenty-nine nationalities are represented; and this is far from a unique case. He has spoken with the utmost clarity on the bearing of Christianity on racial issues:

The Catholic Church has a special responsibility in this endeavour. St Peter came to realise the truth that 'God does not have favourites, but that anybody of any nationality who fears God and does what is right is acceptable to him' (Acts X: 34–5). Subsequently the Holy Spirit was given to those of other races who were not Jews and the apostles came to understand the essentially catholic nature of Christ's Church. By our very definition as Catholic, we must embrace the whole human family, cherishing its diversities and promoting its unity.

Moreover in this country a large proportion of our newcomers are Catholics and come from cultures strongly influenced by Catholicism. Our diocese typifies this situation and we annually celebrate the fact with our multicultural Mass and festival at St George's Cathedral. We must be a multicultural Church, simply to be true to ourselves and to do our pastoral work properly. We can also help our country by giving her an example of what a multicultural community can be like and by taking a lead in trying to build up such a community.

And as usual he has followed up words with deeds.

I asked him what he thought was the gravest, the most urgent question confronting the Church today. He answered without hesitation 'the problem of the family'. In some of his areas there was a majority of children from broken homes. He was labouring to provide far more adequate preparation for marriage. An important diocesan policy document has been drawn up in consultation with the clergy and the laity which contains many practical suggestions regarding preparation for marriage and for marriage enrichment. I pressed him, not successfully, on the question of allowing divorced

Catholics access to the sacraments. He declined to go beyond the official line, which denies such access, though he recognized to the full the need for comfort and compassion of those in this predicament.

He pointed out what I had not grasped previously, that when it comes to individual pronouncements Catholic bishops are not on the same footing as their Anglican counterparts. An Anglican bishop does not have to be a Bishop of Durham to voice, within certain limits, his personal thoughts. The average member of the flock pays much attention to what he has to say, but does not usually feel bound by it. (This, incidentally, makes the task of an interviewer in search of 'copy' a good deal easier in the Anglican case.)

Reflecting on the above, I ask myself whether Anglican bishops 'interfere' in more cases than Catholic ones (I am talking of England and Wales). The fact that there are twenty-six Anglican bishops in the House of Lords and no Catholic bishops there thrusts on the Anglicans a right and duty to speak on matters of current political controversy – a right and duty that the Catholic bishops are spared. The point is underlined by the general consciousness of the Anglican bishops that a special responsibility adheres to them because they are the national Church.

Again, as explained above, the Catholic bishops are so conscious of their collective responsibility that they hesitate to speak on current topics unless they are more or less unanimous. I myself have not been successful in persuading them to come out boldly on the side of penal reform, though I am bound to say that I have not done much better with the Anglicans. In these latter days one must be thankful that capital punishment seems to be ruled out by both kinds of bishops. There are, of course, some well-known Catholic attitudes, for example, on abortion, an unmistakable Catholic interest, where the Catholic Church does indeed speak with one voice, but such cases are not common.

On the ecumenical issue, Archbishop Bowen is his usual practical rather than theoretical self. He does not foresee dramatic progress on the doctrinal plane. The Church of England is much less bound by doctrinal proposition than the Catholic Church, which adds to the difficulties. In his own diocese, however, there has been worked out a very promising covenant in one area with neighbouring churches.

For a moment at least, he thought it was this kind of coming together that was most helpful.

It would be wrong to imply that Archbishop Bowen presents simple answers to the remorseless questions that assail all thinking persons today, bishops not least. The very complicated issues arising from the Warnock Report have led the Catholic bishops to deliver certain judgements, but to leave over some vital areas for further exploration. He confessed that he found himself turning over these unsolved questions again and again. But I am convinced that his own approach will be simple. Someone so obviously devoid of vanity is peculiarly well equipped to follow the two greatest commandments: 'Thou shalt love the Lord thy God with all thy heart and with all thy mind and with all thy soul and with all thy strength.' 'Thou shalt love thy neighbour as thyself.' Those who work most closely to him seem convinced that his leadership reflects a higher guidance.

✿ 17 ✿

Maurice Couve de Murville,
Archbishop of Birmingham

Maurice Couve de Murville, elegant, dancing eyes, full of spon-
taneous response, has had an unusual career on the way to becoming
an archbishop. He was born on 27 June 1929 at St Germain-en-
Laye, near Paris, of Mauritian parents, coming to England at the age
of seven. He was educated at St Andrew's School, Leatherhead,
John Fisher School, Purley, Downsend School, Leatherhead, and
Downside School, Bath. He read history at Trinity College,
Cambridge (1947–50), and was awarded a B.A. degree. He returned
to Paris to study for the priesthood at the Catholic Institute and
received the licence in Sacred Theology in 1957.

He was ordained at Leatherhead for the diocese of Southwark by
the late Bishop Cowderoy on 29 June 1957. He served as a curate at
St Anselm, Dartford (1957–60), and St Joseph's, Brighton (1960–1).
He was appointed Priest-in-Charge of St Francis, Moulsecomb,
Sussex (1961–4). He was the Catholic Chaplain to the University
of Sussex (1961–77). In 1977 he moved to the chaplaincy at
Cambridge University. He has researched at the School of Oriental
and African Studies, University of London, and was awarded the
M.Phil. degree in 1975.

From the above it will be observed that he was a Catholic
chaplain for twenty-one years, sixteen at Sussex University, five at
Cambridge, before being suddenly elevated to the position of
an archbishop, ranking third in the hierarchy of England and
Wales. To understand him, one should never forget this particular
and, I suppose, unique background. While he was a Catholic

chaplain, he was at any one moment responsible at Sussex for two or three hundred souls, at Cambridge perhaps for five hundred. As an archbishop his flock number something like five hundred thousand. He must be deemed to have won such golden opinions as a chaplain that Bruno Heim, the Apostolic Delegate, must have recommended him to Rome as suitable to act as one of the leaders of the Church in England. No doubt this opinion was justified, but he is still very diffident about his qualifications to deal with a mass population.

He came to know, he says, a limited number of people extremely well as a chaplain; now he has a slight acquaintance with a very large number. It is all he can do to get to know the priests at all well. He still thinks of himself as an amateur archbishop. This emerged in 1984. The *Birmingham Post* on 22 March carried a rather sour account of an interview with one of its journalists. One of the headings was 'Slow Steps to an Audience with an Archbishop' and then a little further on 'The Silent Man of St Chad's'. This, the Archbishop's first interview for two years (and I gather that he has not given one since), was clearly a disappointment to the young journalist, who had to submit questions in advance and was not allowed to ask supplementary questions. An extract from the interview will give the flavour:

'After he had read his reply to my question: "Do you find it easy to pray?" I put my first supplementary question: "Is there anything in your own prayer life which you would like to recommend to other people?" The Archbishop replied firmly: "Sorry, it is not on the script."'

When I taxed Archbishop Couve de Murville with his marked reticence and pointed out that Archbishop Worlock, for instance, was far more forthcoming in his dealings with the Press, he replied with one of his engaging smiles: 'He is a professional.' Yet I do not think that anyone would call Archbishop Couve de Murville shy. He is very articulate, but I suppose that in all those years as a chaplain he was able to ignore the Press. There is a sense I think in which he is still a superlative chaplain. He relates issues to individuals, not to men and women in the mass; and he palpably draws from his intimate experience of so many young people, often troubled.

A pastoral letter he wrote on marriage in Lent 1984 bears every mark of this intimate experience of human beings. 'Marriage in our society', he writes,

> is under threat. One out of every three marriages which take place in Britain ends in divorce. There are now two million divorced people in the country and the percentage is still going up. That means that an increasing number of children have had the traumatic experience of seeing their parents' marriage breaking up. This is not something that they can shrug off and forget. It is a terrible blow to a young person, because it is nearly always felt as a rejection. In fact, it has been said that children find it easier to accept the death of one of their parents rather than their divorce. During my years working with young people, I was able to see how often character problems of teenagers are caused by marriage break-up in their home. Teachers tell the same story about the cause of serious disturbance in the children they look after.

There is much more in this same pastoral letter that I wish to quote, but I must content myself with the following passage, which brings out at the same time his strict adherence to official doctrine and his human concern for individuals:

> To those who are divorced and remarried, I say that the Church has not rejected you. There is always a new beginning possible in the path to God and the starting-point has to be where we are now. I would emphasise that you still have a witness to give to the permanent character of marriage, and you do that by not receiving Holy Communion. This can be a very painful thing to accept, but in a way it is your contribution to the struggle of the whole Christian community in the matter of marriage. By accepting that sacrifice you are helping others, and God finds other ways to give you His grace.'

The Archbishop has been criticized to me by a well-informed friend on the grounds of his exceptional fidelity to Papal attitudes, but no one can question the extent and warmth of his practical compassion. This individual approach makes him less ready than one might expect to pronounce on national issues. Adam Smith once said that what is wisdom in a small household can scarce be folly in the affairs of a great nation. Couve de Murville seems to feel that if one gets the personal relationships right, one can't go far wrong. He was as sharply critical of the governmental policies that had produced the horrifying unemployment in his diocese as was his counterpart, Bishop Montefiore. But he does not hesitate to say that divorce, in his experience, is a still graver evil than unemployment. He was ready to entertain my suggestion that the Catholic Church should not keep so quiet when divorce was being made easier and easier by legislation.

On women priests he is, as in all matters, perfectly submissive to the mind of the Church. Like the other Catholic bishops I have spoken to, he by no means excludes the possibility that one day the Catholic Church will agree to the ordination of women, but he considers that so great a change, if it is to come, must come gradually. 'There is', he said with emphasis, 'plenty of time.' He recorded this as one of his fundamental thoughts about the way in which Catholic doctrine develops.

On the ecumenical issue, he agreed that his attitude could be described as cautious. He was desperately anxious that Catholics should not weaken in their own faith in the search for ecumenical consensus. He is passionately concerned with the defence of Catholic education. When he was a university chaplain, he could not help noticing that some of the Catholic students who were most ardently ecumenical finished up in a strange religious limbo, neither Catholic nor Protestant, which was indeed the faith of their Protestant counterparts. Nevertheless, in the Birmingham area he worked in close harmony with Bishop Montefiore and the Free Church leaders.

The intellectual capacity of the Archbishop, possibly not apparent from the above, will easily be appreciated by anyone who reads, for example, his Peake Memorial Lecture for 1985, entitled 'The Catholic Church and the Critical Study of the Bible'. Mr Peake was a methodist scholar and this lecture was given to the Methodist Conference at Birmingham on 27 June 1985 – the first time that a Catholic had been invited to speak. He aroused considerable controversy and surprise by saying that if it could ever be proved by the discovery of bones that the tomb in which Christ was buried was not empty 'I would cease to be a Christian and would instantly resign my archbishopric.' Characteristically he told me with some amusement about the controversy, but not about the wide and deep message in which the remark in question figured incidentally.

He must have obtained a good laugh early on by quoting a remark made in the 1920s by the very Mr Peake whom they were commemorating. It is worth quoting in full:

> If, inspired by a new and sweet humility and a regard for the results of unfettered exegesis and historical research, Rome should renounce her claims to supremacy, her boast of infallibility; if she would revoke all the profane anathemas, repent before the world of her ghastly record of atrocious persecution, and undertake a drastic reform from within, how gladly we should welcome such a triumph of divine grace! But divine grace does not act without the co-operation of the human will; and the will for so splendid a recantation or indeed any recognition that she owes it to humanity is, we must judge, entirely absent.

Couve de Murville did not brush aside Peake's strictures lightly. He was at great pains to explain the various factors that had retarded the development of Catholic biblical scholarship until the beginning of the present century. Since then, there had been remarkable progress, as Peake would have to admit if he were writing today. The Archbishop's fundamental contention, however, was one that Peake might not have found acceptable. Today, maintains the Archbishop, Rome's claim to supremacy and its boast of infallibility in Peake's words is an important defence of Scripture, because it rescues the Bible from being a collection of ancient texts and says firmly that it is the word of God and relevant to every age of the Christian community. Such a claim, he went on, was perfectly compatible with serious critical study, as was shown by the work of leading Catholic scholars, of whom he mentioned some of the most eminent.

He ended on a note that would seem to have appealed strongly to the Methodist Conference, as indeed one would expect:

> The scientific work referred to is really a prolegomenon to the different sort of operation by which the text of the Bible is read and expounded in a believing community, nourishes the spiritual life

of individual Christians, and guarantees the continuity of our faith with the whole traditions of the Church and of Israel. I would hope that this view of Scripture is the most effective bond between Methodists and Catholics in their common search for Christian unity.

So he can pull out the intellectual stops when he chooses, but this does not seem to be his primary interest. As we parted, I asked him whether I was right in thinking that he puts the spiritual welfare of the half-million Catholics in his diocese before all other considerations. He replied that this was so.

❧ 18 ❧

John Aloysius Ward,
Archbishop of Cardiff

As I have remarked elsewhere, all bishops I have met are friendly people. Archbishop Ward's welcome was warm and unselfconscious. His hospitality was what I have been accustomed to among the Franciscans. He himself is a Capuchin. They are no longer bearded, but otherwise seem no different from those who received me into the Catholic Church in 1940. One can easily visualize Archbishop Ward as a wandering friar in the twelfth century.

He is round-faced, jovial, vigorous, and somewhat inclined to stoutness. He is happy to be compared to Friar Tuck. Twice a day he goes for a punishing walk with his dog, with the declared object of keeping his weight under control. He tells me that his best thoughts come to him during these exercises.

He was appointed Archbishop of Cardiff at the age of fifty-four in 1983, moving there from Wrexham where he was Bishop of Menevia. Although born in Leeds his family home was in Wrexham, North Wales. He was educated at the local primary school and at Prior Park College, Bath. He became Guardian of the Franciscan Community and parish priest at Peckham and was elected to the governing council of the Capuchins, becoming Minister Provincial in 1969. In 1970 he was elected an adviser to the Father General of the Order in Rome, with special responsibility world-wide for English-speaking Capuchins. In this role he travelled extensively in Africa, South East Asia, Australia, and America. In 1980 he was episcopally ordained as Coadjutor Bishop of Menevia and he succeeded to the bishopric four months later.

When he was appointed Archbishop he spoke in very stark terms about unemployment. He said that long-term unemployment was 'almost blasphemy against God'. He insisted that 'politicians should on no account treat the unemployed simply as economic factors'. 'It is not enough', he said, 'to have benefits. People need self-respect. Each one of us is made in the image of God. There has to be quality of life [a favourite phrase of his] for that person, and that includes the right to work.'

He has laboured away in this spirit ever since. The most spectacular opportunity occurred during the 1984–5 miners' strike. The situation in Wales was serious enough, but at that time it showed signs of becoming calamitous. He and the other Church leaders in Wales repaired to London to visit Peter Walker, the Minister for Energy. Ward is nice about Walker. He is ready to think of him as a compassionate and brilliant man, but they made no obvious headway on this occasion.

The Welsh Church leaders demanded an independent review where any pits were to be closed. Walker, with the strike already beginning to collapse, gave nothing away, but on his part demanded that the Church leaders should use their influence to promote a ballot in the coal-mines. Archbishop Ward told him that, whatever the original rights and wrongs, men who had made such sacrifices as had the miners for a cause they believed in could not possibly be expected to admit that they were completely in the wrong and accept a ballot. The visit, unproductive on the face of it, achieved wide publicity in Wales and much improved the standing of the Church leaders.

Archbishop Ward's opinions have been equally forthright in regard to the arms race and abortion. He has declared that anyone who believed in abortion could not be a Christian. But it is the relationship of long-term unemployment to the whole identity of Wales that is his special obsession. He is determined to do everything in his power to maintain and enhance the Welsh sense of national identity. He is not himself a Welsh speaker and considers that a few hastily acquired Welsh phrases do more harm than good. But he is urging all new priests to learn Welsh. He is aware that 80 per cent of the population do not in fact speak the language, yet the preservation of it is indispensable to Welsh national self-respect.

Yes, in reply to a question of mine, he accepted the likelihood that there would be extensive pit and factory closures. What he was determined to build up was a national conscience in regard to the human tragedies resulting. Unless one took the brutal view that those who could not find work had better 'get on their bikes', he could see no solution unless more industry was guided into Wales. He saw no great likelihood of this happening under the philosophy of the present government. He did not consider it the role of a bishop to work out a complete economic policy. He had much faith under God in the power of an awakened national conscience to avert the horrors impending.

When he took over as Archbishop, he was thirty years younger than his immediate predecessor, of whom he spoke only with the greatest respect. He had introduced a new and greater thrust towards strengthening and establishing parish, deanery, and diocesan pastoral councils. There were, for example, few parish councils and no special ministers of the type that I can say from first-hand experience can make the whole difference to a parish. He says that the laity must be far more involved in running their own parishes instead of 'leaving everything to the clergy'. He agreed that the hierarchy and the priests should speak out when appropriate. The main responsibility, however, fell on the parishioner. 'They should not be content to wear R.C. on their lapels and fill the churches with ritual Catholics.'

As mentioned above, he speaks out strongly on social questions, but the main object is to form a Christian conscience among the people. Again and again he comes back to his insistence on the quality of life. I have already quoted his passionate dislike of abortion. But he has on occasion told the 'pro-Life' lobby that the quality of life does not refer only to the unborn. The quality of life in Ethiopia should be just as dear to them as it is or should be in Cardiff.

He insists, humorously but very seriously, that the hierarchy of Wales is distinct from the hierarchy of England. (The conference of the bishops of England and Wales is a conference of two hierarchies, not one.) He was at pains to stress the vast area of independence open to a bishop. 'There is a sense in which one can say that a diocesan bishop is only answerable to the Lord and to the Pope.'

The Archbishop is nothing if not compassionate. His *Open Letter to the Lapsed* is indeed moving: 'I wish I had known how to be kinder and more understanding to the lapsed'; he pleads metaphorically with them on his knees: 'Oh that today you could listen to his voice.' But this does not mean that he would ever agree to bend or soften principles. His attitude towards divorced people who would wish to remarry in church illustrates his general position. He is strongly opposed to letting such marriages take place. In his experience serious Catholics who have been divorced would not be easy in their minds after such a ceremony. But he is an active participant in the movement to provide special succour to divorced people. Their plight appeals to him strongly. They should receive far more pastoral care in the future than the past. He does not agree that the divorced who have remarried or live in relationships that cannot have the blessing of the Church should be admitted to communion. There are more honest ways of reaching out pastorally to these sad cases. Experience has taught him that those advised to ignore the Church's clear guidance can rarely do so without violence to conscience. Many have thanked him for clarifying this matter with compassionate understanding.

On Corpus Christi 1985 there was an enormous celebration of the feast in the national stadium at Cardiff Arms Park, where I have incidentally enjoyed myself so hugely in the past. There were three themes, he said, that he would stress in the celebration of Corpus Christi. First, this was International Youth Year, and the youth of the diocese were playing a leading part in the celebration at Cardiff Arms Park: 'The presence of Pope John Paul II with our young people at Ninian Park, Cardiff, affirmed his care for them as Chief Pastor in the Church.' The second theme concerned 'the elderly, the sick, and the handicapped, who occupy a special place in the heart of Christ and in our Church life'. The third concerned 'other suffering members of Christ's Church who might not be present physically on 9 June. Our Catholic people of the diocese have responded magnificently to the call for help from the starving people of Ethiopia, Africa, and others in need.'

Such quotations give, I hope, a small indication of the special flavour that the Archbishop brings to his appointment. It goes without saying that he is heart and soul in the ecumenical movement, though here again there is a long way to go – much further than in some other dioceses. The visit to Peter Walker was significantly the first joint activity of real moment.

The Archbishop strikes me as a very happy man, although he pines at times for the community life of a Franciscan. He is facing in Wales, for reasons explained above, a heavy burden; but Jesus Christ has said that his burden is light, and what Jesus says is good enough for the Archbishop.

⌒ 19 ⌒

Augustine Harris,
Bishop of Middlesbrough

Bishop Harris, appointed to Middlesbrough in 1978, was sixty-eight years of age when I visited him in autumn 1985. He told me that he was the oldest Catholic diocesan bishop. With his still dark hair, roguish smile, youthful figure and movement, he could be in his early fifties. He also told me that all the present bishops in England and Wales have been appointed by the Pope on the recommendation of the retiring Apostolic Delegate, Bruno Heim. He was under the impression that Heim had a strong leaning towards Englishmen of good family. His heraldic expertise pointed in this direction.

Bruno Heim was supposed to be determined that the bishops in England should indeed be English; 'No Irishman need apply.' (It has been pointed out to me that the Bishop of Nottingham is very Irish; perhaps Bruno Heim overlooked him.) The Irish bishops had on the whole sprung from the lower middle classes, while Heim had a penchant for the best public schools. Of the four archbishops, Hume had been at Ampleforth, Bowen and Couve de Murville had been at Downside. There was a story that, when Bowen was appointed to Arundel before being elevated to Southwark, it was thought that his service in the Irish Guards should equip him to cope with the current Duke of Norfolk.

Bishop Harris accepted all this in a jocular way, quite dispassionately. No doubt he would have described it as no more than part of the truth. Many of the new bishops were at local grammar schools. Some of them are of Irish origin one or two generations back. A number of them – Bishops Murphy O'Connor, Kelly, Thomas, Brewer, and

163

Budd – are very good theologians. Bishop Harris himself is completely English, but he has not been to a public school. He was educated at St Cecilia's primary school and St Francis Xavier's College, Liverpool, until 1933, and then went to the Liverpool Archdiocesan Seminary at St Joseph's College, Upholland, to study for the priesthood. He was ordained by Archbishop Downey in 1942 and appointed to St Oswald's, Old Swan, Liverpool, for six months and then to St Elizabeth's, Litherland, 1943–52. He was appointed Chaplain at Walton Prison, Liverpool, 1952–65; was senior Roman Catholic priest, Prison Department, 1957–66; English representative to the International Council of Senior Prison Chaplains (Roman Catholic) 1957–66; member of the Vatican Delegation to the United Nations Quinquennial Congress on Crime, London, 1960, and Stockholm, 1965. He was consecrated Auxiliary Bishop of Liverpool in 1966 and, owing to the illness of Archbishop Beck, had to perform many of the duties that would normally have fallen to the Archbishop. He has therefore been a responsible bishop for twenty years.

He has for many years been President of the Social Welfare Commission of the English and Welsh Hierarchy and Vice-President of its Mass Media Commission with special responsibility for radio and television. He was a member of the Central Religious Advisory Council to the B.B.C. and I.B.A. His comments on the Press, appearances on television, and series on the Terry Wogan morning programme have made him one of the country's better known bishops. For many years, therefore, he has been centrally concerned with the formation of Catholic policy and for relationships with governmental and other official bodies.

I had come prepared to criticize the Social Welfare Commission for lack of impact on public life and activity. He took the words out of my mouth, refuting me in one sense and not in another. He promised to send me a long list of documents that had been issued by the Social Welfare Commission over the year, but readily agreed that they had in all too many cases disappeared into a vacuum. Statements by bishops and commissions are not always noteworthy or in quotable language; sometimes they are not given full value even in the serious Press. Catholic bishops were, for good or for ill, not represented in the House of Lords. He was not, however, making excuses. They really must improve their methods of public information.

Bishop Harris is always candid, whether in regard to Vatican politics or documents for which he himself has a responsibility. He entirely agreed with the strong line taken in the bishops' document about the Warnock Report, 'Personal Origins'. Any use of embryos for any purpose except for the good of the embryo concerned was utterly immoral. But there were some closed minds in Catholic as in other circles; he was alive to the dangers of undue dogmatism in a field where spectacular developments were likely to go on occurring.

I told Bishop Harris that I had found it easier to interview Anglican bishops than Catholic ones. The latter were so reluctant to step out of line that it was difficult to present their individual flavour.

He said: 'That's not so true now as it was. The Catholic bishops have been gaining self-confidence since Vatican II; they are much less defensive nowadays.'

I said that I had not come across notable differences of opinion or even emphasis, to which he replied: 'There are a good many different shades of opinion on a subject like nuclear warfare.'

He had pertinent things to say about the problems of being a bishop. 'A theologian must analyse and explore. A bishop's job is to unify and strengthen the faith of his community.' The Anglican Bishop of Durham had apparently failed to grasp this distinction initially, though he seemed to be grasping it now.

I returned to the charge that the Catholic bishops had been slow to criticize government policy openly, even when it resulted in heavy unemployment, which I knew was repugnant to Bishop Harris and other bishops. He outlined four stages that were necessary for practical solutions to social problems: first, at the basic gospel level, prayer, pursuit of justice, proclamation of the kingdom, love of neighbour; secondly, the development and refinement of the gospel to be found in such documents as Papal encyclicals published during the past 100 years. These two areas are appropriate areas in which bishops (and other Christians) can speak with some authority.

Thirdly, there are many secular specialist interests that all have their particular validity and strength. These would include economics, science and technology, industrial relations, and trade organizations. Then, at the fourth level, the immediate dispute or situation could be tackled against the yardsticks the three previous levels have provided. It sounded to me a code of practice that would prove distinctly cautious in operation.

I do not doubt that on social questions Bishop Harris's instincts would place him on the humanitarian side. He believed that, as far as he could judge, Archbishop Worlock and the Archbishop of York had gone as far as they could reasonably be expected to go in their attempts to reconcile the various parties caught up in the miners' dispute with the National Coal Board.

On the ecumenical side there had been fruitful co-operation with the Archbishop of York. There was steady progress at local level. He was entirely in favour of ARCIC, but he did not see an easy way forward on the plane of doctrine. Long-term national discussions with the Anglicans and the Free Churches were being conducted and were going well.

I mentioned to him that Archbishop Runcie had told me that the question of Anglican Orders would have to be cleared up if real success was to be achieved. Bishop Harris agreed. He thought this particular problem would be solved. What was more fundamental was the question, What is a church? On this point he thought that the Catholics were, at the moment, further on, largely due to the document of Vatican II, *Lumen Gentium*. Hopefully other Churches would take up the same theme.

Naturally I tackled him a shade aggressively about penal reform. I had first come to know him when he was a chaplain in Walton Gaol when, at the request of Cardinal (then Bishop) Heenan, I was visiting an I.R.A prisoner. I had taken to him then and have never forgotten an answer he gave me many years later at a small conference: Jesus Christ was, curiously enough, on the side of the 'baddies'. I have never had any doubt that in penal matters his heart was in what I would call the right place. But through his long association with the Home Office I have feared that his natural impulses might have been blunted. He met my implied criticism with the utmost good humour. He pointed among other initiatives to a statement on penal policy published by the Social Welfare Commission and to the evidence it gave to the May Committee on prisons.

Yes, I retorted, but that was some years ago. 'Surely you must agree that in the last few years the prison situation has sharply deteriorated?'

He entirely concurred and spoke of present government policy with much disapprobation. He was very severe on the policy, now supposedly official, of containment. The idea of holding men and women in prison, denying them their freedom, without any declared attempt to improve them or provide them with better prospects, is downright immoral.

The government's penal policy towards prisoners represented a moral vacuum, a palpable absence of moral motivation and standards. What such a policy failed to take account of was Original Sin. Original Sin can be overcome only by religious conviction or, failing that, by a sense of social responsibility. The present government seemed to bypass this more fundamental approach. But maybe the Churches are failing to play their part in offering alternatives.

He referred to what he called a 'bee in my bonnet'. He bemoaned the destruction twenty years ago of the Prison Commission. With all its faults it cared for prisoners in a fashion of which there have been few signs since the Home Office took over completely. My heart warmed to Bishop Harris as he spoke on these lines, but I could not refrain from once again expressing the hope that the Catholic bishops would be much more articulate in bringing pressure to bear on the government. Archbishop Couve de Murville, whom I had seen the day before, had authorized me to mention him as hoping that the bishops would give penal reform a much higher priority.

On women priests, Bishop Harris, like other Catholic bishops I had interviewed, saw no fundamental objections to women being ordained, though he had said the opposite some years ago. But so great a change could not be expected to come about until there was much more evidence of the Holy Spirit moving the Church in that direction.

As we parted, Bishop Harris told me that he had been much struck some time ago by a saying of Archbishop Ramsey: 'It would be so much easier to come together if we could all go back to our roots.' I said, perhaps rather crudely: 'What would that mean in the case of the Anglicans? Surely not a return to the particular ethos of Henry VIII or even Queen Elizabeth I?'

Bishop Harris replied: 'I think it would mean that we would all have to go back to the Cross.' Assuredly this is where he begins and ends his daily pilgrimage.

167

He has been concerned with many social causes. His lifelong dedication to improving the penal system can best be illustrated by quoting from a lecture he gave in July 1980: 'The Penal System: A Theological Assessment'. He began by provocatively concentrating on three key elements in a penal system that, on the face of it, were anti-God – a contradiction of God's creation. A penal system might seem a contradiction of forgiving. Imprisonment might seem unnatural. Our assumption of the role of judge seems to be assuming a function that belongs only to God. He then proceeded to point the way to a system that represented a Christian aspiration. Imprisonment was immoral unless it contained a real element of rehabilitation – or at least a genuine attempt to provide rehabilitation. Rehabilitation includes obvious needs like accommodation, employment, and clothing. These are the necessary mechanics of rehabilitation.

A theological assessment must probe further. An inmate may be freed from physical containment – his body may be free to walk out of the prison gates – and yet he may still feel trapped. What is his deeper need? Bishop Harris provides a heart-felt Christian answer: 'We have to give the inmate more than an individual number. We must give him an individual identity and that means a dignity. This demands a faith in man, a faith which all but strains us. We need a faith that opens our eyes to the riches that are buried in people, including ourselves.'

Where do our priorities lie? Bishop Harris insists that to answer this we must ask another question: 'Where did, or where do, Christ's priorities lie? The answer is quite mysterious, quite incomprehensible to the acquisitive society.' Christ would leave the ninety-nine and go after the one that strayed; he came to call not the just but the sinners to repentance. He went further: 'Christ not only cared for these outcasts. He identified with them – the downtrodden, the sinner, the rabble, the lost sheep, the little ones, and the captives. We must do likewise, if we are making any claim to be Christians.'

So speaks a man who has had as much contact with prisoners as anyone known to me.

∽ 20 ∽

Alan Charles Clark,
Bishop of East Anglia

Bishop Clark is generally known as Catholic Ecumenical Bishop. He is happy to accept this title as long as it is realized that his primary role is pastoral. To be purely ecumenical could mean to be a kind of hyphen between two religions, which is the last thing he would wish for himself. He has been involved during the last few years in building up a new diocese (of which more below). I would say at once that his jolly personality is analogous to that of Father Brown, though he is in no way overweight. He is ideally suited to such a pastoral task.

He was no more than the auxiliary Bishop of Northampton when invited in 1969 to be the Catholic co-Chairman of the Anglican–Roman Catholic International Commission. In his laughing way he assured me that he was sure he was only the third choice for the position of Catholic co-Chairman!

He was regarded, as he says, as a neutral and uncommitted. The fact that he was no more than an auxiliary at the time seemed to some to limit the commitment of the Catholic Church. It should be mentioned however that he had had twenty years' experience of the Roman scene and was known as a classical theologian of high quality. The Anglican co-Chairman, Dr McAdoo, Bishop of Ossory, later Archbishop of Dublin, was apparently looked on in the same light. In the event the team remained intact for twelve years and, assisted by circumstances, changed the whole ecumenical situation before they handed over to their successors.

169

The final report, published in September 1981, consisted of the following:

'Eucharistic Doctrine', Windsor, 1971.
'Eucharistic Doctrine: Elucidation', Salisbury, 1979.
'Ministry and Ordination', Canterbury, 1973.
'Ministry and Ordination: Elucidation', Salisbury, 1979.
'Authority in the Church I', Venice, 1976.
'Authority in the Church: Elucidation', Windsor, 1981.
'Authority in the Church II', Windsor, 1981.

Asked about the background of ARCIC, Bishop Clark points to the long-standing Anglican exertions in an ecumenical direction. They will always be honourably associated with the name of Archbishop Temple. But Archbishop Temple, with all his exceptional merits, lacked sympathy for Roman Catholicism. Canon Carpenter, a great admirer of Temple, makes this abundantly plain in his invaluable *History of the Archbishops*. He points out, however, that all this was long before the immense change of atmosphere brought by Pope John XXIII. I do not doubt that Archbishop Temple would have responded fervently. Archbishop Temple was always extraordinarily kind to me from the time when he came down to stay with my headmaster, Dr Alington, at Eton. Mrs Temple's labours on behalf of prisoners were another link. I turned to him, and not in vain, for advice immediately before my marriage. But I cannot forget the shadow of pain that passed across his face when I told him, as his guest at Bishopthorpe during the war, that I had been received into the Catholic Church. At regular intervals I turn back to his *Readings in St John's Gospel* and other works.

In a modern sense, the initiative on the Catholic side towards Church unity started with the Second Vatican Council. I can confirm from my own experience the traumatic change in Catholic attitude that followed. In 1961 my brother died. He was a stalwart member of the Church of Ireland Synod, had been a Senator, and had done a lifetime's work for the Dublin theatre. When I went over to Dublin for the funeral, the large gathering of Catholics came together at the grave. They could not enter a Protestant Church for the purposes of a funeral at that time. A few years later I reminded the Archbishop of Dublin, who had presided over the funeral, of this

THE ROMAN CATHOLIC BISHOPS

unhappy situation. He said that he could hardly remember that things had been like that. It had all passed away like a bad dream.

From the Vatican Council of 1962–5 onwards, the Catholic and Anglican streams flowed towards one another. Honoured names in Bishop Clark's catalogue are Pope John XXIII, who summoned the Council, and Archbishop Fisher, who made the daring visit to Rome. I well remember the debate on Christian unity initiated in the House of Lords at the time of the latter's visit. There was general approval. But Clark singles out still more significantly the names of Pope Paul VI, 'the greatest of modern Popes', and Archbishop Ramsey, whose Catholic sympathies were widely recognized. A joint preparatory Commission met at Gazzada on 9 January 1967, in fulfilment of a joint decision by Pope Paul VI and Archbishop Michael Ramsey, expressed in a Common Declaration during their meeting in Rome in March 1966. That Commission, meeting three times in less than a year, produced a report which registered considerable areas of Roman Catholic–Anglican agreement, pointed to persisting historical differences, and outlined a programme of 'growing together' that should include, though not be exhausted in, serious dialogue on these differences. It proclaimed penitence for the past, thankfulness for the graces of the present, urgency and resolve for a future in which our common aim would be the restoration of full organic unity.

The report was endorsed in substance by a letter of Cardinal Bea in June 1968 and by the Lambeth Conference a few weeks later. In January 1970 the signatories of the present report met first as the Anglican–Roman Catholic International Commission. Throughout the next twelve years there was concentration on three main areas of controversy: first, the doctrine of the Eucharist; secondly, ministry and ordination; thirdly, the nature and exercise of authority in the Church. In the concluding statement in 1981 we are told:

The dialogue has been directed not merely to the achievement of doctrinal agreement, which is central to our reconciliation, but to the far greater goal of organic unity. . . . There are high expectations that significant initiatives will be boldly undertaken to deepen our reconciliation and lead us forward in the quest for the full communion to which we have been committed in obedience to God from the beginning of our dialogue.

As I understand it, however, there has never been any intention that the individual Churches would disappear within a larger whole.

Bishop Clark himself would be the last person to single out his personal contribution to the progress made, but no one close to the scene fails to treat it as of the first importance. How far has progress been made under the three headings indicated? On the Eucharist, the agreement appears to have been almost complete. Communion with Christ, says the ARCIC report,

> pre-supposes his true presence effectually signified by the bread and wine which in this mystery become his body and blood. . . . Christ is present and active in various ways in the entire Eucharistic celebrations. It is the same Lord who through the proclaimed word invites his people to his table, who through his minister presides at that table, and who gives himself sacramentally in the body and blood of his Paschal sacrifice. It is the Lord present at the right hand of the Father, and therefore transcending the sacramental order, who thus offers to his Church, in the Eucharistic signs, the special gift of himself.

Substantial agreement on the Eucharist seems to have been such a simple matter that one wonders how, at the time of the Reformation, this was ever such a divisive issue. It should be emphasized that so far the Anglican Church has done no more than 'accept' the ARCIC report. One has yet to learn whether this real presence, as described above, is accepted throughout the Anglican communion.

On the face of it, the second issue, ministry and ordination, was going to be much more awkward. After all, as recently as 1896 the Vatican had stigmatized Anglican Orders as invalid. The members of ARCIC seem to have been far from discouraged. They preferred to tackle the issue obliquely; that is to say they concentrated on the nature of ministry without directly asking the question, Are Anglican Orders valid or aren't they? Their final conclusion is a monument of tactfulness:

> In answer to the question concerning the significance of the Agreed Statements for the mutual recognition of ministry, the Commission has affirmed that a consensus has been reached that

placed the questions in a new context. It believes that our agreement on the essentials of Eucharistic faith with regard to the sacramental presence of Christ and the sacrificial dimension of the Eucharist, and on the nature and purpose of the priesthood, ordination and Apostolic Succession, is the new context in which the questions should now be discussed. This calls for a reappraisal of the verdict on Anglican Orders in *Apostolicae Curae* (1896).

The question of *authority* has long presented, and still probably presents, the most fundamental difficulty. The question of authority in the Church, says ARCIC, has long been recognized as crucial to the growth in unity of the Roman Catholic Church and the Churches of the Anglican communion. 'It was precisely in the problem of Papal primacy that our historical divisions found their unhappy origin. Hence, however significant our consensus on the doctrine of the Eucharist and of the ministry, unresolved questions on the nature and exercise of authority in the Church would hinder the growing experience of unity which is the pattern of our present relations.'

Putting it crudely, how likely is it that the people of England, having had their own Church for more than 300 years, will agree to have their religion dictated to them by an international Church centred in Rome or, for that matter, anywhere else? The members of ARCIC discovered a formula that satisfied them as far as it went. There was agreement concerning a universal Primate. He should exercise, and be seen to exercise, his ministry not in isolation but in collegial association with his brother bishops. 'We have recognised the need in the united Church for a universal Primate who, presiding over the *koinonia*, can speak with authority in the name of the Church.' This conception of a *koinonia* is, as they themselves insist, fundamental to all our statements. It is to be translated as 'communion'.

In the next few years we shall come to know whether this conception of a universal Primate situated in Rome is acceptable to Anglicans and whether what appears to be a whittling down of Papal infallibility is acceptable to Catholics. The Catholic Church has in England and Wales made a very favourable response to ARCIC, but it is by no means clear that the world-wide Catholic Church has as yet accepted its findings. When I talked to Anglican bishops and others about the obstacles in the way of Christian unity their answer varied, but there has been a tendency to look on the present Pope's exercise of authority as creating a difficulty that might not have been present under Paul VI. And yet it was Paul VI who, in his encyclical *Humanae Vitae*, laid down the doctrine that, of all others, has offended liberals in recent times.

There is a disposition among Anglicans sympathetic to Christian unity to insist that the Vatican itself would have to change before unity was possible. Obviously *both* parties in process of convergence will need to change. The difficulty is to discover *together* where the changes must emerge. 'I regard', says Bishop Clark, 'the isolated pursuit of inter-communion as an obstacle to the growth towards the unity of the Churches. In any case, it remains an impasse.' In this he resembles other Catholics and Anglicans I have spoken to. The Bishop, like other ecumenical leaders, is dedicated to communion which exists potentially already and can be realized only by stages, by sharing – and most of all by prayer in common.

❧ 21 ❧

Cormac Murphy-O'Connor,
Bishop of Arundel and Brighton

Bishop Murphy-O'Connor – Cormac to so many of us in his diocese – aged fifty-two, is freely spoken of as the man of the future. He is often tipped as the natural successor to Cardinal Hume as Archbishop of Westminster.

He is a tall man, as I believe are all his family. He and at least two brothers played first-class rugby football, one of them for Ireland. I assumed that he was a lock, but he said that in fact he was a centre. He is at ease in all situations, joyful and sorrowful. He presided with infinite grace over the reception of Malcolm Muggeridge and his wife Kitty in our small Catholic church, with myself and my wife as sponsors. He presided movingly over a little group come together in a private house to mourn the loss of a beloved daughter. He has made his presence felt one way or another throughout our diocese. He has also established the most cordial relations with the Anglican Bishop of Chichester. They paid an immediate visit to Mrs Thatcher after her narrow escape from destruction by bombing in Brighton before the 1984 Conservative Party Conference.

He has been selected more than once for key appointments apart from his present bishopric. After serving as secretary to the present Archbishop of Liverpool, then Bishop of Portsmouth, he held the crucial position for six years of Rector of the English College in Rome. The shades of Cardinal Wiseman, Cardinal Hinsley, and other notables looked down on him. In his revealing book, *The Family*

175

of the Church (of which more in a moment), he has a good deal to say about the lessons that he learned at Rome in the art and science and spiritual role of leadership:

> In Rome I had to exercise authority over 60 or so students for the priesthood. I made many mistakes, but I came out of the experience with certain convictions about the exercise of authority today. The first conviction concerns my belief that authority can only be exercised today in co-responsibility. It was important to convey to the students that we were in this together and that it was not a one-man band. And therefore there had to be constant communication, information, meetings, sharing, listening – above all listening. Somehow decision-making had to be seen to involve everybody, if not decision-taking. There was also the need to make everyone realise that they shared information.

But no one doubts the significance of his final words on the matter: 'It is important to preserve the hierarchic structure. By that I mean one must never allow anarchy to reign; on important matters if anyone is to be blamed, it should be the boss!'

Mrs Thatcher once said to me about another woman politician: 'She is a nice person but she lacks power of decision.' No one would criticize Mrs Thatcher on that score, nor, if one knows him at all, Cormac Murphy-O'Connor.

His conception of leadership as involving partnership goes hand in hand with the main theme of the book already mentioned, *The Family of the Church*. 'In the last twenty years', he says, 'the emphasis in the Church has changed from a very institutional style to the more informal style of a family or people of God.' Like other eminent Catholic leaders, he is a little cagey in answers to the question whether the Catholic Church ever changes at all. However, following Newman, to go no further back, we can all agree that the Church is in a constant state of development. No one can pretend that in the years since Vatican II the development (I had almost said change) has not been extremely rapid.

Speaking as a man in one of his pews, I can testify to the large impact made within his own diocese by his conception of the family. He no doubt would be reluctant to claim originality here, but I am not aware of anyone who has made such use of this particular concept. The following extract from his addresses illustrates his flavour:

> Is your local parish community a truly welcoming one? Do you greet other parishioners and make them feel part of the local family of the faith? Are occasions provided in your parish to meet other Christians at all? If we want non-believers to be interested in our concern, is it not right that we should first be interested in theirs? It was St Ignatius who said that 'one should go in another man's door so that he will come out through yours'!

One might say, 'Pretty obvious stuff', and so it is in the abstract; but what gives it significance in his diocese is the personal drive behind it.

In our own small parish community, our congregation has rapidly increased until we are seriously wondering how we are going to cope with all who join us. A great difference has been made – I have no doubt that this experience is familiar elsewhere – by the establishment of 'extraordinary ministers' who have assisted our dedicated local priest in innumerable ways in mobilizing the faithful and, in addition, those whose faith has been hitherto rather precarious. They are able to carry the sacraments to the sick and themselves conduct a communion service, in our case on Wednesday mornings. Very great care has been taken from the Bishop downwards to equip them for these novel tasks.

I am not suggesting that all this is just a bright idea of Cormac Murphy-O'Connor. He would be horrified and embarrassed by any such suggestion, but I wonder whether the family inspiration has anywhere been given effect to more successfully and energetically than in the part of the country I know best. And, from a Catholic point of view, it is a very difficult area, with Catholics spread thinly over a wide territory.

I mentioned earlier the responsibilities that seem naturally to come his way. At the moment he is Chairman of ARCIC II, the Anglican–Roman Catholic International Commission on the Anglican and Roman traditions, now starting on a second life. The Bishop's co-Chairman Mark Santer is the Anglican Bishop of

Kensington, who has contributed a very cordial foreword to Cormac Murphy-O'Connor's book.

From this point of view the chapter in the book that will be studied most closely is the address on Christian unity, which he delivered at the Anglican Synod, Chichester, 1978. There was much with which every Christian of goodwill could agree, but one passage must have been troublesome to write: 'The Catholic Church does not normally permit other Christians to receive Holy Communion, and this is, I know, often the cause of misunderstanding and sorrow. I would like to say that I truly believe that the situation is becoming equally painful for Roman Catholics.'

He sets out to explain the matter briefly: 'The Eucharist signifies a fullness of common faith and a fullness of unity within the Church. If a fellow Christian receives Holy Communion in a Catholic Church, we understand that in entering into communion with Christ, that Christian is also entering into communion with the faith of the whole Church and thus with the Bishop who teaches and presides over the Eucharist.'

I asked him what really stands in the way at the present time of Anglicans receiving communion in this spirit. He replied that the key thing is 'the feel of the Church, the attitude towards the authority of the Church'. It may well be that a number of Anglicans will already have this 'feel'. But until they share it collectively, it is difficult to see how they can, as Anglicans, desire or be qualified to receive Catholic communion. Will the time come when this difficulty will be surmounted? He is optimistic about the possibilities within his own lifetime, but progress will come by stages.

I told him the Bishop of London was reported as saying that there was no theoretical objection to the primacy of the Pope in a universal Church, but the Papacy itself would, from an Anglican point of view, need reform. Bishop Murphy-O'Connor prefers to say it is not the Papal authority, but the use made of it, that will require to be modified. If anyone known to me on the Catholic side can pave the way to inter-communion and beyond that to unity, he surely is the man.

‿ 22 ‿

Tomas Seamus O'Fiaich,
Cardinal Archbishop of Armagh,
Catholic Primate of All Ireland

If there were a competition for the friendliest bishop, there would
be a dead-heat between many of the candidates, with Cardinal
O'Fiaich well fancied; for the jolliest bishop the Cardinal might
emerge on top with strong challenges from the Anglican Bishop of
Bradford and the Catholic Archbishop of Cardiff. For the most
expansive and candid, Cardinal O'Fiaich would be a clear winner.

I had been received by him before now and entertained royally to
lunch at his comfortable house in Armagh behind the Catholic
cathedral. This time I was motored from Belfast airport by a lady
whose husband is a militant Protestant Loyalist. Foolishly as I now
think, I had not liked to ask whether the Cardinal would allow her to
join us at lunch. In the event she called for me at 3 p.m. to take me
back to the airport. Hearing this, the Cardinal dashed down the
steps of his house and engaged her in lively conversation. It was
difficult to tear them apart. This temperament of his must be borne
in mind, along with his background, in assessing the wisdom of some
of his pronouncements.

He has enjoyed and he still enjoys – if that is the right word – an
unflattering Press in England. Yet when I have seen him in England,
for example on the occasion of the canonization of Oliver Plunkett,
he got on remarkably well with everybody. He has many Protestant
friends in Northern Ireland, including Dr Armstrong, the Protestant
Primate, as I know from talking to the latter. Mr Ken Livingstone
has said about himself that no one who knows him can dislike him;

the same could be said with still more truth of Cardinal O'Fiaich. As most people know by now, he comes from the Crossmaglen area of Northern Ireland, that strange Nationalist peninsula which sticks out into the Republic. British soldiers who have served in Northern Ireland know it all too well as hostile territory. He was in fact born, north of the border, at Cullyhana, near Crossmaglen in South Armagh on 3 November 1923.

But in the Cardinal's recollection, although there was a strong local culture and it was a great area for Irish music, 'there was no religious tension'. In fact 'some of our closest friends were Presbyterian families' – one family in particular, Nelson was the name; 'we were constantly up and down to their house. People find it hard to believe about South Armagh, but I have never seen any religious bigotry there.' The Cardinal has said, moreover, which would surprise most people:

Perhaps I should put this on the record, but I have to smile sometimes when I see references to Crossmaglen and its great Republican tradition. Back in the 1930s and 1940s we looked at Crossmaglen as almost a garrison town – it didn't have a British garrison, but about half the middle-aged people there had served in the British Army in the First World War. Crossmaglen was looked on at that time as very English culturally and politically.

Nevertheless the Cardinal would hardly be human if he did not feel a special sympathy for the families of Crossmaglen when their young people were in trouble, however reprehensible their conduct.

It is necessary at this point to emphasize the brilliance of his academic record. In this respect he is far from being the average man. His father was a schoolteacher, later the principal of the elementary school where the Cardinal and his elder brother received their primary education. At St Patrick's College, Maynooth, besides the normal seminary courses in philosophy, theology, and scripture, he did Celtic studies, for which he received a B.A. degree with first-class honours in 1943. From 1948 to 1950 he studied early and medieval Irish history at University College, Dublin, taking an M.A. degree with first-class honours. A further two years at Louvain University in Belgium culminated in a licentiate in historical sciences (Lic.Sc.Hist.) *avec la plus grande distinction* in 1952. He has travelled widely, researching the work and influence of the early Irish monks abroad, on which he is an acknowledged authority. He speaks French and German.

In 1953 he was appointed lecturer in modern history at Maynooth, and professor in 1959. He became Vice-President of Maynooth in 1970 and was the popular choice in the college when appointed President in 1974.

As Catholic Primate of All Ireland, his first duty is to the Catholics of all thirty-two counties, but he must also pay proper regard for the interests of the Protestants, a small minority in the South and a two-to-one majority in the North. At this point his temperament comes in. It would simply not be in his nature to suppress his convictions concerning, for example, the maltreatment for many years of the Catholics in the North and about a united Ireland. He has spoken out on occasion in a manner critical of the British and the Northern Unionists. He has denounced violence repeatedly, but this has not been much attended to in England.

A few quotations out of many. One statement, described by the *Guardian* as 'the bravest words on the I.R.A.', was issued jointly with the Bishop of Derry, Dr Edward Daly, after a bombing in which two children were victims: 'Only completely ruthless and heartless men, without any feeling for human rights or the sacredness of human life, could do such a thing. . . . Under no pretext can such murderous attacks be excused, or membership of the organization responsible be condoned.'

When in June 1978 the I.R.A. claimed responsibility for the murder of a retired postman, Patrick McEntee, from the Cardinal's native area of Crossmaglen, alleging he had been 'an informer', Dr O'Fiaich did not conceal his anger. 'Who will be next? Will there be a next?' he asked in a homily at the funeral Mass:

Already threats have been issued to other people in the area. It poisons the whole atmosphere, destroys normal friendships, and breeds fear and terror in a people. . . . My dear friends, let no one try to suggest that this crime has anything to do with patriotism. . . . No cause is advanced by murder, and no Irish cause can receive anything but dishonour from the slaughter of a brother Irishman,

Protestant or Catholic. If those responsible for this deed will not listen to me then let them listen to the words of the leaders whose cause they sometimes claim to serve, but whose cause they have foully dishonoured. 'We place the cause of the Irish Republic under the protection of the most high God . . . and we pray that no one who serves that cause will dishonour it by cowardice, inhumanity or rapine.'

In August 1978 he issued a statement that was far less agreeable to English opinion. After spending a day visiting Long Kesh Prison, Cardinal O'Fiaich drew attention to the conditions in which prisoners in H-Blocks 3, 4, and 5 were living, comparing them to the slums of Calcutta. He revealed that there were 200 from the Archdiocese of Armagh among the 1,800 prisoners in Long Kesh and that this was equivalent to all the young men of a similar age group in a typical parish of his diocese. The British government reacted with a statement saying that the prisoners were responsible for their own condition. Speaking as one who visited Long Kesh Prison and talked to prisoners, though not in the H-Blocks, I could understand both points of view.

Cardinal O'Fiaich aroused still more controversy – being criticized this time not only by the British but also by the Irish government – when he explicitly declined to say that it was morally wrong in principle to support the Sinn Fein Party, the political wing of the I.R.A. The Cardinal's answer was not in fact about the use of violence, though both governments later tried to imply that it was. The question he answered was about 'supporting a political party whose spokesman supported the use of violence by a supposed army', to quote the commentator Feargal O'Connor.

Naturally I asked Dr O'Fiaich whether he still justified his statement that it was morally possible for a Catholic to support Sinn Fein, in spite of its role as the political wing of the violence-loving I.R.A. He had no doubts about his answer. It was morally wrong for anyone to join Sinn Fein to show approval of the use of force to achieve a united Ireland. It need not, however, be morally wrong if one is convinced that it is more likely than any other party to promote social welfare and that one's membership will not be used as support for violence.

182

I do not rank him with the Bishop of Durham in these widely criticized pronouncements, though both are equally sincere. I credit the Bishop of Durham with a long-standing tendency to provoke argument, if necessary by shocking his hearers. Cardinal O'Fiaich says what he thinks, whether it is diplomatic or the reverse.

I asked him what was the most serious problem he faced, taking Catholic Ireland as a whole. He did not hesitate. It was the falling-off of church attendance; in some areas this was painfully noticeable. It appeared, however, that over 86 per cent of Catholics still say that they go to church once a week. Perhaps the Cardinal was referring to apprehensions about the future, rather than to any calamity that had already occurred, because the percentage among urban dwellers has fallen by nearly 10 per cent during the past decade.

As regards priestly vocations, there had been a serious decline for many years after Vatican II. This seemed to have been checked. Possibly a plateau had been reached. Ireland was still self-sufficient in priests, but the days were over when it could liberally supply the needs of other lands.

I pressed the rather awkward question, Why should Vatican II, which all sensible Catholics applaud enthusiastically, have led to a decline in priestly vocation? The Cardinal suggested *inter alia* that the new freedom of priests to be laicized and then married (a right now suspended) had damaged the prestige of the priesthood. In Ireland in past years there had been enormous pride in having a priest in the family. But once it became clear that one could leave the priesthood at will and marry, if one felt like it, the whole office was devalued, the gilt was knocked off, the glamour much diminished. If time had permitted, I am sure that the Cardinal would have gone into the matter more deeply.

We discussed the influence of the Catholic Church in the Republic, and the way it had recently been exercised – a matter of relevance to the prospect of unity among the Churches, and political unity in Ireland. He corrected the idea that the Church had taken up arms from the beginning in the abortion controversy. The initiative had come from various groups of laity, no doubt imbued with their own form of Catholic devotion. The Church had admittedly played an important part at the end, but the initiative had come from elsewhere. He wanted me to realize that the Catholic Church in

Ireland, as a general rule, did not desire to impose its religious views on the population by means of criminal sanctions.

A definitive statement approved on 15 March 1978 by the Episcopal Conference expresses in firm language his own view:

> The question at issue is not whether artificial contraception is morally right or wrong. The clear teaching of the Catholic Church is that it is morally wrong. No change in state law can make the use of contraceptives morally right, since what is wrong in itself remains wrong, regardless of what state law says. . . . No one can by passing a law make what is wrong in itself become right. This teaching is binding on the conscience of Catholics.

What followed next is of special interest:

> It does not necessarily follow from this that the state is bound to prohibit the distribution and sale of contraceptives. There are many things which the Catholic Church holds to be morally wrong, but which it has never suggested should be prohibited by the state. Those who insist on seeing the issue purely in terms of the state enforcing, or not enforcing, Catholic moral teaching are therefore missing the point.

However, he continued, there is a public and social aspect, and he proceeded to argue against artificial contraception along fairly familiar lines. The statement called attention to great progress all over Ireland in recent years in setting up services of instruction and advice regarding natural methods of responsible parenthood. The whole emphasis of this statement was not on saying good Catholics must regard artificial contraception as immoral because the Church says so, but on saying that careful thought and study should lead to the conclusion that artificial contraception is not in the interests of society.

We talked about divorce. I assumed that the Catholic Church was opposed to any change that made divorce legally possible in Ireland. He agreed that this would still be true. But there were signs of movement. Nearly two-thirds of the population appeared to be in favour of divorce law reform. He was reluctant to make any forecast about the future.

As regards unemployment, no one could have been more forthright than the Cardinal. He regarded with horror the present level of unemployment, alike in North and South. He had taken what personal steps were open to him. He had called on all clergy to provide work directly for a few unemployed at least. He himself had provided work directly for twelve young people.

We talked a good deal about relations between Catholics and Protestants. He was aware that I had been brought up as an Irish Protestant. He had been interviewed not long before by Kieran Moore for *The Universe* and made one of his controversial remarks in passing: 'Unfortunately you still have an awful lot of bigotry. I think 90 per cent of the religious bigotry is to be found among Protestants . . .' The accompanying statement was little noticed: '. . . whereas the bigotry one finds among Catholics is mainly political.'

A passage from that interview should be quoted here. He repeated the gist of it to me:

It is not a religious war. Side by side with the violence you have a considerable amount of ecumenical activities. Something which is not well known in England is that the religious leaders in Ireland meet every month. We pray together, we read the Scriptures together. . . .

Having now interviewed the Cardinal and the Protestant Primate at some length, I feel able to testify to the sincerity of their friendship. Cardinal O'Fiaich is a man of God first and last. But in his case it is virtually impossible to avoid 'political' utterances. He is an all-Ireland patriot. He is an inflexible supporter of Irish unity. He is convinced that in some shape or form it will come about one day. Meanwhile he has the responsibility of diocesan and national leadership. He is utterly opposed to violence; but not a few of his flock are actively involved in it. He remains concerned for their souls. Anyone who thinks of him as a bogeyman should meet him.

Of the Anglo-Irish agreement reached in November 1985 he said: 'I hope that it will make a genuine contribution to peace and reconciliation in Northern Ireland.'

185

∽ 23 ∽

Thomas Joseph Winning,
Archbishop of Glasgow

It is impossible not to begin with an outrageous pun. No one could be more winning than Archbishop Winning! A smile full of sincerity, a readiness to meet anyone half-way; a slight Scottish accent, but a universalist kind of approach, that would put his interlocutor at home anywhere.

I had not realized when I met him that he was the son of a miner, though it is well known all over Scotland. He is strongly built, rather taller than the average miner. He was educated in the state system in Motherwell. He moved backwards and forwards to Rome, completing his education. Born in 1925, by 1953 he was attaining a D.C.L. *cum laude* at the Gregorian University, Rome, though he plays down his academic distinction.

From 1966 to 1970 he was parish priest at St Luke's, Motherwell. He was nominated Titular Bishop of Louth and Bishop Auxiliary of Glasgow, October 1971. From 1972 to 1974 he was parish priest at Our Holy Redeemer, Clydebank. He became Archbishop of Glasgow on 23 April 1974.

Now that the senior Archbishop, Cardinal Gray of Edinburgh, is retired, it is generally assumed that Archbishop Winning will become a cardinal. He is the elected President of the Bishops' Conference of Scotland. Naturally I asked him about this prospect, and just as naturally he set the question aside, leaving it in the hands of God. He did not commit the affectation of pretending that it was an unlikely possibility.

His career seems to represent an inevitable progression from small

186

beginnings to a great position. It must be assumed that he was soon picked out as a man destined for leadership. When I interviewed him he was mainly concerned to describe his far-reaching plans for the renewal of the Catholic life in Scotland. He is clearly accustomed to take long views. For two and a half years the ground has been surveyed. The point has now been reached when a ten-year programme will be embarked upon.

He is neither under-confident nor over-confident about the prospects. He has a great fundamental belief in the Catholics of the West of Scotland. He is aware that there is a saying in Scotland that every true Scot is a Presbyterian. A high proportion of the Catholics in his diocese, which includes a third of the Scottish capital, have come from Ireland in relatively recent times. They are aware that the older inhabitants regard them as aliens. I told him that my eldest daughter had married a Fraser, an ancient Catholic family, and that I had six Scottish grandchildren. He congratulated me, but pointed out that that was not typical of his own diocese.

What was a more serious threat to his flock were the secular influences that had done so much to undermine religion in recent years. For every two Catholic priests who retired, there was only one to replace them. But the Archbishop communicated to me a burning zeal that I feel sure he disseminates throughout his flock.

He is a passionate believer in Christian unity. On the face of it, Scotland is not a very promising area. The Episcopal Church covers only one per cent of the population. On paper the gap between the Catholic and the Presbyterians, the Church of Scotland, who are roughly equal in numbers, is very wide. From the angle of the book, it is no good looking for bishops in the latter Church. But the Archbishop does indeed seem to have narrowed the gap in terms of human friendship. He was the first Catholic leader ever to address the General Assembly of the Church of Scotland. He told me that in terms of social class the Catholics tend to be more at home with the Presbyterians than with the 'Piscies'.

I told him that I was in Scotland shortly before the Pope's visit in 1982, promoting my own book on the Pope. I was warned that the Pope's reception there was likely to be unenthusiastic. He told me that in the event the Pope had said that he had received a warmer reception in Scotland than anywhere else except Poland. I have been

187

told that the Archbishop played a notable part. In the many addresses he has given in the last ten years, he has stressed what might be called the obvious Catholic theme; but he has done so with a directness and immediacy all his own.

Archbishop Winning has a way of asking the old questions with a new urgency, for instance:

What is our vision of the objectives we are striving to reach? What is the purpose of Catholic education? How does this differ from society's view of education? What is the family today? What is a school? What are these two institutions in partnership for? What are the challenges of today that have to be met by family and school? What is the way ahead? Can family and school see the vision of her mission which is for us paramount? While I promise not to begin with Creation, I cannot bypass these essential preliminaries.

The answers that he gives can be summed up in his insistence that the family and the school should act as partners in education, and at all times he comes back to a definition of Catholic education that he derives from a 1977 Synod: *to teach is to love*. There's a wealth of thought in that dictum, and it is enhanced by a further thought that the Catholic faith is essentially about relationships – with God, ourselves, and all others.

One cannot help recalling here the Church's vision of herself, as expressed in the opening lines of *Lumen Gentium*: 'By her relationship with Christ, the Church is a kind of sacrament or sign of intimate union with God, and of the unity of all mankind. She is also an instrument for the achievement of such union and unity.'

The Archbishop is quite reasonably pugnacious. He has aroused some controversy in the past in standing up for his community or his Church against what he took for a criticism from Prince Charles. The latter had made some comment on the fact that Princess Michael had not been permitted by the Pope to be married in church because a previous marriage had not been dissolved. Archbishop Winning bluntly asked Prince Charles how he justified the rule that a Catholic could not ascend the throne of Britain. He made it plain, however, afterwards that there was nothing personal in his rejoinder; in fact, he much admired Prince Charles.

A side of him that appeals to me very much, not always associated with doughty fighters, is his intense feeling for the handicapped. He has expressed this in word and deed very often. In a famous letter, 'Education and the Handicapped', to be read at all masses on Catholic Education Sunday, 1 February 1981, he made abundantly plain his sympathy not only with the handicapped but with their parents also:

> The physically handicapped are not mentally impaired, and it is important to remember this. They suffer from a physical disability, but are very often highly intelligent. A mentally handicapped person may be severely or only mildly disabled.
>
> You may find it difficult to relate to the mentally handicapped and are reticent or uncomfortable in their presence. Such feelings come from not having known mentally handicapped people. The more you get to know them as persons, the less their handicap affects you. For they are human beings like the rest of us, with the same hopes and fears, the same reasons for joy and sorrow, the same need for loving support, the same desire to be accepted as persons in their own right.

Nothing in the foregoing must give the impression that the Archbishop is an easy-going obliging sort of person who is incapable of standing up for the rights of his community. When he speaks out he sometimes causes surprise by the vehemence of his pronouncements. In his archdiocesan newspaper, *Flourish* (February 1985), he caused surprise and dismay in some quarters by his uninhibited support for the striking teachers. He referred to 'the only remedy the teachers had'. 'The faceless civil service', he wrote, 'has decreed that education in the nineteen-nineties will be done on the cheap'. This time he was speaking on behalf not merely of his beloved Catholic schools, but of all members of the teaching profession. 'To me', he said, 'they are first-class people, part of the cream of society.'

The article followed a joint statement from the Church of Scotland and the Catholic Education Commission supporting an independent review of teachers' salaries and calling for an investigation of the 'grievances' that have caused a caring profession to withdraw its co-operation. But the Archbishop obviously felt that the statement was not strong enough and issued his own outspoken attack on the government who, he says, 'pay lip-service to consultation, but rarely conclude that the customer is right'.

One argument he uses for insisting on the maintenance of separate Catholic schools appeals to me in the English as well as in the Scottish connection: 'We are seeking', says the Archbishop, 'to preserve Catholic schools because it is the most effective way of teaching *Christian* values' (emphasis added). He points to the feeble condition of religious education in the state system in Scotland. The same could be said with still more truth in England. Yet, even on this subject, he is less dogmatic than might have been expected.

The journalist Stewart Lamont has interviewed Archbishop Winning perceptively more than once. On one occasion he inquired: 'So are Catholic schools here to stay?'

The Archbishop replied: 'Not necessarily. . . . You see', he said,

we are no longer talking about the defence of the faith. We passed that point some time ago. Separate Catholic education is not a timeless truth. The only timeless truth is the Kingdom of God. Catholic schools have existed for the propagation of that truth. If there came a time when we felt that that truth would be better served in Christian schools – not non-denominational schools – then so be it.

He becomes passionate, though never raising his voice, when he speaks about the social deprivation of the people of Glasgow. An appeal for £1,600,000 to renovate his cathedral was dramatically abandoned in 1977. It would have been grossly insensitive to go ahead 'when so many of our fellow citizens in Glasgow are suffering so much'. As he told Stewart Lamont, his dream is to see 'Glasgow a less deprived city – people are crushed by the system, losing the dignity of human beings'. He calls Glasgow 'my part of the vineyard' and he is desperately involved in its cultivation.

When he said things of this kind to me, I raised with him the question that I am always inclined to put to bishops. 'How far are you prepared to come out into the open and condemn the government, which has no small responsibility for the situation?' I am aware of course that a prudent bishop does not readily divide his flock by taking sides in the political struggle. Archbishop Winning added the thought that no party was in a position to throw stones at their rivals in these matters, even though the great majority of Catholics in Glasgow voted Labour.

Theologically he is a traditionalist; he has no time for liberal theologians like the brilliant dissident Hans Kung who might blur the distinctive nature of historic Catholic doctrine. But I would not regard him as having a closed mind to future possibilities – in the example quoted above, for instance, the possibility of Catholic schools being transcended by something still better.

If I tried to sum up Archbishop Winning – always a hazardous enterprise – I should say that he has enormous energy and an unremitting intention of bringing about reforms that are in his power. I would say that he has an equally strong sense of the unlimited possibilities open to the Holy Spirit in the field of doctrine. He is a well-integrated Christian man.

Conclusions

What then of the twenty-three bishops interviewed and studied? No generalization will cover them all, except that there is a common devotion to Christ and to pastoral work in his service. There is the fact too that they have been selected by the authorities as well suited to carry the heavy responsibility of diocesan leadership.

Let us first look at the Anglicans.

The Anglican bishops

Leaving out doctrine for the moment and accepting the common devotion mentioned above, what comparison if any can I draw between the Christian Anglicans? Physically they are of all shapes and sizes, though none of them are overweight or, for that matter, skinny. The Bishops of Birmingham and Salisbury are a good deal taller than I am, in other words six feet and several inches. The Bishop of Durham is probably the shortest, but with his powerful head and shoulders he could not be described as a small man. David Sheppard, Bishop of Liverpool, still looks the part of an England cricket captain. Dr Runcie, himself no mean cricketer in his time, is large and powerful. The Bishop of Norwich (till his retirement in 1985), who was a commando chaplain, has kept in trim. So, as far as I could perceive, have the others.

The Bishop of Bradford makes the modest claim that he is the only bishop without a degree; the others all went to Oxford or Cambridge and in most cases obtained first-class honours. They had all had some parish experience, but before becoming bishops their main achievements have lain in the world of universities and theological colleges – three of them, Durham, Salisbury, and Chichester, at Oxford; and three others – Canterbury, York, and Birmingham, at

193

Cambridge. Their manner might be described as slightly academic, but not noticeably clerical.

Their ability to get on with so-called ordinary people has been enhanced by, in nearly every case, a period in the services. The Second World War, and the national service that followed after it, supplied them with an advantage enjoyed by few of their predecessors.

The average age of the eleven selected Church of England Anglicans was, when I interviewed them in 1985, sixty. On their own ground they are all friendly, outgoing, hospitable people. In the House of Lords they get on well with other peers, but most of them do not mix as freely in the social life as one could wish. In the 'Interlude' between Parts I and II of the book I have touched on their performance in the Chamber. Their influence there has increased, I should judge, in recent years. Ministers in Mrs Thatcher's government might say they have become more of a nuisance. The presence of a large number of independent peers (over 200) adds a dimension to the House of Lords that is unparalleled elsewhere and obviously lacking in the House of Commons. The bishops are intellectually and morally a notable element in that grouping, but the difficulty of deserting their diocese in order to attend restricts the quantity, though not the quality, of their offerings.

In 1982–3 Mr Graham Turner produced some brilliant articles in the *Sunday Telegraph* about the bishops today. I cannot, however, agree with his final words. He watched the Bishop of London trying to play a tune for a child on a makeshift musical instrument. 'The tune was uncertain and the instrument was plainly not a trumpet. Thus, as it seems to me, our beloved bishops.' Entertaining, but unfair.

I think that Graham Turner was too much inclined to take the bishops at their own humble, Christian self-evaluation. Another reason, said one of the bishops, why the bishops hadn't taken more of a stand over the past twenty years was the chaotic state of doctrinal and moral theology in the Protestant Churches. 'The Church of England couldn't even decide how it wanted to use the Bible': I've no doubt that the bishop used these words to Graham Turner. He certainly did not use them to me. Perhaps each of us found what he was looking for.

I hoped to find a tone of confident Christianity among the bishops, and I was not disappointed. But of course these highly intellectual men are aware of all sorts of intricate problems. Graham Turner, however, has done a splendid job in summarizing the present living conditions of the bishops. The reader should be referred to his *Telegraph* article of 30 December 1982 for a summary. A few examples can be quoted here. In Salisbury, the palace has become a school for 140 boys. The former bishop's house in Chester is now a Y.M.C.A. hostel. The palace in Lincoln has been transformed into a commodious conference centre and hotel. Part of Hartlebury Castle, the Bishop of Worcester's seat, is now a county museum. The Bishop of Winchester shares Wolvesey with a firm of quantity surveyors. And so on.

I have said something in the essay about the Bishop of Bath and Wells of the exceptional use he makes of his famous 'plant', and the fact that his wife does most of the housework. In this respect she is similar to a good many of her episcopal sisters. The bishop's salary today places him on a level with a comfortable professional man, but does not begin to rank him with the 'top' people.

What of the views they express? The results of the elections for the new general Synod were announced in October 1985. All forty-four dioceses had been having elections of clergy and laity. The new representatives will sit until July 1990. In most dioceses, the elections were strongly contested. The main topics at issue were the ordination of women to the priesthood and the orthodoxy of belief in the Church of England. This latter has often been referred to as 'the Durham controversy'. Approximately 1,300 candidates stood for the 445 diocesan places up for election – three for every seat.

Forty per cent of the elected members of the old Synod did not stand for re-election and, with fifty-one sitting members losing their seats, half the faces in the Houses of Clergy and Laity are new. The result of the elections to the House of Bishops has been even more striking. There, the forty-four diocesan bishops who sit in the Synod ex officio are joined by nine suffragan bishops elected by the suffragans of the two Provinces. Seven out of the nine suffragans are newly elected.

The new Synod is distinctly younger. The average age of the

elected clergy is forty-eight and that of the laity fifty. In the House of Laity those under forty years of age account for 17 per cent of the total compared with 9.6 per cent in the Synod of 1980, whilst those over sixty when elected have declined to 16 per cent from 32 per cent in 1980.

The proportion of women has been rising steadily since synodical government was introduced in 1970, when it was 22 per cent. Now it is virtually double at 43 per cent. It must not be assumed that the ordination of women will have benefited substantially. A number of the women who were successful were regrettably, as I would think, *against* the ordination of women.

The official view conveyed to me is that it is impossible to predict how the new Synod is likely to vote on any issue. The most that can be said is that a number of well-known Synod members who occupy the middle ground have lost their seats. In his presidential address to the new Synod, the Archbishop of Canterbury deliberately left the prospects open:

A Christian Synod is not so much a place for assertion as for listening and discovery. We seek to know the will of God for his people, and this means listening not just to each other in the local situation, but to the whole Church which has a wisdom and a breadth greater than any individual, group, or nation. We in England may be justly proud that we have become the mother-Church of a great communion but we have to realise that today we are but one national Church within a great partnership of autonomous Churches.

The Church of England awaits, as Scott-Fitzgerald would have said, 'its intricate destiny'.

This book is about bishops. Who is there, even if he be the Archbishop of Canterbury, who would care to sum up the state of doctrinal opinion in the Church of England in 1986? That applies not least to opinion among the bishops. The Church of England traditionally allows a very wide range of thought and expression to all its members. There seems, for example, no movement to recommend unfrocking the Reverend Don Cupitt, though he has expressed himself in his television talks with astonishing disregard of orthodox Christian opinion. Every now and then, however, a bishop causes excitement and indignation by publicly expounding a view that would have passed unnoticed in someone less eminent. And the Bishop of Durham, by virtue of his position, is a very senior bishop.

Among the bishops I spoke to, the retiring bishop of Norwich, Maurice Wood, repeated his public insistence that the Bishop of Durham should not express such views about the Virgin Birth, the Incarnation, and the Resurrection, and remain a bishop. He has spelt out a powerful argument in a book published since I interviewed him, called *This Is Our Faith*. Among other bishops there was a disposition, understandable enough, to play the issue down; to say that it was the presentation, rather than the substance, of the Bishop of Durham's views that could be regretted. It is, however, a fact that these same views of the Bishop of Durham that have caused so much controversy were widely known before he was appointed a bishop. The Archbishop of York obviously considered, and still considers, that his views lie well within the limits permitted to Anglicans. Nor can one pin the responsibility on the Archbishop of York alone. We must suppose that in the higher reaches of the Anglican Church the same attitude is prevalent. Yet, on the face of it, Maurice Wood and the Reverend David Holloway, author of *The Church of England: Where Is It Going?*, have strong grounds for saying that the views of the Bishop of Durham were contrary to accepted Anglican doctrine.

The doctrine of the Church of England, says David Holloway, as spelt out in Canon A.5, The Church of England (Worship and Doctrine) Measure 1974 (5.1), makes it clear that this is the Canon above all Canons for defining Anglican doctrinal statements. Nor is this some ancient text from the Reformation period. The new Canons were agreed during the 1950s and 1960s and came into force as recently as 1969. Canon A.5 says: 'The doctrine of the Church of England is grounded in the holy Scriptures and in such teaching of the ancient Fathers and councils of the Church as are agreeable to the said Scriptures. In particular such doctrine is to be found in the Thirty-nine Articles of Religion, the Book of Common Prayer and the Ordinal.'

Holloway goes on: 'How do we interpret this Canon A.5?' Therein lies the rub. To quote what I have said earlier in my essay about the

197

Archbishop of York: 'There is no doubt about *his* belief in the Incarnation and the Resurrection. "The doctrine of the Incarnation and the Resurrection are not in doubt among the leadership of the Church." But as usual he will not let us off with a simple statement. "There is", he says, "a liberty of interpretation about the precise way in which they are historically grounded." ' The question that I posed there reasserts itself remorselessly. How much liberty of interpretation is to be permitted to an Anglican layman, to an Anglican clergyman, above all to an Anglican bishop?

Most men and women 'in the pew' have a fairly simple idea of historical fact; it either happened or it didn't happen, like the battles of Hastings or Waterloo. But theologians tend to make distinctions of their own that may befuddle the layman, even the highly intelligent layman, and annoy most of all perhaps the man or woman of simple faith. I much admire, for example, the Reverend John Marsh's commentary on St John's Gospel, but he makes a distinction between theological and historical truth, which leaves me and many others asking, 'Did it, or didn't it happen? Are you saying that Jesus did or did not say these things?' The Archbishop of York seems to be drawing a similar distinction in defending the Bishop of Durham, although it would appear that his own views of what did or didn't happen at the time of the Resurrection are in a historical sense quite orthodox.

We must never forget, which the bishops themselves never forget, that we and they are concerned here with great mysteries. Nothing simple will ever represent the truth to a highly sophisticated mind.

Where do the bishops stand on the issue that more than any other is said to have dominated the elections for the Synod in autumn 1985: the question of women priests? Three of those I interviewed were strongly opposed to the ordination of women – the Anglo-Catholic Bishops of London and of Chichester, and the stout evangelical, Maurice Wood, the retiring Bishop of Norwich. Dr Runcie voted the last time round against the ordination of women but has since, I gather, accepted the case for ordaining them. The others were all in favour of ordaining them; some, like the Bishop of Liverpool, almost passionately so. The Bishop of Bradford, incidentally, differs on this issue from his fellow evangelical, Maurice Wood.

All three opponents of the ordination of women denounced it as internally divisive. The Bishop of Norwich (Maurice Wood) spoke movingly against such ordination of women in terms of theological principle. The Bishops of London and Chichester certainly disliked it on those grounds. But they were primarily opposed to any unilateral movement in that direction because it would nullify the claims of the Church of England to be part of the universal Church. Neither they nor the Catholic bishops I spoke to ruled out the possibility that the ordination of women would one day be accepted by the Church Universal. But for the moment any unilateral move was viewed with horror by the three Anglicans in question.

On the theology at least, the most profound discussion that has come my way is that of the Bishop of Salisbury, Chairman of the Church of England Doctrine Commission. In an article in *Theology*, September 1985, he spelled out at greater length what he had told me when I went to see him. 'What', he asks, 'is it specifically about blessing, absolving, and celebrating the Eucharist which means that they cannot be performed by a woman? Why indeed should it be these three tasks, of all others, which cause so much concern? Are they not, after all, ones which depend least on our own human qualities?' He points out that by contrast other ministerial activities, such as teaching, preaching, counselling, and pastoral care, all palpably require human capacities of one sort or another that are not necessarily found in everyone. Ironically, of course, teaching, preaching, counselling, and pastoral care are activities that have been widely entrusted to women in the Church of England, which is divided on whether or not to admit them to perform the three priestly functions. I agree with the implication that there is something paradoxical and even ridiculous here.

The Bishop accepts the fact that until recent times it was the universal practice of the Church to restrict ordination for men. But he raises the whole question of whether there is any fundamental and inexorable principle behind this tradition. If there is not, there is no reason why half the human race should be excluded from one particular function when in every sphere of life there has been a complete liberating revolution.

He considers that the deepest objection is the view that since Jesus Christ is a man the priest who represents him in offering the Host should also be male. But here he finds a serious misunderstanding. The priest who offers the Host is an agent of Christ, not Christ

199

himself; representative, not a representation. There is no reason therefore why he should be of the same sex as Jesus. I myself find all this very convincing. Admittedly, I was ready to be convinced.

The Bishop quotes more than one Papal pronouncement on his side of the theoretical argument. Of the Catholic bishops I interviewed, none considered it inconceivable that the time would come when the Catholic Church itself would accept the ordination of women. The arguments from 'TRAD' (tradition) remain, but if they were to be treated as Holy Writ there could be no development of the kind on which the Church of Rome and the Church of England are both prepared to pride themselves.

It is harder to sum up the individual attitudes with regard to the movement towards Christian unity. With the possible exception of Maurice Wood, all the bishops appear in principle to favour such a movement. But David Sheppard, Bishop of Liverpool, told me that in spite of his very intimate collaboration with Archbishop Worlock he could not agree to any movement towards Rome that meant a movement away from the Free Churches. More than one other bishop agreed with this formulation.

The Bishop of London, a strong Anglo-Catholic, has insisted that the Papacy must be considerably reformed before the Church of England could ally itself with it and accord the Pope a universal primacy. Dr Runcie left no one in any doubt at the time of the Pope's visit of his own powerful desire for unity with Rome. His sense of the Anglican Church as truly international and not just the Church of a single country, England, seems to motivate him powerfully in the direction of an international unity. He considers that the question of Anglican Orders must be cleared up before large progress is possible. The Roman Catholic bishops I have spoken to do not find an insuperable objection here. All concerned seem to be waiting for the Holy Spirit and meanwhile are collaborating on local levels with much cordiality.

During the 1984–5 miners' strike an extreme tension amounting to antagonism developed between the episcopacy and the government. It appeared to die down, but the mutual suspicion has seemed to remain. The abolition of the G.L.C. and other metropolitan councils in 1985 saw the bishops, or most of them, fighting strenuously on the losing side. At the end of 1985 the bishops, supported by the leaders of the other Churches, offered vehement opposition to the government's proposals to abolish all restrictions on Sunday trading. At just about the same time appeared the report of the Archbishop of Canterbury's Commission on Urban Priority Areas (U.P.A.s), entitled *Faith in the City*.

In advance of its publication, a government spokesman was denouncing it as a product of 'Marxist theology'. Norman Tebbit, Chairman of the Conservative Party, described the report as 'muddled, old-fashioned Labour thinking'. He said that the medicine had been tried before and it had failed. So there is no disguising the conflict between what appears to be the social philosophy of the Church of England and that of Mrs Thatcher's government.

The Vice-Chairman of the Commission on U.P.A.s was David Sheppard, Bishop of Liverpool. It must be assumed that the Archbishop of Canterbury was well aware, when he appointed him, of the Bishop's views and had studied carefully his book, *Bias to the Poor*. The Archbishop of Canterbury, representing the Church of England, must be deemed to have expected and indeed hoped for the kind of report that he has received.

What is there about this report that has so infuriated the Conservative leaders and, it would appear, many Conservative M.P.s before they had even read it? The answer to this in the simplest terms is that the Commission insists that far more must be done to help the U.P.A.s than the government shows any signs of doing. Running throughout the report, there is a passionate demand for action, and this alone might render it unattractive to any government well satisfied that its existing policies are the best available.

But let us distinguish the main propositions submitted in the report, and ask ourselves how far they are bound to be anathema to Mrs Thatcher's supporters. The picture of the inner-city U.P.A.s is, up to a point, uncontroversial; the report describes the symptoms and signs of economic decline, the physical decay, and the social disintegration, and asks: 'Are "two nations" being recreated?' It concludes that there is an increasing and disturbing degree of polarization between the U.P.A.s and housing and social conditions in other, more prosperous, areas.

So far, one might feel, there could be some general agreement.

This prospect becomes weaker when it is evident that these unpleasant aspects of the life of the inner cities are in no small measure due to government policy. It is, however, when we turn to the fundamental presuppositions of the report that the underlying conflict is revealed in its nakedness, although even here the first steps can be taken in unison. Who can object to the following formulation? 'There are two obligations laid on the Christian – the personal (charity, service and evangelism) and the social (action to change the circumstances which cause poverty and distress).' These are often presented as alternatives, but the report argues that a Christian is committed to a form of action embracing both.

Such a formulation can mean little in the abstract. The dividing line is drawn when there is an attempt to apply such principles. Two underlying themes permeate the 354 pages of the report; both are inimical to the social philosophy of Mrs Thatcher's government, though not necessarily to that of other Conservative leaders, of Mr Heath, or the so-called 'wets' for example. The main assumption, the report tells us, on which present economic policies are based is that

> prosperity can be restored if individuals are set free to pursue their own economic salvation. The appeal is to economic self-interest and individualism, and freeing market mechanisms through the removal of 'unnecessary' governmental interference and restrictive trade union practice.
>
> Individual responsibility and self-reliance are excellent objectives. The nation cannot do without them. But pursuit of them must not damage a collective obligation and provision for those who have no choice, or whose choices are at best forced ones. We believe that at present too much emphasis is being given to individualism and not enough to collective obligation.

The attitudes indicated are clearly opposed to those of Mrs Thatcher's government. So is the emphasis laid throughout the report on more equality in the distribution of resources, as between rich areas and poor areas, rich people and poor people. The Church of England today, supported it would seem by the other Churches, favours a considerably more equal society.

202

This is not to say that the Labour Party can claim the report as a socialist document. (The description of it as Marxist is of course ludicrous.) It would seem to represent a majority opinion among the clergy of the Church of England at present. The *Sunday Times* (8 December 1985) discovered a general support for the document among the Anglican bishops. It also records the results of a Gallup poll among Anglican clergy. It appears that 57 per cent of Anglican churchmen supported the Liberal–S.D.P. Alliance, with 25 per cent for the Tories, and 16 per cent for Labour.

Briefly, in the words of the *Sunday Times*, the report calls for an urgent response to the acute problems in the inner cities. Among other things, it advocates more government spending on inner cities; a major examination of housing spending, including mortgage tax relief, and a review of the relationship between income support and pay and taxation. The benefits and burdens, it warns, must be shared more equally, otherwise there will be 'more suffering, bitterness, and social disintegration'. This is good Alliance policy. It falls a long way short of socialist aspirations. But any Labour government coming into power should be happy if it carried out in a single term the recommendations of the Archbishop's Commission.

A gifted Catholic writer, Peregrine Worsthorne in the *Sunday Telegraph* (8 December 1985), and a resolute Thatcherite spokesman, David Hart in *The Times* (9 December 1985), have wheeled out the oldest argument in the world against religious concentration on social issues. They have insisted that the Churches should be concentrating on the salvation of souls. A very different figure is the Reverend David Holloway, but he reaches similar conclusions. He is an evangelical, one of eight Chairmen of the General Synod, and a proponent of the traditional Church teaching of personal salvation. He presides over a 600-strong congregation. To him, the report is, in its advocacy of political and financial solutions to inner-city problems, an abnegation of the Church's responsibility to offer spiritual solutions to life's problems.

'The danger is', he says, 'that if we take these things on board, the Church forgets what it's really there to preach – that the good in society will be achieved only when there is repentance.'

For half a century I have been all too familiar with this argument. I was personal assistant to Sir William (later Lord) Beveridge when he captured the imagination of the world with his plan to abolish want (the 1942 Beveridge Plan). I was disconcerted when I went into my Catholic church to hear a priest (and he was not the only one) proclaiming the message that 'Beveridge is not enough.' No one who has read Matthew XXV, or for that matter the Gospels as a whole, can fail to recall the words of Christ: 'Insomuch as you have done it to the least of these my brethren, you have done it to me.'

But of course it is possible to be a Christian and a Thatcherite Conservative. Many years ago I read a leading article in *The Times* that began with the sentence: 'Unfortunately wealth is like heat; it is only when it is unequally distributed that it performs what the physicists call work.' My task at the moment is to point out that the bishops of today would appear to be rejecting this doctrine.

The question arises as to what the proposals of the Commission on the inner cities would cost. Can we, the wealthy British nation, afford them? Sir William Beveridge when asked this question about his Report used to reply: 'We can't not afford it.' This I hope is the answer that will be given ultimately by the people of England to the proposals of the Archbishop's Commission.

On 11 December 1985 a major debate was held in the House of Commons about the inner cities. Somewhat naturally it became a contest between the opposition parties denouncing the government for not doing anything like enough to assist the inner cities, and the government defending its record. Mr Tebbit, the Chairman of the Conservative Party, attempted to distract attention at the end of the debate by a vehement assault on the militants of Liverpool and the failure of the Labour Party to deal with them. Dispassionate students will concentrate on the opening speech of the minister, the Secretary of State for the Environment, Mr Kenneth Baker. Stripping his speech of its inevitable debating contentions, I quote what seems to me a significant closing passage:

I accept that we are not debating the Church of England report, but it is the hidden hand behind the debate. It makes 38 recommendations to the Church and 23 to the state. I find it surprising that all its recommendations are made to institutions and none to individuals for the very basis of Christian teaching is that grace flows through individuals, not through institutions.

It is not an alibi that seems likely to commend itself to the Church of England in the 1980s.

The Church of England Year Book for 1986 appeared when this book was going to press. It does not mince words about the reaction of the government to the report; it describes it as 'partly hysterical and entirely confused'. It refers to the breaching of the embargo on publication, with a 'strong rumour of an official hand in it'. 'The vituperation levels rose even higher when Mr Norman Tebbit and his lieutenant Mr Jeffrey Archer, entered the lists, with attempts to discredit the Chairman of the Commission (Sir Richard O'Brien) and other members of the Commission.'

Of other matters dealt with, the debate on belief was treated as the most significant. The retiring Bishop of Winchester had helped to steady the nerves of those whose instinct was that the Church of England had to be comprehensive. On the other hand the Rev. David Holloway 'was uncompromising and stark'. There were 'patient, middle-ground speeches' from the Archbishops of Canterbury and York.

With the matter referred to the House of Bishops, who were expected to bring their considered thoughts to Synod in July 1986, 'the rumble of gunfire' was still heard.

'Perhaps' said the Year Book, 'the Bishops' report would help in resolving contradiction. But the debate in July promised to be stormy.'

The Synod of the Church of England discussed *Faith in the City* on 6 and 7 February 1986. I was privileged to be present for part of the time in the Press Gallery. Clifford Longley's *Times* report sums up the outcome: 'With only minor reservations, the Anglican report highly critical of government policy in the inner cities was adopted as official policy by the General Synod of the Church of England yesterday.'

There was no consolation therefore for the government in the vote recorded by the Synod. I myself listened from the gallery to the impressive opening and closing of the debate on the first day by the Archbishop of Canterbury. He did not retract a syllable from the report, but his attitude towards the government was conciliatory. He referred to a meeting he had had with the Minister for the Environment and to an indication that some new assistance would be given to the inner cities.

For the purposes of my own education, I was glad to have listened to two speeches vehement in criticism and not lacking in eloquence from two Conservative gentlemen, one an M.P. The M.P. informed the Synod that he was not surprised by the report; the Commission was obviously of left-wing flavour. The other Conservative speaker denounced the interference of the clergy in politics: 'I sat under my parson for twenty years', he told us. 'I never discovered what his politics were. He had the sense to keep his mouth shut' (loud laughter – at him, rather than with him).

I came away with a better appreciation of the difficulty of any Archbishop of Canterbury. No doubt David Sheppard expressed the profound desire of the vast majority of the Synod to bring help to the inner cities in the spirit of Christ. 'I was hungry and you gave me to eat – insomuch as you have done it to the least of these my brethren you have done it to me.' But out of those who actively play their part among the Church of England laity, half at least must be supposed to be of conservative temper, whatever their immediate party preference. No shepherd of the flock can simply ignore so many devoted sheep. The Archbishop, in my opinion, understands all these things at least as well as anyone else. He is determined, as is the Church of England, that Thatcherism should at the least be brought under intense moral scrutiny. There was considerable concern about the so-called inadequate theological basis of the report. In the circumstances this seemed unreasonable, but it was perhaps just as well that it should be expressed.

Something else should be added here. The Catholic bishops' conference, held in Chelmsford, Essex, in January 1986, devoted two days to the report. They recorded their gratitude for the great service that had been carried out. They commended the report to their clergy and people for study and local action.

The Catholic bishops

There is one transcending difference between Church of England bishops and Catholic bishops in England and Wales, Scotland and Ireland. The former can be far more independent in arriving at their doctrines; they are far less subject to any control outside themselves. The Church of England is part of a far-flung communion with something like 70 million members, but when it comes to deciding on doctrine it does not seem that the opinions of the Anglican Churches overseas are a very significant factor.

Admittedly the present system of government in the Church of England is described as 'synodical'. The Synod, apart from the bishops, is an elected assembly. The bishops cannot go ahead on their own; but they can make their views individually and collectively plain. The Church of England is still some way from accepting the ordination of women, but the bishops have not hesitated to vote in its favour by forty-one votes to six. Admittedly again, the Church of England, as the established Church of the country, is still subject to some residual parliamentary interference. A limited choice of bishops is still left to the Prime Minister. But these restrictions are small compared with those inherently attaching to any national member of the world-wide Catholic Church.

There are perhaps 5 million Roman Catholics in England. They are usually referred to as 10 per cent of the population. There are perhaps 700 million Roman Catholics in the world. The Catholic Churches in these islands can make a vital contribution, as was shown at the November 1985 Synod in Rome, to the development of policy. The ultimate seat of authority remains in Rome.

Connected with this, the Roman Catholic bishop considers that he approaches his life work with a slightly different emphasis from that of his Anglican brother. He sets out with the positive objective of promoting the unity of the whole Church. His local pastoral mission is seen as an expression of that unity. He does not regard his vocation as in any sense individualistic. Not surprisingly, it is harder to distinguish the respective attitudes and contributions of the Catholic bishops. The contributions are in some cases well known. Bishop Harris of Middlesbrough is looked to for guidance on penal matters, and to some extent on social welfare generally. Archbishop Worlock, apart from his strategic insight and remarkable gifts as a draftsman, provides a unique example of day-by-day collaboration with the leaders of the other Churches. Bishops Clark and Murphy-O'Connor, as successive Chairmen of ARCIC, provide specialized leadership in inter-Church relations. The Archbishop of Cardiff rules the roost in Wales. So, in a wider sense, does Cardinal O'Fiaich in Ireland, where conditions are not very similar to those in England.

On matters of social doctrine, the bishops have spoken out

uncompromisingly on behalf of traditional Catholic values, notably in regard to abortion and the newer issue of embryo research. They are generally understood to be more tolerant in the area of contraception than the present official line of the world-wide Church. The same would apply to their attitude towards the access to the sacraments of divorced people who have remarried. The question of women priests, which is so agitating the Church of England, does not arise today in the Catholic Church. None of those I have spoken to on this subject, however, asserted a fundamental theological objection to the ordination of women.

In the realm of theology, I found nobody remotely equivalent to the Bishop of Durham. Those who discussed the matter with me, Bishop Harris for example, drew the sharpest of distinctions between the duty of a bishop, which is to promote the unity of the Church and to strengthen the faithful, and the duty of a theologian, which is one of scholarship and exploration. All of them agree that over the years and centuries the doctrine of the Church develops under the guidance of the Holy Spirit. No one has explained to me precisely how this process works. The *consensus fidelium*, the consent of the faithful, has always played an important part. Since the Second Vatican Council more and more emphasis is being laid on the role of the laity. Anyone who attends a parish church is aware that consultation is being carried wider and deeper.

Saturday after Saturday a little group of us in our village have been meeting as part of a world-wide process of eliciting the views of the laity. To take some of the typical questions put to us: How does being a member of a parish help us to cope with daily life? In what ways do we feel that the parish contributes to a sense of community? How can we help to build up community spirit? We have discussed such parochial issues as how our coffee mornings after Mass could be made more popular, and I have come away with an increased awareness of the ability of a small local group to say something valuable about their own little area. All this, repeated world-wide, will be of enormous assistance to the 'Synod on the Laity' of 1987. But the decisions will always rest with the leaders of the Church, that is to say the Pope and the bishops.

I would not say that the movement towards Christian unity is stronger among the Catholic than the Anglican bishops. Nor would I say that it is weaker. In each case the ARCIC process is in dedicated hands. One thing at least can be asserted with absolute confidence; the bishops, led by Cardinal Hume – but their sentiment is unanimous – are passionately concerned to do all in their power to make Vatican II a reality and to carry its fulfilment ever further.

This brings us to the Synod held in Rome at the end of November 1985. It would be less than frank not to recognize the existence within the Church of some quite severe criticisms of trends in official policy and assertions of decline where there ought to have been growth. Father Michael Winter, in his book *Whatever Happened to Vatican II?*, summarizes most of the criticisms; but even he admits that for those who are still committed members of the Catholic Church there has been a 'widespread maturing of the commitment to faith in Christ'.

Archbishop Worlock acknowledges that in England there has been some decline in attendance at Mass, but does not agree that this represents a weakening of Catholicism. Measured in terms of people now actively involved in the life and mission of the Church, the Catholic Church is stronger than ever in England, and there are many parts of the world where this would be still more true, where there has been remarkable expansion.

I am an avid reader of anything written by Peter Hebblethwaite about the Church today, no longer a Jesuit but still a devout Catholic. In his latest work, *In the Vatican,* he paints an expert but highly unattractive picture of the *Curia.* I cannot dispute with him there. In my view, however, he does far less than justice to the world-wide spiritual influence of the Pope, alike among Catholics and non-Catholics.

It is still unclear why the November 1985 Synod was called. Archbishop Worlock suggested to me that the simplest explanation is this: the Pope has a passion for anniversaries. It suddenly occurred to him that in November it would be twenty years since the ending of the Vatican Council. Why not call a Synod to commemorate the anniversary? Why not indeed? No sooner thought of than done. The fact that the Synod on the Laity planned for 1986 had to be postponed to 1987 indicates that this was a truly impromptu decision.

All through 1985 fears were growing that here was an attempt to undermine Vatican II and to 'put the clock back'. Cardinal Ratzinger, Head of the Holy Office, one of the two most powerful cardinals, seemed to confirm such suspicions in a lecture followed by a book. A very well informed bishop told me that it was wrong to say that the Pope wanted to 'put the clock back', but he did want to slow up the rate of change. In the event, nothing of the sort occurred. To quote the *Catholic Herald* of 6 December 1985: 'The Synod got away to a fine start on November 25th when the Belgian Cardinal Godfried Danneels presented his summary of the episcopal conference's responses to the Synodal Secretariat's questionnaire. It made clear that the world's bishops, while admitting difficulties in the past twenty years, wholeheartedly endorsed the more positive, open attitudes introduced by the Council.'

Who can say how the Pope would have reacted if the messages received from the bishops all round the world had been different, or less enthusiastic than Vatican II? As it was, he was careful to avoid giving a strong lead to the Synod or seeking to influence its conclusions. By the end, he would appear to have accepted their overwhelming verdict of commitment to carrying further the philosophy of the Second Vatican Council.

Apart from a general enthusiastic support for Vatican II, what message emerged from the Synod? A key passage from its final report runs as follows: 'The reason for the summoning was to celebrate, reaffirm the meaning, and carry forward the work of the Second Vatican Council. We are grateful to see that with God's help we have achieved these aims.' Whatever may have been the apprehensions beforehand, there was no doubt about the final decision in favour of carrying the work of the Council further and further.

The most valuable section of the final report is 'The Church as *Communio*'. The words are so technical and yet so fraught with spiritual meaning that one must quote a few sentences verbatim, although doing so inevitably takes them out of context:

What does the complex word 'communio' mean? Fundamentally it is a matter of our communion with God through Jesus Christ in the Holy Spirit. This communion exists through the word of God and the Sacraments. Baptism is the door and foundation of the

210

Church's communion: the Eucharist is the source of the whole of Christian life and its summit (cf. *Lumen Gentium II*). Communion with the Body of Christ in the Eucharist signifies and brings about or builds up the intimate union of all the faithful in the Body of Christ, which is the Church (cf. Cor. X: 16 seq.).

Those who were looking for a renewed stress on the aspiration on the unity with other Churches and for increased participation by the laity will find it here. But the idea of *communio* is linked more obviously with the principle of collegiality. We are told that the ecclesiology of *communio* provides a sacramental foundation for collegiality. 'Collegial action', we are told, 'implies the activity of the whole college, together with its Head, directed at the whole Church.' In practical terms this takes us back to a point made earlier; the Catholic bishop is dedicated to the unity of the whole Church and exists intrinsically as part of it. To quote from the final report: 'The College, together with its Head, but never without its Head [i.e. the Pope] has full power over the Universal Church.' The message is one, no doubt, of great spiritual potentiality, but it is not for many of us as meaningful as it is for the Synod.

Cardinal Hume, whose own speech on *communio* carried much weight, has shown no doubt about the success of the Synod. He says: 'The Synod should be seen as a positive achievement. It said "Yes" to the Council. It acknowledged that the Holy Spirit is still at work in the Church. It was a good preparation for the Synod on the laity.' He considered that the emphasis laid on *communio* was of great significance: 'I expect to see in the years to come further theological attention directed to this concept and its consequences. It will be of very great importance for progress in Christian unity between the Churches.'

Many loose ends remain, as was inevitable in a Synod so hastily convened and so rapidly conducted. 'It is far from clear', to quote the *Catholic Herald* again, 'what are the respective roles of Roman curia, cardinalate college, Synod, and national episcopal conferences.'

There is some anxiety about the recommended preparation of a catechism. It is feared that if prepared by Cardinal Ratzinger's congregation it might become something of a strait-jacket. But by and large, the Catholic bishops in this country rejoiced at the outcome. They seem confident that the forces of decentralization will be strengthened; more autonomy will be available for the national Churches.

Bishop Agnellus Andrew, for four years Head of Communications in the Vatican, has stressed to me the ever-mounting pressure from the Third World for indigenization, i.e. the demand that African Churches, for example, should be allowed to express themselves through an African culture, rather than through the traditional idioms of Greece and Rome. Coming closer to home, there is no doubt that the bishops in England have been less than happy with the centralizing pressures of the *Curia* in recent years. They expect life to be easier and more fruitful as a result of the 1985 Synod.

I have no doubt that it was the emphatic endorsement of Vatican II before the Synod met that produced its forward-looking conclusion. The part played by the bishops of England, Wales, Scotland, and Ireland must be reckoned of high importance.

Christian Unity

An important press conference was held on Monday 3 March 1986. The joint co-Chairmen of the Second Anglican–Roman Catholic International Commission, the Anglican Bishop of Kensington and the Roman Catholic Bishop of Arundel and Brighton, presented correspondence between ARCIC II and Cardinal Johannes Willebrands, President of the Vatican Secretariat for the Promotion of Christian Unity. The Cardinal restated the reasons why the Roman Catholic Church has not been able to recognize Anglican Orders. These rested on the judgement that the doctrines of the Eucharist and of the Priesthood ·contained in the Church of England's sixteenth-century service books were not in accord with the Catholic doctrine. He saw hope for a solution to the problem in the Agreed Statements on Eucharist and Ministry already produced by ARCIC I. These statements will now be evaluated by the two Churches.

The Cardinal also noted the theological and liturgical developments of recent years which had brought the Churches closer together.

The joint chairmen of ARCIC II replied at length. Two sentences only can be quoted here: 'Your letter was especially helpful and timely.' They drew much obvious encouragement from it. Towards the end of their letter they stated in the most unequivocal terms: 'Our goal is full ecclesial union.'

But neither they nor any well-informed person supposes that it will come overnight.

A Final Word

Christianity is the religion of love. It is that or it is nothing. John Henry Newman, alike in his Anglican and Catholic days, saw the real struggle of the century as one between belief and unbelief. The other divisions and dissensions were subsidiary to this one and mainly of significance in their bearing on it. Those who in the flesh or on television saw and listened to the Pope and the Archbishop of Canterbury when the former visited Canterbury in 1982 must have felt that in the sight of God the divisions between the Church of Rome and the Anglican Church were of secondary importance.

The present author, thirty-five years an Anglican (Church of Ireland and C. of E.), forty-six years a Roman Catholic, married to a woman also a Catholic convert who was brought up a Unitarian, should be ashamed of himself if he adopted a sectarian attitude. But I am more convinced than ever that Jesus Christ founded a Church and that the Catholic Church today is its visible continuation. I am more convinced than ever that the Holy Spirit is at work within it and that its message and its sacraments are alike of divine origin.

It is not for me to distinguish the presence of divine grace outside the Roman Church. The Church of England bears many marks of evident sanctity, and this is not true of the Church of England alone.

Turning to ethics, I find a unique value in Christian conceptions of humility and forgiveness. Most elevated doctrines advocate love in some form or other, but Christians possess a unique motivation in the life and death of Jesus Christ. 'Love one another as I have loved you'; 'Inasmuch as you have done it to the least of these my brethren you have done it to me.' In agony on the Cross: 'Father forgive them for they know not what they do.' No other faith possesses an equal responsibility. The leaders of the Christian Churches carry indeed

214

a stupendous responsibility in trying to live up to the mandate received from the Founder.

In this book I have concentrated on the local aspect of the world-wide struggle. I have concerned myself primarily with England and to a lesser extent with Wales, Scotland, and Ireland. I refrain from a dogmatic pronouncement as to how Christianity is progressing at present. Taking the world as a whole, it would be easy to be optimistic; harder, in the case of Britain, but even there pessimism is out of place.

I was born in 1905; I was an undergraduate from 1924 to 1928, a don from 1932 to 1939 and again from 1953 to 1955. I see no convincing evidence that Christianity was any stronger in Great Britain or Ireland at any of these dates than it is today. I cannot, of course, deny that church attendances have been much reduced during the present century, but they are no clear indication of true piety. So shrewd a judge as Archbishop Worlock assures me that the devotion of active Catholics is as great as ever. I think that the Anglican view is the same. We have never had a more popular monarch than the present Queen, or a more religious one. The last six Prime Ministers have all been genuine Christians. When was this last true in Britain?

The interest of this book does not, I submit, stand or fall by such unquantifiable estimates. It consists of short sketches of samples of leading bishops in these two islands. It is not a sociological study of episcopacy, but it will I hope contribute to such a study. The whole point of the authority of a bishop is that it is an authority inherited from Jesus Christ, initially through the instrumentality of the Apostles. The essence of episcopacy, Catholic or Anglican, is hierarchical; the power comes from above.

Today, in Britain and Ireland, we live in an age of expanding democracy. Neither the Catholic nor the Anglican Church has been unaffected. The Church of England's government is described as episcopal, but also as synodical – that is to say, to some extent democratic. The Church of Rome is still said to be authoritarian, with a personal leader, the Pope, as its head. But Archbishop Worlock, to quote him again, considers that one of the most far-reaching insights of Vatican II is a new understanding of the role of the laity. 'One mission, different ministries, and an equality of dignity.' The tensions between authority and democracy, already visible in the Anglican Church, may be expected in due course to reveal themselves in the Roman Communion.

Was the Reformation a gigantic mistake, an unmitigated disaster? Was the corruption of the Roman Church a principal excuse or explanation? Answers to questions such as these must await the Day of Judgement. In the meanwhile all serious Christians, Catholic and Anglican, must pray for an ever greater measure of unity between their Churches. There are theological differences in regard to authority, social divergencies on matters such as divorce and birth control. They will make amalgamation impossible in the foreseeable future. But we are not talking today of amalgamation; we are talking of the kind of relationship illustrated for a brief moment by the Pope and the Archbishop of Canterbury in Canterbury Cathedral. Having interviewed thirteen Anglican and ten Catholic Bishops – a very rare experience – I am confident that *their* Churches, and not only their Churches, are indeed determined to draw closer and closer together in seeking to practise the religion of love.

Select Bibliography

Anglican–Roman Catholic International Commission, *The Final Report*, C.T.S./S.P.C.K., 1981.

Archbishop's Commission on Urban Priority Areas, *Faith in the City*, Church Information Office, 1985.

Baker, John Austin, *The Foolishness of God*, Darton, Longman & Todd, 1970.

Barnes, F. W., *The Rise of Christianity*, Darton, Longman & Todd, 1947.

Church of England Board for Social Responsibility, *The Church and The Bomb*, Hodder & Stoughton, 1982.

Personal Origins: Report of the Working Party on Human Fertilization and Embryology, Church Information Office, 1985.

Duggan, Margaret, *Runcie, The Making of an Archbishop*, Hodder & Stoughton, 1985.

Habgood, John, *A Working Faith*, Darton, Longman & Todd, 1980.

— *Church and Nation in a Secular Age*, Darton, Longman & Todd, 1980.

Harris, Murray, J., *Easter in Durham: Bishop Jenkins and the Resurrection of Jesus*, Paternoster Press, 1985.

Holloway, David, *The Church of England: Where Is It Going?*, Kingsway Publications, 1985.

Hume, Basil, *Searching For God*, Hodder & Stoughton, 1979.

— *To Be A Pilgrim*, S.P.C.K., 1984.

Longford, Frank, *Pope John Paul II*, Michael Joseph/Rainbird, 1982.

Montefiore, Hugh, *The Probability of God*, S.C.M. Press, 1985.

Moore, Peter, *Bishops, But What Kind?*, S.P.C.K., 1982.

Murphy-O'Connor, Cormac, *The Family of the Church*, Darton, Longman & Todd, 1984.

Robinson, John, *Honest To God*, S.C.M. Press, 1963.

Roman Catholic Bishops of England and Wales, *The Easter People*, St Paul Publications, 1980.

Sheppard, David, *Bias to the Poor*, Hodder & Stoughton, 1984.

Warnock Committee, *Report of the Committee of Inquiry into Human Fertilization and Embryology*, H.M.S.O., 1984.

Welsby, Paul, *History of the Church of England, 1945–1980*, Oxford University Press, 1984.

Wood, Maurice, *This Is Our Faith*, Hodder & Stoughton, 1985.

Worlock, Derek, *Give Me Your Hand*, St Paul Publications, 1977.

Index

219

Commission on Urban Priority Areas, inner cities, *Faith in the City*, 19, 26, 59, 60, 145, 201–6
Commons, House of, 117
communio, 210–11
Communion, *see* Eucharist
contraception, birth control, 104, 135, 136, 184, 208
Corpus Christi (1985), 161
Couve de Murville, Maurice, *see* Birmingham, Archbishop of
Creeds, 13, 26, 43
Crosland, Anthony, 18, 19
Crossmaglen, 180
Crossman, R. H. S., 78
Cross Appointments Commission, 13
Cupitt, Rev. Don, 89, 196–7

Daly, Dr Edward, *see* Derry, Bishop of
Danneels, Cardinal Godfried, 210
d'Arcy, Father Martin, 46, 73
de Valera, Éamon, 102
death penalty, *see* capital punishment
Derby, Bishop of, 116
Derry, Bishop of (Dr Edward Daly), 181
devil, personal, 45, 110
Dimbleby Lecture (1984), 56
disabled people, handicapped people, 148, 189
divorce, 50, 65, 113–14, 149–50, 154–5, 184
  remarriage of divorced people, *see under* marriage
Docherty, Father, 147
doctrine, 12–13, 21–2, 36–7, 90, 96–7, 195, 196–8; *see also* Bible; Creeds; Thirty-nine Articles; *also* Resurrection *and other subjects*
Doctrine Commission, 22, 90
Duggan, Margaret, 17, 18, 24–5
Durham, Bishop of (David Jenkins), 6, 14, 21–2, 77–83, 99–100
  appearance, manner, 41, 78, 99, 183, 193–4

criticism of, doubts concerning, 4, 8, 15, 27, 33, 36–7, 65–6, 75, 77–83 *passim*, 89, 165, 197
  a sound Christian, 36–7, 79, 89, 197
  Gospel stories, his view of, 80–1
  Ireland, no impact in, 102
  speeches in the Lords by, 77, 117
  at 1985 Synod, 8
Durham, bishopric of, 29, 77
'Durham controversy', 195

East Anglia, Bishop of (Alan Charles Clark), 64, 169–74, 207
Easter in Durham, 36, 81
Easter People, The, 123
ecumenical movement, *see* unity, Christian
education, schools, teachers, 42, 188, 189–90
Einstein, Albert, 37
embryo research, Warnock Report, 8–9, 26, 34, 67, 74, 124–5, 132, 133, 151, 165
episcopacy, *see* bishops
Episcopal Church of Scotland, 12, 106–107, 187
ethics, morality, 5, 214
  medical, 30–1; *see also* embryo research
  sexual, 6, 135–6; *see also* abortion; contraception
Eucharist, Communion, 125, 154, 171, 172, 173, 178, 211, 212
evangelicals, 14, 15, 62, 70
Evans, Dr Sydney, 85
evil, 45–6, 110

Faith in the City, see Commission on Urban Priority Areas
Falklands war, 7, 20, 35, 115
Family of the Church, The, 175–6, 176
family problems, 149; *see also* divorce; marriage
Farrer, Austin, 13, 108

INDEX

INDEX

Welsby, Paul, 3, 5, 23, 24, 27

Welsh language, 159

· Westminster, Cardinal Archbishop of (Basil Hume), 98, 127–37, 211

Whale, John, 29, 30

Whatever Happened to Vatican II?, 209

Whitehouse, Mary, 6

Whitelaw, Lord, 18, 77

Willebrands, Cardinal Johannes, 212

Williams, Dr Ronald, 6

Williamson, Anne, 69

Williamson, Rev. John, 60

Williamson, Robert (Roy), *see* Bradford, Bishop of

Winchester, Bishop of, 195

Winning, Thomas Joseph, *see* Glasgow, Archbishop of

Winter, Father Michael, 209

women, ordination of

support for, 9–10, 14, 51–2, 59, 70, 74, 97–8, 102, 198–200

opposition to, 9, 14, 24, 43–4, 51–4, 63–4, 196, 198–200

need for consensus, gradualism, 24–25, 26, 44, 52, 53–4, 64, 97–8, 155, 167, 198–200

other references, 6, 16, 50, 108–9, 195, 200

Wood, Margaret, 61, 64

Wood, Maurice (former Bishop of Norwich), 14, 49, 61–7, 113, 193, 197, 198–9, 200

Worcester, Bishop of, 195

Working Faith, A, 30

Worlock, Derek, *see* Liverpool, Archbishop of

Worsthorne, Peregrine, 203

York, Archbishop of (John Habgood), 29–38, 81, 166, 193–4, 197, 198

Young, Lord, 38

Young, Hugo, 130

Your Suffering, 62